Disability Matters

Disability Matters

Legal and Pedagogical Issues of Disability in Education

Paul T. Jaeger and
Cynthia Ann Bowman

BERGIN & GARVEY
Westport, Connecticut • London

Library of Congress Cataloging-in-Publication Data

Jaeger, Paul T., 1974–
    Disability matters : legal and pedagogical issues of disability in education / Paul T. Jaeger and Cynthia Ann Bowman.
        p. cm.
    Includes bibliographical references and index.
    ISBN 0–89789–909–1 (alk. paper)
    1. Children with disabilities—Education—Law and legislation—United States.
    2. Children with disabilities—Education—United States. I. Bowman, Cynthia Ann, 1958– II. Title.
    KF4210.J34 2002
    344.73'0791—dc21   2002025207

British Library Cataloguing in Publication Data is available.

Library of Congress Catalog Card Number: 2002025207
ISBN: 0–89789–909–1

First published in 2002

Bergin & Garvey, 88 Post Road West, Westport, CT 06881
An imprint of Greenwood Publishing Group, Inc.
www.greenwood.com

Printed in the United States of America

The paper used in this book complies with the Permanent Paper Standard issued by the National Information Standards Organization (Z39.48–1984).

10 9 8 7 6 5 4 3 2 1

To my parents, whose influence on me is profound and beyond measure. Mom, thank you for all the encouragement and support through the writing of this book. Dad, if only you had lived to see this . . . no one would have been happier or more proud.

—Paul

To my mom, who taught me that disability did not have to impact my hopes and dreams. Your courage and love were my inspiration!

—Cindy

Contents

Introduction:
Disability Matters to Everyone

This book is an introduction to and an analysis of the legal and pedagogical issues related to disability and education. The information in this book is necessary for every general education teacher, special education teacher, and administrator in schools, both public and private. The book provides information about the rights of students with disabilities in any level of school, from elementary school to graduate school, and the rights of teachers and administrators with disabilities. Further, this book is designed to function as a reference work for anyone (educator or lawyer) doing introductory research in disability law and education by providing analysis of relevant statutes, cases, legal scholarship, and education research.

As a teacher or an administrator, no matter the kind or level of school, you will work every day of your career with students who have disabilities. The popular movements for integrating students with disabilities into general education classrooms, as well as the bevy of legal protections provided under the law in the last three decades, have brought the disabled into every classroom. In spite of the recent progress made in disability rights, the education of educators has not kept pace. We have found that many pre-service teachers who do not specialize in special education often get little or no training about the legal, pedagogical, and human dimensions of working with disabled students. Once in the field, educators are often without a reference as to how to deal with their disabled students, as required by law and as dictated by principles of education.

This book is designed to provide a resource for everyone involved in the education process to understand the legal rights and the social positions of the disabled individuals in their school community. As a result of integration, a teacher, whether he or she teaches general education or special education, cannot avoid teaching students with disabilities. To adequately meet the needs of students with disabilities, it is the duty of each pre-service teacher, teacher, administrator, and education professor to understand what it means for an individual to have a disability in this society and what the laws protecting these students do and why.

This book is also intended as a guide for education majors, teachers, and other school employees with disabilities to understand their rights and their roles in the education profession. The disabled have traditionally had a very limited role as educators, often being limited to teaching disabled students. This phenomenon is worthwhile for educators, disabled or not, to understand; it demonstrates how this society has historically limited the potential of individuals with disabilities.

Providing an accurate description of the law and its relation to the education system and individuals with disabilities is a daunting task for several reasons. In the United States, the law can change rapidly, especially in the areas of civil rights and protections of minorities. The year in which this book was written saw a potentially dramatic change to the scope of one of the major disability laws, the Americans with Disabilities Act, when the Supreme Court of the United States limited the uses of the law against state and local governments (*Board of Trustees of the University of Alabama v. Garrett*, 2001). This decision, a part of the Supreme Court's much-debated campaign to limit the liability of states to suit from private individuals, has been looming for several years. Though the exact impact of that decision will only become clear over the long term, there does not appear to be another issue of the same magnitude regarding the rights of the disabled which the Supreme Court will have a chance to address in the next few years. It is entirely feasible that another legal challenge to federal laws protecting the disabled may be raised in the near future; however, there is no major issue currently working its way up through the appeals process which seems to have the potential to drastically alter the rights of the disabled in education.

Further, lower courts are incessantly tinkering with the meanings of various laws that affect the rights of the disabled, often changing the interpretation or the application of some relatively minor aspect of one of the federal disability laws. These small alterations, however, do not change the general meaning and impact of the law from the standpoint of the educator or the student. Despite the constant potential for major or minor changes to disability laws by the courts, the overall scope and importance of the laws ought to be fairly stable for the teacher and the student in this context. Appendix A, "How to Understand and Use Legal Sources," provides an explanation of the mechanics associated with the legislature and the judiciary that are relevant to this text, as well as how to find the official text of the cases and the laws described in this book. Appendix B, "A Guide to Relevant Legal Acronyms and Abbreviations," provides a list of definitions of legal acronyms and abbreviations for laws and legal citations used in this text.

LEARNING THE LAW: A LIFELONG PROCESS

Prior to delving into the substance of the laws that affect the education of students with disabilities, a discussion of some extremely general principles about the law seems in order. We live in a society ruled by law. Though a bit of a cliché, the assertion of justice for all does indeed hold true. In the United States, there are laws about virtually every aspect of life. There are federal laws, state laws, and local laws. The diverse local, state, and federal courts are constantly interpreting these various laws. Living with the law is a part of daily life in the United States.

The law, however, is not some unchanging, easily defined set of rules. The legislature that passes a law will often modify, change, or repeal that law over time. The individual state legislatures and the federal legislature must respect the powers of one another to make laws as delineated by the Constitution. The various levels of courts, in reviewing and interpreting the laws within their jurisdiction, often greatly alter those laws. Changes in society, political climate, technology, science, and many other elements that affect legal principles can significantly alter the interpretation or the application of a particular law. The bottom line is that the interpretation and application of any law is rarely a static concept. The most common changes to laws are minor ones, preserving the major principle of the law, altering only a small part of the law. But occasionally, an action of either the legislature or the judiciary will radically change a law or repeal it altogether. Lawyers must put great effort into staying current in any area of specialization because the law is in a constant state of evolution.

Keeping the ever-evolving nature of the law in mind when dealing with legal issues is immensely important. Learning about a legal issue at a particular time does not mean that what you learned about that legal issue remains correct indefinitely. Laws can be changed in minor ways or in significant ways by legislatures or by courts at any time. As noted above, both the courts and the Congress seem to be incessantly refining federal disability laws. Understanding any legal issue is an ongoing process that requires active effort. One of the best ways to keep current in an area of the law is to follow the progress of relevant cases as they proceed through the courts.

Just because you read this book does not mean you can stop learning about disability law and how it affects your job as an education professional. This book provides an introduction to and overview of the federal laws that relate to students with disabilities in schools. It provides a great deal of information about legal obligations and teaching strategies and techniques that can help to meet these legal obligations. It also offers historical and social elements to help you understand the meaning of being disabled in the United States. This book, however, is not your ticket to stop learning disability law and education.

In particular, the focus of this book is on the federal disability laws that affect students and schools. These federal laws establish a set of standards with which all states must comply. However, a state may pass further laws regarding students with disabilities, as long as those state laws do not conflict with the federal laws. A full compendium of all the various state laws related to students with disabilities would be several times the size of this book. You should make the effort to learn the substance of the state laws related to students with disabilities where you live and work.

Bearing in mind the potentially changing nature of laws, this book was written to remain as current as possible without risking becoming time-locked. Any book about legal issues, of course, runs the risk of being affected by a major change in the law. Barring a very major change in the disability laws that affect education, the material in this book should remain current. If there is a major change in the law, then we will have to write a new edition of the text, but such is life for law and education professionals.

Every situation under the law is unique and heavily dependent on the particular facts of the situation. A small difference in detail can make for a large difference in the outcome of a case. For that reason, as well as for many others, this book should not be viewed as a reference guide for those seeking to take a legal action related to the topics covered by this book. An attorney should be consulted whenever a legal action of any sort is considered.

Due to the special nature of this text, it has two separate sections for cited materials. The first section, "References," contains the full citations for all education materials, journal articles, books, and secondary legal sources. The second section, "Table of Legal Authorities," contains the full citations for all statutes, cases, and regulations. The primary reason for having these separate reference sections is to facilitate the efforts of those, educators or lawyers, who use this text to do legal research.

DISABILITY WILL CONTINUE TO MATTER

This book is an introduction to the federal laws related to students with disabilities, to teaching strategies for working with students with disabilities, and to the social, cultural, and emotional elements of disability. Introducing you to laws, teaching strategies, social issues, and individual stories, this book balances the legal, the pedagogical, and the human factors affecting students with disabilities. Hopefully, you will consider this book your gateway to continuing to learn about the issues affecting individuals with disabilities. Now that the integration of students with disabilities is the law of the United States, all current and future teachers, regardless of what they teach, will be working with students with disabilities.

Prelude: The Name Game

Ted, an idealistic education major, enters the grounds of the school where he has been assigned to student teach. After signing in at the front office, Ted proceeds to what will be his classroom. The first student he encounters in the hallway asks him a strange question.

"You here to teach the boxes?"

The befuddled education major does not know how to respond. Ted didn't think students would be this hard to understand before even setting foot in the classroom.

"You're a box. So you gonna teach the boxes?" the student asks again, this time with a hint of annoyance.

Ted, it should be noted, has an obvious physical disability. He, however, fails to put together that a box means a person with a disability. By this point, the student has wandered off muttering about teachers never knowing anything, so Ted timidly makes his way to his assigned classroom. Upon meeting his cooperating teacher, Ted quickly asks what box means and why he is one. The cooperating teacher tells him that "box" is another name for disabled students. The special education classes at this school are taught in portables that resemble boxcars, resulting in the students with disabilities being called boxes.

Ted is disturbed to find that his cooperating teacher and the other teachers use the term, as though it were perfectly acceptable. During the course of his time there, Ted finds himself frequently being referred to by students and teachers as a box. He broaches the issue at three different faculty meetings but is told that the term means no harm and he shouldn't be so touchy. When Ted tells administrators at his university about the term and how uncomfortable it makes him feel and how much he fears it may be hurting the students with disabilities at the school, the administrators tell Ted "not to make trouble" even though "that's what you handicapped people do." Ted is told he should be grateful for the opportunity to do his internship and not be so sensitive about what he is called.

The language used to refer to individuals with disabilities in many quotations in this text may surprise you. Writers, critics, state governments, the federal government, and the courts have not always described individuals with disabilities in the kindest of terms. In some cases, the usage has improved over the years, but in other cases, the persistent use of derogatory terms to describe individuals with disabilities is jaw dropping. Yet, the language provides insight into the discrimination faced by individuals with disabilities. Members of the judiciary, who do so much to interpret and shape the laws affecting the disabled, often have used outdated terminology in opinions. Though the United States Congress has stopped using the term "handicapped" in legislation, it only got around to doing so in about 1990. We have opted not to indicate the use of offensive terminology in quotes in this text simply because it would be a rather constant procedure. This decision, however, should not be taken as any sort of tacit endorsement of any derogatory terms used to describe individuals with disabilities. In each case an inappropriate term appears in a quote, the offense and outrage are simply to be assumed.

Some may feel this emphasis on usage of certain terms to describe individuals with disabilities is overly sensitive. However, those who feel this way are asked to consider how all historically oppressed groups have been assigned many designations they find deeply offensive or inappropriate. Many of these groups have made significant progress in changing attitudes regarding what terms are appropriate to use. Minorities of all kinds have had difficult struggles to escape the burdens of certain derogatory terms that had been socially acceptable. It is now virtually unthinkable that an educated person would use the disparaging terms these groups have worked so hard to shed. Certainly no teacher could ever in good conscience use such words to describe these groups in the classroom or refer to a member of the class by one of these terms. Nevertheless, usage of derogatory terms to describe the disabled remains commonplace and institutionalized, in schools and in innumerable other places. Derogatory terms about most groups have been stricken from legal and legislative dialogues, but are still frequently used when referring to individuals with disabilities (Perlin, 1992). How do you refer to students who receive special education? What do you call a parking place especially reserved for individuals with mobility impairments?

To be perfectly clear, don't ever refer to an individual with a disability as "handicapped," "invalid," "crippled," "retarded," "mental," "abnormal," "unhealthy," "backward," "differently abled" or any other term that conveys or implies a sense of inferiority. Further, don't address or describe a disabled person in a manner that equates the impairment and the person with impairment, such as "cripple" or "handicap." Individuals with disabilities have disabilities; they are not defined by their disabilities. When talking to or about individuals with disabilities, use common sense and treat them with the same respect that you would accord any other minority group.

In writing this text, we have tried to use the terms preferred by each group of individuals with disabilities. For example, a person who employs a wheelchair to get around is a wheelchair user. Trying to be precise in the terminology may not always work. As a friend of one of the authors of this text once sighed: "I started out blind, then I became legally blind, and now I'm visually impaired. Being visually impaired sounds more pleasant, but I still can't see." The terms change and progress with time and alterations to social attitudes. Yet, the use of the most neutral terms may not make everyone happy.

In interacting with members of the disability community, you may find some have taken to referring to themselves with certain slurs as an attempt to gain a certain sense of empowerment over the discriminatory terms. One author once asserted that the best word for describing himself and other people with mobility impairments is "cripple, a word which I prefer to either *handicapped* or *disabled*, each of which seems to me a euphemism for the realities facing us" (Kriegel, 1982, p. 52). Though he may prefer that term, many people with similar impairments would find that same term terribly offensive. That author, however, is taking a term meant to inflict hurt and turning it into an affirmation of the reality of the self. This technique has been effectively employed by a number of groups, including the African-American community and the alternative lifestyle community. To subvert the pain and discomfort associated with the most offensive slur directed at their community, some African Americans refer to themselves and other members of their community by certain terms. Similarly, members of the alternative lifestyle community have turned several derogatory terms into terms of empowerment within their community. Not all members of these communities approve of such language, but enough do to have brought about a new usage for these discriminatory terms.

Inspired by these other groups, some members of the disability community have taken to using certain derogatory terms in a self-referential manner. Fairly common examples are the phrases "Crip is Hip" and "Crip Power," which have adorned signs, logos, and t-shirts for some disability rights groups. Please realize, though, that if a member of a minority group uses a derogatory term in a self-referential manner, it is not an open invitation for people who are not members of that community to use the term in any fashion.

One of the quickest ways to cause people to lose interest in your ideas is to be negative. Unfortunately, many important topics do not get the study and understanding they deserve because people discussing the situation focus too much on what was and is wrong. That is not the approach of this text. Despite the preceding few pages on the name game, this book won't harangue you. This book won't guilt you. This book won't tell you that you're a bad person. What this book does do is present the legal and sociological realities of being disabled and working with the disabled in the United States. Some of the material will probably shock you. Other parts will likely depress you. That is an unfortunate part of the reality, however. This nation, for all its wonderful accomplishments, has done some terrible things to the disabled population, especially in the area of education. Some gigantic problems still remain. There is considerable room for hope based on the tremendous progress made since 1975, but 25 years is hardly enough time to undo the oppression and bias of many centuries. However, things really are getting better and the authors of this book are optimistic about the situation.

Disability Matters

Chapter 1

The Relationships between Disability, Education, and the Law

A 12-year-old boy in a wheelchair arrives for his first day at his new middle school. Because the school district does not have an accessible bus for him to ride, his mother has to rearrange her work schedule to get him to school. When he arrives at the school, he can't get in. The school is an old building, and the only entrance is at the top of a flight of concrete stairs. He cannot get his chair up the many steps. He cannot even get in his own school.

The parents of a 6-year-old deaf girl are told she cannot start kindergarten. The school district thinks educating her would be too expensive. The parents are told the district only spends money on "the healthy, normal children." Trying to teach someone who could not hear would be "a waste of money." She is not allowed to enroll in school.

Leslie graduated at the top of her class in Secondary Education. She had excelled in her coursework and successfully completed her practicum experiences and her student teaching internship. She could not find a school district willing to hire a visually impaired English teacher.

These scenarios may sound unthinkable, but they are accurate representations of sad events which have been repeated innumerable times in the United States. Think back to your first day of school, or your first day as the new kid at a school. Everyone clearly recalls the feelings of nervousness, anticipation, and excitement. You hope you will make friends quickly. You hope you'll like your classes. You hope to get good grades. You hope your teachers won't be too intimidating. You hope you remembered to bring your lunch. And if you have a disability, you hope the school allows you to attend. Not many people who read the previous sentence can relate to it. For most of American history, however, the central fear for disabled children in going to school was not being provided the basic dignity of entering the building and being allowed to learn. At various times, the disabled have been deemed uneducable, been sent to segregated institutions that were more like prisons than schools, been subject to sterilization rather than education, and been denied access to public schools for being too expensive and too much work. These are just a few of the historical biases that prevented the disabled from becoming disabled students in any real sense.

The reasons for this history of discrimination are varied, reflecting the biases of the nation changing with time. Though the requirement that each disabled student receive a free appropriate public school education is now legally mandated, discrimination in education against the disabled is still rampant, affecting both disabled students and disabled teachers. Three major federal laws protect the disabled: the Rehabilitation Act, the Americans with Disabilities Act, and the Individuals with Disabilities Education Act. Many individual states provide other types of legal protection for the disabled. All of these laws are designed to prevent discrimination.

Such laws are still quite recent developments in the history of the United States. This nation went almost 200 years, 197 years to be precise, without offering any meaningful legal protections to the disabled. Laws protecting the disabled, however, have become a central part of every public school. All individuals who are going to teach in a public school, whether or not they have a disability, must be familiar with these laws and how they affect the disabled individuals, students and teachers, in the school community. To understand the origins of the need for protection of the disabled in public schools, it may be best to start at the history of American education, since it is impossible "to explain the present *by* the present" (Ladurie, 1979, p. 119).

A BRIEF HISTORY OF EDUCATION AND DISABILITY IN THE UNITED STATES

In the United States, the movement in favor of free public common schools did not even begin in earnest until after 1830 (Rippa, 1992). To the contemporary mind, it may seem surprising to note that the very first public high school in the United States was established in Boston in 1821, teaching exclusively male students (Rippa, 1992). The movement toward providing free public education was initiated by the unlikely alliance of humanitarian activists and labor unions, eventually prompting generally apathetic parents to demand egalitarian common schooling (Curoe, 1926).

By 1860, the free public school movement had gained complete acceptance in most northern American cities, with more than 100 free public high schools in Massachusetts alone (Rippa, 1992).

These free public schools did not welcome disabled students, however. The term *special education* did not emerge until the 1880s, with Alexander Graham Bell popularizing the use of the term (Winzer, 1993). Systematized education for those with disabilities barely predated the creation of the term. The first private education for the blind in the United States was offered in 1812, and private schooling for deaf individuals first began in 1817 (Shapiro, 1993). These disabled students could receive education only at separate residential institutions, which were nothing like the schools other students attended (Winzer, 1993). The residential schools were "warehouses where people were isolated from society. Children with disabilities apparently were not worthy of investment" (Smith, 2001, p. 15).

In the education of all groups, the United States lagged behind many nations. For example, the Republic of Poland–Lithuania established the first state department of education in 1773, while one of Napoleon's first acts after becoming emperor of France in 1804 was to create a state educational system run by a centralized education ministry (Davies, 1998). Paraguay, upon gaining independence from Spain in 1814, immediately introduced free, compulsory elementary education for all children from age seven (Landes, 1998). Even with these differences in evolution of general public education, the United States was strikingly far behind many European nations in providing educational opportunities to disabled students; for example, in France, deaf students were first schooled in 1748, blind students in 1782, and mentally impaired students in 1832 (Winzer, 1993). Denmark mandated compulsory education for children with sensory impairments in 1817 (Hansen, 1916). By 1893, both France and England had legally mandated free primary education for disabled children (Winzer, 1993). In Canada, free compulsory education was first provided for blind and deaf children in the 1880s (Winzer, 1993). In the United States, the first special education training classes for teachers were not offered until 1905 (Smith, 2001).

Before the latter part of the nineteenth century, the only attempts to educate disabled individuals were made by brave private tutors, the earliest recorded being in 1679 when a teacher named Phillip Nelson attempted to teach a deaf child (Fay, 1899). Nelson had to stop when the local church denounced his work as blasphemy for attempting to perform a miracle (Fay, 1899). Obviously, the concept of teaching the disabled faced stiff, though not quite rational, opposition in the United States. Part of this situation resulted from the prevailing attitude in the colonial era that individuals with disabilities were a social detriment best deported and forced to return to England (Shapiro, 1993).

From the beginning of European settlement in America, town schools

sprang up in New England (Rippa, 1992). Though nothing like public
schools of today, these private Latin grammar schools in the Northeast
offered an education mainly to boys. When free public education was first
offered in northern cities, hundreds of years after private education was
available, not only were disabled individuals excluded from the public
schools, the vast majority of disabled individuals did not yet have the opportunity to be educated anywhere at all.

Before the disabled of the United States would get a chance to participate
in public education, they would first have to survive the nineteenth-century
movements of segregation, sterilization, and legislation intended to control
or eliminate the disabled population, each heavily influenced by the theory
of eugenics. Sir Francis Galton, the English scholar who launched the science of meteorology with his 1863 book *Meteorographica*, spearheaded
the movement in favor of eugenics, the practice of selective human breed-
ing. In a series of very popular books, such as 1869's *Hereditary Genius:
Its Laws and Consequences*, Galton wrote of the need to improve human
standards by eliminating undesirable elements, best accomplished by not
allowing some people to procreate. His theories were based on no science
whatsoever, powered only by racism and other onerous cultural biases. In
spite of this fact, or perhaps because of it, eugenics became popular in the
late nineteenth century and early twentieth century in the United States,
leading to many disturbing proposals by legislators and other policymakers.
Some of these horrifying ideas included forcibly preventing the disabled
from having children and placing all disabled individuals on islands by
themselves, isolated by gender. The less threatening proposals included simply locking away all disabled individuals or segregating them from the rest
of society in an isolated part of a sparsely populated state.

In the United States, educational opportunities came slowly and sporad-
ically for individuals with disabilities. Kentucky established the first state
school for the deaf in 1823; Boston established the first day school for deaf
students in 1869 (Weintraub & Ballard, 1982). Deaf students were the
most likely to receive an education of all students with disabilities. In 1864,
President Lincoln signed into law the bill creating Gallaudet College, a
college for deaf individuals. The first certification programs for special education were created in Minnesota in 1915, and the first cooperative agreements between school districts for provision of special education were
created in Pennsylvania in 1919 (Weintraub & Ballard, 1982).

In the early twentieth century, education of students with sensory disabilities was gaining limited acceptance, though nine states still did not provide education for blind students as late as 1930 (Winzer, 1993). In 1950,
fewer than 20 percent of disabled children were receiving an education
(Ballard, Ramirez, & Weintraub, 1982; Winzer, 1993). By 1962, only 16
states educated the mildly mentally impaired; into the mid-1970s, some

states simply did not allow disabled children to attend public schools (Smith, 2001). The states that did allow disabled students to attend public schools still had exclusionary practices; for example, in 1958, the Supreme Court of Illinois held that state law could not be interpreted to allow a mentally impaired child to attend public school (*Department of Public Welfare v. Haas*, 1958). A 1969 study found that only seven states were educating more than 51 percent of children with disabilities (Zettel & Ballard, 1982). Prior to the 1970s, education of the disabled depended on the "generosity of private charity and the largess of state and local governments" and those few disabled children who were allowed into the public schools faced "widespread neglect and abuse from schools" and "isolation and minimal services" (Tweedie, 1983, p. 49).

State courts spent much of the twentieth century holding the disabled to be without any meaningful educational rights. In 1893, the Supreme Judicial Court of Massachusetts permitted the state to expel a student who was labeled "weak in mind" (*Watson v. City of Cambridge*, 1893). In 1919, the Wisconsin Supreme Court held that a child who drooled, had a speech impediment, and suffered facial contortions should not be allowed into public schools in spite of the fact the student had demonstrated the ability to academically and physically benefit from school (*Beattie v. Board of Education of City of Antigo*, 1919). In 1934, a father unsuccessfully sued to have his mentally disabled son admitted to public school in Ohio (*Board of Education v. State ex rel. Goldman*, 1934). State courts frequently upheld the institutionalization of the disabled on either the grounds of "protection of society" (*Ex Parte Zeigler*, 1944) or prevention of procreation (*In re Masters*, 1944). In 1927, the United States Supreme Court actually held that involuntary sterilization of the disabled by state authorities was constitutional to "prevent our being swamped with incompetence" and to "prevent those who are manifestly unfit from continuing their kind" (*Buck v. Bell*, 1927, p. 207). This case has never been over-ruled; even in the last 20 years, involuntary sterilization of the disabled has persisted as an issue in some states (*In re Moe*, 1982; *In re Terwilliger*, 1982; *Poe v. Lynchburg Training School and Hospital*, 1981). More than 60,000 people in 30 states were victims of sterilization laws. In 2002, Governor Mark R. Warner of Virginia issued the first official apology from any of the states that practiced sterilization.

THE JUDICIARY STEPS IN, PART I: INITIAL RECOGNITION OF THE RIGHTS OF THE DISABLED

Brown v. Board of Education (1954) stated that "it is doubtful that any child may reasonably be expected to succeed in life if he is denied the opportunity of an education" and such an opportunity "is a right which must be made available to all on equal terms" (p. 493). Though *Brown* addressed the rights of all children to an equal public education regardless of race, the Supreme Court was, for the first time, establishing that the American public schools were open to all and that everyone deserved to receive equal treatment in them. The Court's holding embodies the principle that the public schools of the United States are meant to provide an equal education to all. However, the extension of this principle to disabled students of the United States has been a very difficult process.

An early-1970s case about Pennsylvania law was the first instance of the judiciary specifically holding that disabled students had a constitutional right to receive a public education. In *Pennsylvania Association for Retarded Children (PARC) v. Commonwealth of Pennsylvania* (1971), the federal district court held that the exclusion of mentally disabled children from public school was unconstitutional. Since the state had endeavored to provide a free public education to all the children in the state, Pennsylvania could not deny access to that free public education to students with disabilities. The Court established an evaluation process for level of educability and appropriate placement for each mentally disabled student, ranging from mainstreaming into general education classes to placement in a special education classroom. The court stated that only in the most extreme circumstances could home schooling or another setting outside school even be considered. The ground-breaking *PARC* case immediately inspired disabled rights groups in 36 other states to file suits against their state governments (Spring, 1993).

Disabled students, as a group, first began to gain specific federal rights to public education with the decision in *Mills v. Board of Education* (1972), invalidating the District of Columbia's policy of excluding exceptional children, including those who would now be considered to be disabled, from attending public schools. The school district had been excluding, expelling, reassigning, and refusing to admit exceptional students with no due process of law; over 18,000 disabled students had been denied an education as a result of this policy. The court held this policy was a clear violation of the students' rights to receive a public education. The court established the mandate that all disabled children deserve a public education, harshly dismissing the school district's claims that it did not have enough funding to educate disabled students:

If sufficient funds are not available to finance all of the services and programs that are needed and desirable in the system, then the available funds must be expended equitably in such a manner that no child is entirely excluded from a publicly supported education consistent with his needs and ability to benefit therefrom. The inadequacies of the District of Columbia Public School System, whether occasioned by insufficient funding or administrative inefficiency, certainly cannot be permitted to bear more heavily on the "exceptional" or the handicapped child than on the normal child. (p. 876)

The court further established detailed due process rights for disabled students and gave parents a right of notice and appeal for hearings and decisions regarding the education of their children. The holding in this case provided the basic framework for most state and federal legislation for protecting the interests of disabled children. This court provided the first great victory in the fight for educational rights for the disabled.

The Rehabilitation Act

In 1973, Congress passed the Rehabilitation Act to protect the rights of the disabled from outdated and biased perceptions and laws to which the disabled were subject and to educate a populace that was unfamiliar with and insensitive to the obstacles confronting individuals with disabilities. The Rehabilitation Act is codified at 29 U.S.C.A. sec. 701 *et seq.*; Section 504 of the Rehabilitation Act is primarily codified at 29 U.S.C.A. sec. 794. The Rehabilitation Act protects anyone who "(i) has a physical or mental impairment which substantially limits one or more of such person's major life activities, (ii) has a record of such impairment, or (iii) is regarded as having such an impairment" (34 C.F.R. sec. 104.3(j)). Section 504 of the Rehabilitation Act specifies: "No otherwise qualified individual with a disability in the United States . . . shall, solely by reason of his or her disability, be excluded from the participation in, be denied the benefits of, or be subjected to discrimination under any program or activity receiving Federal financing assistance" (29 U.S.C.A. sec. 794). Since all public schools receive federal funding, they are all subject to the regulations of the Rehabilitation Act. Under the act, "program or activity" includes all operations of state educational agencies and local educational agencies, regardless of whether the particular action involved directly received federal funding (29 U.S.C.A. sec. 794). The Rehabilitation Act establishes and protects the basic rights of disabled students and disabled teachers to fair and equal treatment in public schools.

The Rehabilitation Act makes schools responsible for identifying students with disabilities and for providing parental notice of the identification and placement for the identified students (29 U.S.C.A. sec. 794). Section 504 specifies five mandated principles that establish the protection of the rights of disabled children to receive a public education: (1) location and notification, (2) free appropriate public education, (3) educational setting, (4) evaluation and placement, and (5) procedural safeguards (34 C.F.R. sec. 104.3). The guarantees of rights by Section 504 established the basic set of legal rights for disabled students to receive an equitable public education. However, the procedural protections under the Rehabilitation Act are more limited than under other laws; for example, the notice of a hearing does not have to be in writing and there is no parental consent requirement for the placement to occur (34 C.F.R. sec. 104.3).

For teachers with disabilities, the Rehabilitation Act is also tremendously significant. As all public schools are covered by the requirements of the Rehabilitation Act, a public school cannot discriminate against an otherwise qualified teacher with a disability simply because he or she is disabled. Section 504 is violated if a person with a disability is denied a position "solely by reason of his disability" (29 U.S.C.A. sec. 794). This means that a public school cannot refuse to hire, promote, or otherwise employ a teacher with a disability because of the disability. Under the act, disabled individuals must first establish they are otherwise qualified for the position and that the employer can reasonably accommodate the special needs of the individual (29 U.S.C.A. sec. 794). In the context of education, this process is fairly simple. A graduate of an accredited college with a degree in education and a teaching certificate likely would meet the otherwise qualified requirement. The special needs are usually reasonable so long as they do not result in prohibitive expense or endanger the well-being of others. In the context of schools, a determination of reasonable accommodations for a disabled individual who can "perform the essential functions of the position in question without endangering the health and safety of the individual or others" includes "the reasonableness of the cost of any necessary workplace accommodation, the availability of alternatives therefor, or other appropriate relief in order to achieve an equitable and appropriate remedy" (*Wood v. Omaha School District*, 1994, p. 669). An unreasonable accommodation is something that would impose undue hardship on the operation of the program at issue.

Second, the disabled individual must establish that the reason for the employment decision was a result of the disability. This second requirement is more difficult, but still fairly clear in the context of education (29 U.S.C.A. sec. 794). Courts have been willing to infer that negative employment decisions against disabled public school employees, unless the public school can clearly demonstrate to the contrary, are a result of discrimination based on the individual's disability. The legal victories of two disabled teachers demonstrate how the Rehabilitation Act can protect teachers. In 1974, a blind English teacher, who held a Professional Certificate from the Pennsylvania Department of Education, won the legal right to take the Philadelphia Teacher's Examination after having been previously denied the opportunity because the school district claimed blindness excluded her from the right to teach (*Gurmankin v. Costanzo*, 1977). She passed the exam and became a teacher in the school district (*Gurmankin v. Costanzo*, 1980). The school district apparently did not learn its lesson, as it then refused to award her seniority at the proper time, for which the district received an order granting the teacher retroactive seniority and a severe reprimand from the federal court (*Gurmankin v. Costanzo*, 1980).

In 1987, the Supreme Court specifically held that if an individual is otherwise qualified to teach, the individual cannot be prevented from teaching as a result of a disability (*School Board of Nassau County v. Arline*, 1987). Gene Arline was an elementary teacher in Nassau County, Florida between 1966 and 1977. In 1978, she suffered a relapse of tuberculosis which she had contracted as a child and which she had been free of for more than two decades; in 1979, she was fired for having tuberculosis. At the hearing for her dismissal, the school board actually stated that Arline was being discharged "not because she had done anything wrong," but because she had a "continued reoccurence [*sic*] of tuberculosis" (p. 276). The Supreme Court, while refraining from commentary on the poor grammar of the school district, did hold the firing was a violation of the Rehabilitation Act because Arline was otherwise qualified to teach and the school district specified that it fired her because of her disability. The Court did leave open the possibility that she could properly be dismissed if the school demonstrated that her condition posed a serious health risk to her students or co-workers.

The principles in the Rehabilitation Act have survived intact over the past 30 years, still comprising the core statement of rights for disabled students and disabled teachers in public schools.

From EAHCA to IDEA

The Individuals with Disabilities Education Act (IDEA) was first passed in 1975 as the Education for All Handicapped Children Act (EAHCA), which established the standard of a "free appropriate public education" for disabled children. The statute codifying IDEA is located at 20 U.S.C.A. sec. 1400 *et seq.* and the federal regulations for the implementation of IDEA are located at 34 C.F.R. sec. 300 *et seq.* The act compels schools to place disabled children in the least restrictive environment possible and to integrate the disabled children into classes with non-disabled children as often as possible (34 C.F.R. sec. 300.550–300.552). The placement of the disabled student is to be as close to the child's home as available and appropriate (34 C.F.R. sec. 300.550–300.552). The act establishes that public schools on the state and local level would be held accountable for failure to properly educate disabled students (20 U.S.C.A. sec. 1400–1485). EAHCA was amended in 1986 when Congress passed the Handicapped Children's Protection Act, which awards attorney's fees and costs to parents who successfully litigate a dispute over the status of a disabled child (20 U.S.C.A. sec. 1400, 1415). Parents also have the right to sue for compensatory education, damages, and other appropriate relief (20 U.S.C.A. sec. 1415).

These acts created some significant protections of the rights of disabled students. However, the flaws in the statutes created new forms of discrimination. Rather than being simply excluded from public schools, many disabled children faced isolationist or inhumane circumstances at public schools. Because EAHCA did not require parental consent to the placement and required schools merely to mainstream disabled students when the school determined it was beneficial, many disabled students found themselves in difficult situations. The problems were likely most pronounced at public schools in small communities that had rather small populations of disabled students. The parents of these students were often faced with the choice of removing their child from public school or accepting the school's treatment of the child.

IDEA, a modified and renamed version of EACHA, was designed to rectify many of the flaws that the previous versions of the law had allowed to occur (20 U.S.C.A. sec. 1400–1485). The act was based on extensive congressional findings that emphasized the need for further improvement in the education of the disabled. The act prioritizes educating disabled students in as normal a situation as possible by including disabled students in general classrooms to the maximum extent feasible (IDEA regulations, 34 C.F.R. sec. 330.550). IDEA also provided for more parental involvement in the placement and education of the student (20 U.S.C.A. sec. 1414). Rather than simply being informed of the school's decision regarding the education of their child, parents were given a greater right to participate in the decisions regarding the education of their children (20 U.S.C.A. sec. 1414). IDEA also added due process requirements and appeal procedures to protect the rights of disabled students (20 U.S.C.A. sec. 1414–1415; 34 C.F.R. sec. 300.503–300.528). The greatest advance provided by IDEA, however, was the grant of the right of private action against state agencies not complying with IDEA (20 U.S.C.A. sec. 1414–1415; 34 C.F.R. sec. 300.503–300.507). Parents were given a legal avenue to enforce the rights of their disabled children when dealing with discriminatory school systems.

The right of private suit against the states makes IDEA a significant tool for improvement of the education of the disabled, as parents were given a heightened enforcement technique to protect the rights of their children. If a school system is not providing the appropriate accommodations or is providing no accommodations at all, the parents have the ability to sue the school district in order to assure the free appropriate public education for the disabled child, designed to meet the specific needs of the individual child (20 U.S.C.A. sec. 1414). Under IDEA, an "individualized education program" (known as an "IEP") has to be created for the disabled child and reviewed annually (20 U.S.C.A. sec. 1401–1415; 34 C.F.R. sec. 300.340–300.349). A disabled child must be placed in the least restrictive educational environment possible, being mainstreamed into general education classes as much as possible (20 U.S.C.A. sec. 1400–1485). To protect the rights of the disabled student, IDEA has a series of substantial safeguards, including parental access to relevant school records; requirement of written notice to parents of proposed changes in their child's educational program; a full, fair and impartial hearing, with legal counsel if so desired, for educational decisions; the opportunity to appeal any decisions to the courts; the right of the child to remain in current placement while hearings are pending (known as the "stay-put" provision); and the ability of parents to be reimbursed for legal costs and fees if they prevail (20 U.S.C.A. sec. 1414–1415).

One other important advance of IDEA is that a disabled child has the right to an education without having to demonstrate that the educational program will be definitively beneficial. IDEA has created a "zero-reject" situation where every child "regardless of the severity of their handicap" deserves an education (*Timothy W. v. Rochester, New Hampshire School District*, 1989, p. 960). Zero-reject embodies the principle that no student will again "be subjected to the deplorable state of affairs which existed at the time of the act's passage, in which millions of handicapped children received inadequate education or none at all" (pp. 960–961). The court concluded that IDEA "mandates an appropriate public education for all handicapped children, regardless of the level of achievement that such children might attain" (pp. 960–961).

In its present form, IDEA delineates and codifies many specific rights and protections for disabled students in public schools. Thus far, IDEA has provided a patient accumulation of successes in improving the conditions for disabled students in public schools.

The Americans with Disabilities Act

Enacted in 1990, the Americans with Disabilities Act (ADA) prohibits discrimination against persons with disabilities by various private and public institutions, including state governments, and provides a mechanism for legal protection and remedies (42 U.S.C.A. sec. 12101–12213). The ADA works in conjunction with the rights and protections granted by the Rehabilitation Act (29 U.S.C.A. sec. 701 *et seq.*). The ADA defines a disability as a "physical or mental impairment that substantially limits one or more major life activities; a record of such an impairment; or being regarded as having such an impairment" (42 U.S.C.A. sec. 12102(2)). The Department of Justice regulations derived from the ADA specify disabilities as "any physiological disorder or condition, cosmetic disfigurement, or anatomical loss" affecting, among other body systems, neurological functioning, and "[a]ny mental or psychological disorder" (28 C.F.R. sec. 35.104). Title II of the ADA instructs the instrumentalities of local and state governments that "no qualified individual with a disability shall . . . be excluded from participation in or be denied the benefits of the services, programs, or activities of a public entity" (42 U.S.C.A. sec. 12132). The Rehabilitation Act provides those same protections for federal agencies and any agency receiving federal assistance (29 U.S.C.A. sec. 794). Ultimately, these statutes are intended to prevent discrimination in government, employment, education, physical accessibility, health services, welfare, and social services (42 U.S.C.A. sec. 12101 *et seq.*).

According to the ADA, a person who has a "physical or mental impairment" which "substantially limits" any major life activity is considered disabled under the ADA (42 U.S.C.A. sec. 12102). When an individual cannot perform a major life activity, such as "caring for oneself, performing manual tasks, walking, seeing, hearing, speaking, breathing, learning and working," the individual is a member of the legally protected class of the disabled (29 C.F.R. sec. 1630.2). To protect these individuals, the ADA was enacted with separate sections, known as Titles, meant to address three different areas of discrimination. Title I addresses employment discrimination by private employers; Title II addresses discrimination by state and local governments; and Title III addresses discrimination in places of public accommodation and commercial facilities, ranging from parks to stores to licensing agencies (42 U.S.C.A. sec. 12181(7)). Title III also applies to each "nursery, elementary, secondary, undergraduate, or postgraduate private school, or other place of education" (42 U.S.C.A. sec. 12181(7)(J)). Title II, in covering "any State or local government" and "any department, agency, special purpose district, or other instrumentality of a State or States or local government," clearly serves to prohibit discrimination in public schools (42 U.S.C.A. sec. 12131).

Title II of the ADA has been determined to protect access to and use of such disparate public entities as universities (*Darian v. University of Massachusetts Boston*, 1987), courts (*People v. Caldwell*, 1995), and prisons (*Saunders v. Horn*, 1996). The ADA, however, has not had that dramatic effect on disabled students in public schools. The primary reason for this limited impact is the substantial overlap between Title II of the ADA and Section 504 of the Rehabilitation Act. When the ADA was enacted, the Rehabilitation Act already prevented discrimination against the disabled by any entity receiving federal financial assistance. As all public schools are partially funded by the federal government, they were already prohibited from engaging in discrimination against the disabled. Further, IDEA already existed to designate the rights of the disabled in public schools.

THE JUDICIARY STEPS IN, PART II: LIMITATIONS ON THE RIGHTS OF THE DISABLED

Not all of the recent legal decisions about disability have been a help to individuals with disabilities, especially several decisions of the Supreme Court of the United States that limited the rights of the disabled. The federal laws that were established by Congress to protect the rights of the disabled, especially the ADA, have been curtailed by Supreme Court holdings. The first indication that the Supreme Court would not give the same value to the rights of the disabled as Congress came in 1982. Implementation of EAHCA was tempered by the Supreme Court in *Board of Education of the Hendrick Hudson School District v. Rowley* (1982). In *Rowley*, the Court held that the laws protecting disabled students did not mandate that they be provided every form of assistance possible to improve their chance of receiving an equal education. Instead, the Court decided that schools need only provide some educational assistance to make the educational environment somewhat more conducive to learning for the student. Under *Rowley*, making the educational environment a little bit closer to equal was good enough to pass constitutional muster.

In *City of Cleburne v. City of Cleburne Living Center, Inc.* (1985), the Supreme Court addressed the rights of the disabled to seek general legal protection as a group. Though the case dealt only with the mentally impaired, the ruling is the only time the Supreme Court has addressed such significant disability rights issues. In *Cleburne*, the Court ruled that "the large and amorphous class of the mentally retarded" did not constitute a class of citizens protected by the equal protection clause (pp. 445–446). A group that is considered a protected class under the equal protection clause receives the highest level of protection provided by the judiciary against discrimination. By deciding the mentally disabled were not a protected class under the equal protection clause, the Court made clear that the disabled would not receive the same kind of legal protection from oppression that has been given to other minorities. The Supreme Court has recognized national origin (*Korematsu v. United States*, 1944), race (*Brown v. Board of Education*, 1954), alienage (*Graham v. Richardson*, 1971), gender (*Craig v. Boren*, 1976), and illegitimacy (*Trimble v. Gordon*, 1977) as being classes covered by the equal protection clause. A persuasive argument can be made that individuals with disabilities should be covered by the equal protection clause (Burgdorf & Burgdorf, 1975). In *Cleburne*, the Court did not acknowledge all of the mentally impaired individuals in the nation as a protected class, mainly because it constituted a "large and amorphous class" (pp. 445–446). The Court did, however, assert, "legislation that distinguishes between the mentally retarded and others must be rationally related to a legitimate governmental purpose" (pp. 445–446). The *Cleburne* ruling does not clearly settle the question if smaller, more definable groups of disabled, such as those with the exact same condition, could qualify as a protected class. The ruling does, however, help define how legislation may be used to affect the disabled. In *Cleburne*, the Supreme Court emphasized the requirement of a rational relationship to "a legitimate government purpose" for limitations on the rights of the mentally impaired (pp. 445–446).

The Supreme Court's next limitation of the rights of the disabled came in 1999 with a set of cases issued on the same day. *Sutton v. United Air Lines, Inc.* (1999), *Murphy v. United Parcel Service* (1999), and *Albertsons, Inc. v. Kirkingburg* (1999) established a new limitation on who qualifies for protection under disability laws. Under these cases, the Court established the standard that an individual can only qualify for legal protection under disability law if the individual is limited in a major life activity after the maximum corrections and mitigating measures are taken. For example, one cannot be considered disabled under the ADA for having profound loss of eyesight if that sight problem can be corrected into the normal range through lenses or surgery. In *Sutton*, the Court wrote: "Congress did not intend to bring under the statute's protection all those whose uncorrected conditions amount to disabilities" (p. 484). This set of cases places a burden on the disabled to prove that they remain disabled in spite of whatever corrective measures might exist. If an individual has profound loss of eyesight that cannot be corrected into the normal range with any available measures, then that individual qualifies for protection as a disabled individual. The individual, however, may be put in the position of having to demonstrate that he or she would remain disabled no matter what corrective measures were taken.

In 2001, the Supreme Court significantly limited the impact of the ADA. In *Board of Trustees of the University of Alabama v. Garrett*, the Supreme Court modified Title II of the ADA, the section of the ADA that makes state and local governments liable for violations of the rights of the disabled. The Court held that state and local governments were not liable to suit for monetary damages under the ADA, but still could be forced to comply with the act. Though this may not sound like a large difference, the effect is sizable. Instead of having to fear paying out large sums of money for violating the rights of the disabled, state and local governments now only must contend with the rather insignificant threat of being told to stop discriminating by the courts. Whether this will impact the education of the disabled has yet to be determined.

THE DISABLED IN SCHOOLS TODAY

Over the course of the struggle to win rights for disabled individuals in schools, public attitudes have not necessarily changed as much as we would like to think they have. A veteran educator recently described special education as still being "a life sentence of ostracism and humiliation" from the rest of the student body (Gatto, 2000, p. 7). In *Alexander v. Choate* (1985), the Supreme Court observed that discrimination against the disabled is "most often the product . . . of benign neglect" resulting from "apathetic attitudes rather than affirmative animus" (pp. 295–297). In *Pushkin v. Regents of the University of Colorado* (1981), the Tenth Circuit observed that discrimination "often occurs under the guise of extending a helping hand" (p. 1385). One disability-rights activist has recently identified a trend among state and local governments to use legislation to act as "a functional block" to solutions to disability issues (Crawford, 1999, p. 7). These varying perceptions are all accurate assessments of the current state of attitudes toward the disabled in the United States, especially in the area of education. The major federal laws do provide a guarantee of some level of educational rights for disabled individuals; however, a great many more steps must yet be taken.

Though social attitudes toward the disabled population have improved, the disabled are still very much a minority in status and social power. "Disabled people are marginalized and excluded from mainstream society. . . . Disabled people represent one of the poorest groups in Western society" (Kitchin, 1998, p. 343). No longer can a school deny a disabled child physical access to a school or refuse to educate a disabled child. Some significant progress has been made. Over the past decade, the number of students with disabilities educated in general education classrooms has increased consistently, while the number of students with disabilities in resource rooms has declined (McLesky, Henry, & Hodges, 1998). However, disabled students and disabled teachers in public schools still face tremendous challenges. Students with mild disabilities are still dramatically more likely to be educated in general education classrooms than students with more profound disabilities (Hobbs & Westling, 1998). The largest portion of students with disabilities in separate schools are students with serious emotional disorders, multiple disabilities, and deaf-blindness (McLesky, Henry, & Hodges, 1999). Further, as the age of a student with a disability increases, the likelihood of placement in separate classrooms, schools, and facilities also increases (Hobbs & Westling, 1998). Many of the current challenges for disabled students and teachers in schools are less obvious than the challenges that have been corrected by the federal laws, but they are just as real.

In *Plyler v. Doe* (1982), Justice William Brennan, speaking for the United States Supreme Court, wrote:

Education provides the basic tools by which individuals might lead economically productive lives to the benefit of us all. . . . We cannot ignore the significant social costs borne by our Nation when select groups are denied the means to absorb the values and skills upon which our social order rests. (p. 221)

Teachers have the greatest ability to ensure that students with disabilities receive a meaningful education. If teachers, administrators, parents, and other members of the school community do not actively work to preserve the legal rights given to students with disabilities, those rights are of little value. To fail to adequately and correctly educate students with disabilities is to ignore the social costs Justice Brennan feared and to run the risk of allowing education of the disabled to slip back toward the opprobrious level of the past. Every current and future educator must understand and apply the legal mandates regarding the education of students with disabilities for these rights to be maintained and for students with disabilities to receive a fair, appropriate public education and participate fully in society.

CROSS-EXAMINATIONS AND REBUTTALS

What can the historical treatment of the disabled teach:

- Educators?
- Administrators?
- Students?
- Parents?
- Society?

What are *your* legal responsibilities under the ADA and IDEA?
Which case resonated with you personally and professionally? Why?

Chapter 2

Defining Disability

Who is disabled, anyway? It seems as though it should be a fairly straight-forward question. Formulating a definition for disability, however, presents a staggeringly difficult challenge. Take a moment and think about what you might include in a comprehensive definition of disability. While reading this section, keep in mind this initial definition you created. You will be surprised by how difficult the task at hand truly is.

In random interviews of children, teens, college students, and teachers, we received the following definitions of disability:

- Not being able to do something that others can do
- Anything that causes someone to struggle
- A challenge to overcome
- When someone has to have help
- Something that keeps a person from learning or achieving
- An impediment that the majority do not possess
- A challenge that builds courage
- A physical, mental, inflicted, learned, or inherited problem
- A handicap or hardship that may hinder someone but can make them stronger

There was a consistent difficulty by all respondents in formulating, and communicating, a definition of disability as well as a reticence to discuss disability as an educational issue; however, to initiate change, we must be willing to break down barriers of silence, misunderstanding, and prejudicial mindsets.

The following story illustrates the difficulties in discussing and understanding disability.

One of my dearest friends, a middle school teacher, invited me to come to her class to discuss disabilities with a group of students labeled at-risk who refused to read *Flowers for Algernon* or *Freak the Mighty*. I had been in the school many times, supervising student teachers, and I knew these students had seen me on campus and in classrooms. I sat in the middle of a double horseshoe arrangement of desks and began by asking the students how many of them had seen me before. When several hands went up, I smiled and said, "I thought so" and told them how happy I was to be visiting them. I then asked how they would describe me when they told their friends throughout the day they had a guest speaker in English language arts.

One young man immediately replied, "Short."

Another boy directly behind him said, "Really short." I laughed and told them they had done a good job establishing that I was short and asked what other qualities would describe me.

One young lady answered, "You have brown curly hair."

They boy next to her added, "And your hair is short, too."

One young girl said, "You have a lot of energy."

Another responded, "You are nice."

The boy next to her whispered, "How do you know she is nice? She might be really mean."

Across the room a boy shouted, "And you are funny."

The girl next to him added, "You seem happy. Are you?" I interrupted with a laugh and told them that this was a good stopping point and praised them for saying such nice things. I said, "You know, there is one thing you didn't mention when you were describing me that most people mention."

Tentatively, a student said, "Oh, you mean your handicap."

The girl next to her whispered, "That's not nice."

I responded by saying, "Thank you for being so honest. I came here today to talk with you and share things I have never told anyone."

The classroom became silent as the students leaned forward anxiously in their desks. Adolescents need the truth; they deserve the truth, in an environment that allows for an open and safe, non-judgmental, discussion. I asked them to please feel free to ask questions or offer ideas as I began . . .

"When I was five, I was running and playing with my friends, just like you. One day I could do anything; the next day I was totally paralyzed. My mom and dad were really scared and took me to the doctor right away. Our family doctor didn't know what was wrong and sent me to another doctor. That doctor thought I might have polio but the tests showed I did not. He told my parents to take me to the Cleveland Clinic, so my dad and I set off for Cleveland while my mom stayed home with my baby brother. After a week of tests, I was diagnosed with Juvenile Rheumatoid Arthritis. The doctors told my parents that I would never have a normal life—I wouldn't be able to go to school, drive a car, go out with friends, or live alone."

All of a sudden a little boy in the back slammed his fists on his desk and yelled, "That pisses me off. How could they say such mean things?"

Everyone turned and looked at him and back at me. He continued with his tirade against the doctors while one young girl asked what my parents did. Before I could answer, another student interjected with a series of questions such as, "But you TEACH school and I've seen your car . . ."

Another student asked if my car was normal. I smiled and told the students I would take one question at a time, as they were all so important.

I explained to the class how necessary it was for the doctors to be honest with my parents and me because we needed to know what to expect. I shared information on Rheumatoid Arthritis and explained how it affected each joint and limited many of my activities.

One girl said, "So, when you get up in the morning, what do you do?"

A young man replied, "She gets out of bed, duh."

Another young man said, "I bet you take drugs."

I wasn't prepared for such interest in my daily activities and allowed their questions to guide my sharing. They ran through a list of tasks to see which ones were problematic and asked if I ever needed help. I started laughing and asked how many of them liked asking for help. No one raised a hand, so I told them how I had to ask their teacher, when we were attending a conference together, to zip up my dress. They looked at their teacher, then at me, asking if we felt embarrassed. I told them I would have been more embarrassed if I would have had to go around all day with an unzipped dress, and I didn't mind asking for help when I knew the person cared about me. The teacher asked the students how they felt when they helped someone, and, almost in unison, the class responded, "Good!" She explained how happy she was that I asked for her help because she knew it meant that I trusted her. I asked the students if anyone had ever made fun of them. The room was alive with stories of broken friendships, hurt feelings, anger, disappointment, and pain. I then asked if they had ever made fun of anyone, and after a moment of awkward silence, they asked if anyone had ever made fun of me. I told them about the little boy in sixth grade who quacked whenever he saw me walk, the boy who walked all the way home on my heels, and the girls who made fun of my orthopedic shoes. Once again, the young man who had gotten so violently angry earlier, jumped out of his desk, put his arm around my shoulder and promised he would take care of anyone who ever made fun of me again. I hugged him and asked the whole class how we could help the world become more understanding. As they started brainstorming ideas, I wrote them on the board, marveling at the wisdom of these adolescents labeled at-risk. Their solutions included:

- Talking to people
- Smiling
- Offering to help
- Explaining the disability
- Remembering that everybody has problems
- Learning about different disabilities
- Being honest
- Treating kids like people

This conversation initiated a sharing of their personal stories concerning disability, cruelty, frustration, and empathy. Their comments and questions resonated with sensitivity and intensity.

"How do you feel when you see people doing what you can't do?" asked a quiet boy in the corner.

"Do you get mad or do you want to kill yourself?" added a girl across the room. I replied honestly and told them that sometimes I wanted to cry when I saw someone running or biking, but I have to remember that there are things that I can do that some people can't and those people might feel the same way about me. As the bell rang to begin the next class and I prepared to leave, trying to talk to all the students wanting to personally share their life stories of pain, friendship, and diversity; a seventh grade student thanked me for helping him understand that disability isn't something to fear or avoid.

Part of the difficulty in defining who is disabled comes from the fact that a disability is not necessarily an immutable or static condition. Unlike gender or race, disabled people cannot be identified by a single common characteristic, such as an ancestral, a biological, or a physical trait. Disabled people do not share a common birthplace, skin color, language, or heritage. Often times, you cannot look at someone and tell that they have a disability. Disabled people are not even unified by the nature of their disabilities or how they became disabled. Some people are born with disabilities, while others become disabled by accident, by degenerative condition, or by advancing age. Some disabilities are genetic, while others are caused by external circumstances. Occasionally, some fortunate people who have disabilities cease to be disabled when medical science finds a way to alleviate their conditions.

The other significant difficulty in creating a simple definition of who is disabled results from the massive range of conditions that are disabilities. Physical impairments, such as loss of sight, loss of hearing, or loss of mobility, seem to generally be accepted as disabilities. Similarly, certain mental impairments, such as the inability to think beyond a certain basic level, are commonly understood as disabilities. Problems arise from the precision of the definitions of even these conditions that are commonly thought of as disabilities. How much sight loss makes a person disabled? What level of difficulty in mobility makes the individual disabled? How far below the average ability to learn must a person be to qualify as having a mental disability? The definition challenge becomes exponentially more complex when other conditions are considered. Beyond the wide array of physical and mental conditions, a definition of disability must consider diseases, learning disabilities, addictions, emotional conditions, and behavioral conditions. Even if each of these varying problems is not included in a definition of disability, they must at least be assessed when formulating the definition. Which conditions are included, and which are not, significantly shapes the definition.

The final dilemma in defining disability is an odd by-product of modern culture. As the disabled have been afforded more legal rights in the United

States, some people have taken unexpected liberties with the concept of disability, either out of selfishness or ignorance. The simplest example of this occurrence is the perfectly healthy person with the disabled parking tag, who pulls into the disabled parking place and then gamely jumps out of the car, dashing off somewhere. The fleet-footed individual in the disabled parking space may be taking advantage of the situation to save time or the individual may genuinely, though incorrectly, feel they have a disability. How they got the parking tag is a separate question entirely.

Some people see identification as disabled as a means of personal gain, whether for advantage and convenience, such as the parking tag or in order to gain sympathy. Anyone with an obvious impairment has had the strange experience of being told by a perfectly healthy individual that he or she also has a disability, such as a corn on his or her foot, near-sightedness, an inability to digest walnuts, allergies to pine pollen, trouble sleeping more than seven hours a night, or innumerable other silly complaints that people have misidentified as a disability. Why people do so is confounding, but it may derive from the attention that can be garnered by sounding woeful; saying you deserve pity is a much easier way to gain attention than performing a few minutes of decent standup comedy. Though identifying an insignificant problem as a disability may get attention from some people, it has negative social consequences beyond simply insulting people who actually are disabled. Ultimately, the result of people claiming petty problems as disabilities is a further confusion in society as to what a disability really is.

People with disabilities do share two things in common. First, people with disabilities are unified by the fact that they have a condition in their physical or mental constitution which society deems unusual. However, this is very imprecise, since many conditions fit that definition without being considered disabilities. Having naturally red hair is an unusual physical condition statistically speaking, but no one considers naturally red hair a disability. A genius level I.Q. is an unusual mental condition, but hardly a disability. Neither red hair nor a genius level I.Q. would meet the second commonality shared by people with disabilities: the fact that the unusual physical or mental condition causes the individual to be discriminated against. Persons with red hair or genius level I.Q. scores are not the victims of social discrimination for their unusual conditions. Persons with disabilities, however, are the victims of discrimination. When signing the ADA into law in 1991, then-President George Bush announced: "Let the shameful wall of exclusion finally come tumbling down" (Shapiro, 1993, p. 140). It seems fairly clear that persons who are disabled possess unusual physical or mental conditions that cause some other people to discriminate against them. This observation, however, is not a definitive statement of who is disabled.

The truth is that there is no consensus definition of who is disabled.

There is not even a consensus as to how many disabled people there are in the United States. The only real consensus seems to be that the disabled face a great deal of discrimination in society, especially in the field of education. When modifying IDEA in 1990, Congress noted in the findings section that more than half of the disabled children in the United States did not receive appropriate educational services, over 1 million disabled children were excluded entirely from the public school system, and an alarming number of disabled children did not succeed in school because their disabilities went undetected (20 U.S.C.A. sec. 1400(c)). The current version of IDEA notes in the findings that the implementation of IDEA "has been impeded by low expectations and an insufficient focus on applying replicable research on proven methods of teaching and learning for children with disabilities" (20 U.S.C.A. sec. 1400(c)(4)).

Not surprisingly, formulating a legal definition of disability has proven a difficult process. Lawmakers have been forced to confront this problem anew each time a law regarding the disabled is considered. After all, why bother creating laws to protect the disabled without knowing who is protected? Fortunately, the general meanings of disability under the Rehabilitation Act and the ADA are similar. The meanings from these two acts have been used in other anti-discrimination acts meant to protect the disabled, such as the Fair Housing Act of 1988 (42 U.S.C.A. sec. 3602) and the Air Carrier Access Act (49 U.S.C.A. sec. 41705). IDEA, which employs different definitions and uses of disability, will be examined separately later in this section.

Under the definitions and meanings of the term disabled in the Rehabilitation Act and the ADA, an individual is considered disabled if he or she meets any one of the following three conditions: (1) having a physical or mental impairment that substantially limits one or more of the individual's major life activities; (2) having a record of such an impairment; or (3) being regarded as having such an impairment. The first of the three conditions is of the highest significance in most contexts, including education. The second condition is for individuals who have had an impairment that substantially limited a major life activity, but which no longer does. The most common example of the second condition is an individual who has a history of cancer, but the individual is cured or in remission. Other individuals who may qualify under the second condition include people with a prior history of mental illness, heart disease, or other treatable diseases. The third condition is for individuals who do not have an impairment that significantly limits a major life activity, but they have been mistakenly identified, classified, or treated as if they were disabled. Some examples of this condition include people being mistakenly treated as disabled for being a carrier of the Hepatitis B virus, having asymptotic HIV, or having minor physical ailments such as minor knee or back pains.

To fully understand the scope of who is included in the first condition, the meanings of certain terms must be discussed. Major life activities include "caring for oneself, performing manual tasks, walking, seeing, hearing, speaking, breathing, learning and working," as well as sitting, standing, lifting, reaching, and engaging in mental or emotional processes such as "thinking, concentrating, and interacting with others" (29 C.F.R. sec. 1630.2(i); EEOC Compliance Manual No. 198, sec. 902.15). In short, a major life activity must be major. It is an activity in which an individual engages numerous times, if not constantly, over the course of each day of the individual's life. An impairment of an activity that is not a major life activity, such as the ability to digest dairy products, is not a disability. Pregnancy is not considered to impair a major life activity, so it is not a disability.

The other significant part of the definition of disability derives from the requirement that the impairment create a substantial limitation of a major life activity. In general terms, an individual who is substantially limited in a major life activity is unable to perform that activity at all or can only perform the activity in severely limited fashion compared to other individuals performing the same activity (29 C.F.R. sec. 1630.2). For example, an individual who has very limited hearing, even with the use of hearing aids, when compared to how the average person hears, is disabled. A common misconception is that people who are disabled cannot engage to any extent in the activity in which they are impaired. People who are legally blind often have some amount of sight, though it is significantly reduced. People can be deaf without being profoundly deaf and unable to hear anything, even with hearing aids. An individual can be disabled for having mobility impairments, yet still be able to walk unaided for limited distances in some circumstances. A substantial limitation can be either an inability to engage in an activity or a significant reduction in the ability to engage in an activity.

A physical or mental impairment, according to the Department of Justice regulations for enforcement of the ADA, is "any physiological disorder or condition, cosmetic disfigurement, or anatomical loss" affecting any one or more major body systems, such as sensory functioning or neurological functioning, and "[a]ny mental or psychological disorder" (28 C.F.R. sec. 35.104). This means that a physiological disorder or condition, cosmetic disfigurement, or anatomical loss that does not substantially impair the function of a major body system is not a disability. Left-handedness, though an atypical physiological condition, is not a disability because it does not substantially impair a major life function. Bad acne or scarring from chicken pox can be seen as cosmetic disfigurement, but neither is a disability since no major body system is involved. The removal of an appendix is an anatomical loss, but it is not a disability since the loss of the appendix does not impair the function of any major body system. Finally, any illnesses that are transitory or brief are never considered disabilities. Being in bed with a bad case of the flu does not make you temporally disabled, no matter how unpleasant an experience it may be.

Disabilities, the physical and mental impairments that do substantially limit major life activities, include a wide range of conditions. Some of the more common physical disabilities include hearing impairments, visual impairments, mobility impairments, multiple sclerosis, muscular dystrophy, chronic fatigue, immune dysfunction syndrome, Crohn's disease, and cardiac problems. Some types of physical impairment can be a disability or not depending on whether a major life activity is being limited. HIV, AIDS, and AIDS Related Complex can be disabilities, but commonly are not disabilities when treatments prevent the disease from limiting any major life activities. A mental impairment, to be considered a disability, must be diagnosed by mental health professionals as a condition that constitutes impairment of a major life activity. Many mental health conditions are impairments that do not substantially limit any major life activities. Manic depression, autism, apraxia, organic brain syndrome, and schizophrenia can all be disabilities, but only if the individual with the mental impairment is substantially limited in a major life activity due to the condition.

Ironically, the lawmakers seem to have been more interested in deciding what is not a disability. Under the Rehabilitation Act and the ADA, a strange and varied list of conditions are deemed not to constitute disabilities under any circumstances: homosexuality; bisexuality; transvestitism; transsexualism, pedophilia; exhibitionism; voyeurism; gender identity disorders not resulting from physical impairments; any other sexual behavior disorders; pyromania; compulsive gambling; kleptomania; current alcoholism; obesity; and psychoactive substance use disorders resulting from the current illegal use of drugs (42 U.S.C.A. sec. 12211).

IDEA, as it deals specifically with the educational rights of disabled children, protects only children who are educationally disabled. Not all children with disabilities are protected by IDEA. The statute actually provides an extensive list of the disabilities that are recognized under IDEA: "mental retardation, hearing impairments including deafness, speech or language impairments, visual impairments including blindness, serious emotional disturbance, orthopedic impairments, autism, traumatic brain injury, other health impairments, or specific learning disabilities," (20 U.S.C.A. sec. 1401(3)(A)). By including a specific, exhaustive list of which disabilities are covered by IDEA, there is a reduction of doubt as to who is protected by the statute. However, some groups have felt certain conditions were inappropriately excluded from the list. For example, there has been some controversy as to whether attention deficit disorder (ADD) should be added to this list. Legislation to have ADD added to the list has not succeeded, and the Department of Education has found no reason to place ADD on the list, since it can be described under "other health impairments." Further, if a child has a disability that is not specifically protected by IDEA, the child is not left defenseless in school. A disabled child who is ineligible for assistance under IDEA can still receive assistance under the Rehabilitation Act.

For the majority of the pre-service teachers with disabilities we interviewed, those college students preparing for a career in teaching, it was not until the semester of student teaching that they became frustrated and concerned about their own disabilities. Many cited the student teaching applications as a source of anxiety—how to disclose to a potential cooperating teacher that they possess a disability? Some, however, did not encounter problems until they had difficulties being placed or had their initial meeting with the cooperating teacher, who showed directly or indirectly a lack of confidence in the student teacher's ability. Others experienced no problems until student teaching began; and then they faced issues of accommodation, whether it was the physical layout of the school or more personal accommodations for learning, emotional, or social disabilities. The distinctions between disability and discrimination become blurred by societal attitudes, perceptions, and financial considerations.

CROSS-EXAMINATIONS AND REBUTTALS

How did your definition of disability compare with the legal definitions of disability?

Which, if any, of the conditions considered disabilities surprised you?

Do you have any disagreements with the courts? Why or why not?

Which disabilities do you expect the students in your classes to possess?

How are you prepared to deal with the students with disabilities?

What accommodations might be necessary for students with:

- Hearing impairments?
- Visual impairments?
- Mobility impairments?
- Emotional disorders?
- Learning disabilities?

Chapter 3

Defining Discrimination

Mark was in a wheelchair as a result of an automobile accident. In spite of the difficulties he faced maneuvering his wheelchair across the campus, even in the ice and snow, he met his obligations with more responsibility than the majority of his classmates and possessed a classroom presence of a veteran teacher. No one considered an accessible school for his student teaching experience.

The first day of a new semester and I was experiencing the vulnerability of meeting my students for the first time from a wheelchair, uncomfortably placed in a university computer lab. Computer monitors hid the faces of the 28 pre-service teachers who had entered the lab avoiding any eye contact or introductions. From the back of the room I heard, "I didn't know there were any education professors in wheelchairs," and in response, "Yeah, this should be some class."

My initial reaction was disappointment that these pre-service teachers one semester from student teaching, one year from their own classrooms, possessed so little understanding and compassion. My second response was anger that a few students inferred inferior teaching from a professor in a wheelchair. At the end of class, when no one offered assistance or inquired as to whether I needed help getting to my office, the disappointment and anger shifted to alienation and isolation. When a fellow teacher-educator knowingly let the door slam on my efforts to exit the building, I began to doubt the ethics and integrity of the teaching profession.

People with disabilities face many barriers every day, from physical obstacles to systemic barriers in employment and civic programs. Often, the most difficult barriers to overcome are attitudes other people carry regarding people with disabilities. Whether born from ignorance, fear, misunderstanding or hatred, these attitudes keep people from appreciating, and experiencing, the full potential a person with a disability can achieve. Fifty-four million Americans have one or more physical or mental disabilities, and this number is increasing as the population as a whole is growing older. The number of students receiving some form of special education usually exceeds 5 million (Vanderwood, McGrew, & Ysseldyke, 1998). Studies have documented that people with disabilities, as a group, occupy an inferior status in our society and are severely disadvantaged socially, vocationally, economically, and educationally. Society doesn't expect people with disabilities to perform up to standard, and when people with disabilities do, they are perceived as heroic or courageous. This attitude has the effect of patronizing people with disabilities rather than empowering them to demand equal pay, equal benefits, equal opportunity and equal access to the workplace.

With a more precise and comprehensive understanding of what a disability is, we now turn to another difficult yet essential term: discrimination. In a practical sense, discrimination has a wide variety of meanings, many of which are not actually negative. However, forms of discrimination against certain groups of people are inherently bad for the individuals and for all of society, leading to violations of civil rights. These forms of discrimination are banned under the law and are known as legally impermissible discrimination. To understand the difference between the forms of discrimination, it may be beneficial to examine the ways in which the ability to discriminate are a part of everyday life.

If you were to consult a dictionary, you would find that to discriminate means to sort, to distinguish, or to observe differences. The ability to discriminate between objects is essential to survival, allowing you to tell the difference between walls and floors, red lights and green lights, garden hoses and rattlesnakes, and innumerable other useful distinctions. Discrimination between kind is also quite beneficial. This form of discrimination is important in consumption of food, as you might otherwise find yourself trying to ingest many items similar to things we do eat, but that are inedible, noxious, or poisonous. You can eat a leaf from a lettuce plant and be perfectly fine; eat a leaf from any random plant, such as hemlock, and you could endanger your life. Discrimination between kind not only proves useful, it partially defines each person as an individual, informing your style of dress and grooming by your discerning what types of garments you think you look good in and the colors you prefer to wear. Discrimination between kind also determines the types of people you like to be around and are attracted to. In a certain sense, each person routinely makes discriminatory judgments against individuals. People constantly make choices, such as which individuals to spend time with, to argue against, to kiss, to fear, and to dislike, based on forms of discrimination between individuals. If you take a moment and think about it, you will be able to identify important characteristics you require in your friends, your colleagues, and your significant other.

A perfect example of making choices that require discrimination between individuals is deciding whom to trust. The average person does not trust everyone in the world, does not share secrets with everyone within earshot. Instead, a person uses certain characteristics as criteria to discriminate between people to determine their levels of trustworthiness. Imagine yourself lost in an unfamiliar airport. You need directions to get to the appropriate terminal so you do not miss your flight, which is about to board. The line at the information desk is so long that you'll never get to the front in time. You decide to ask someone for directions. Behind you in line is a man with a worried look on his face, muttering about how confused he is, who you saw running frantically around the airport before he got in the information line. Sitting ten feet to your left is an experienced-looking airline captain, relaxing before a flight. You will choose whom to ask, and it will likely be the experienced airline pilot, who has probably been in the airport numerous times before and can tell you exactly where to go. Asking the man in line behind you will do you no good, since he's clearly lost, too. In making this choice, you have discriminated between two options, choosing the one most likely to help you. You have based your decision on which could successfully give you the directions you need. This type of discrimination would be permissible.

However, discrimination between people can have insidious motives as well. Picture yourself still in the line at the airport. The confused man behind you is white, and the airline pilot is an African-American woman. Maybe you would ask the confused man in line because you believe women are never very good with directions. Or maybe you would ask the confused man because you don't trust African Americans. Or maybe you would ask the pilot, not because the man is clearly befuddled, but because you believe white men are only concerned with their own interests. In making any one of these choices, you would have discriminated between the two individuals, but not based on their individual characteristics. You have discriminated between the two people based on discriminatory views toward the groups to which the two individuals belong.

The first form of discrimination, based on their individual qualities of confused versus knowledgeable, would be legally permissible, allowed under the law. The second form of discrimination, based on the social group memberships of African-American woman versus white man, would be legally impermissible, not allowed under the law. This distinction may seem very precise, but it is of utmost importance.

In the airport, whoever is not asked for directions will likely never know that you chose not to ask them, much less the reason why you chose to ask someone else. It probably didn't matter at all to the confused man or the pilot whether you asked one or the other. If you had discriminated against one based on racial bias or gender bias, it would have had no impact on the life of either. But what if it was something important? What if the man and the woman were applicants for a job, and you had to decide whom to hire? The decision of who got the job would be important, affecting both their lives. It is in such cases that laws prohibiting discrimination against members of certain groups based on their membership in that group are of utmost importance. In schools across the world, discrimination is continually occurring. The discrimination may manifest as who is selected for academic or athletic teams, who is invited to parties and field trips, and who is singled out for suspension.

In 1964, Congress enacted a new version of the Civil Rights Act (42 U.S.C.A. sec. 1981 *et seq.*). It was the first truly comprehensive federal legislation outlawing discrimination in all aspects of society based on membership in certain social groups and replaced a much more limited Civil Rights Act from 1956. The Civil Rights Act prohibits discrimination in many areas, such as commerce, provision of accommodations, and participation in government, as well as prohibits employers, unions, and employment agencies from discriminating in employment-related decisions (42 U.S.C.A. sec. 1981). Discrimination is prohibited against individuals based on their race, gender, national origin, religion, and color. The act also created the Equal Employment Opportunity Commission (EEOC), a federal agency with the agenda to enforce the Civil Rights Act of 1964. These protections have been reinforced and expanded by further federal legislation, including the Pregnancy Discrimination Act of 1978 (42 U.S.C.A. sec. 2000(e–k)) and the 1991 amendments to the Civil Rights Act.

Based on these pieces of legislation, if you were making a hiring decision between two candidates, you could not consider their race, gender, national origin, religion, or color when deciding whom to hire. To use any of those traits as the reason for your employment decision would be a case of legally impermissible discrimination. Membership in any of those protected groups has little, if anything, to do with the ability to perform a job. You can hire the candidate who is better qualified and better educated, who has superior recommendations, who is friendlier and more outgoing, or uncountable other reasons that are related to job performance. That form of distinguishing between people is obviously permissible. The same distinction holds true for other types of public forums. A restaurant could not refuse to serve Asian-Americans, a department store could not refuse to sell items to Catholic customers, and a local government could not prevent all women from serving on juries.

A perceptive reader will note that discrimination against the disabled has not yet been mentioned. The Civil Rights Act of 1964, in fact, does not mention the disabled at all. Until the passage of the ADA in 1990, Congress failed to comprehensively address disability-based discrimination in society on a general level. When enacting the ADA, Congress stated, "historically, society has tended to isolate and segregate individuals with disabilities and, despite some improvements, such forms of discrimination against individuals with disabilities continue to be a serious and pervasive social problem" (42 U.S.C.A. sec. 12101(a)(2)). The areas of discrimination the ADA was intended to address include discriminatory practices in businesses, stores, housing, lodging, places of entertainment and public gathering, schools, recreation facilities, social service centers, and transportation facilities. The areas of employment, public accommodations, and local government functions are the most obvious and frequent places of discrimination against the disabled that the ADA was intended to address.

In employment, statistics clearly explain the situation. The employment rate for individuals who do not have a disability is usually about 80 percent; the employment rate for individuals with disabilities who want to work is as low as under 30 percent for those with severe functional limitations and approximately 20 percent for those who need personal assistance to perform a life activity (Colker & Tucker, 1998). Further, most individuals with disabilities who are employed are stuck in low-level jobs with little chance of advancement (Colker & Tucker, 1998). In passing the ADA, Congress stated such discrimination "denies people with disabilities the opportunity to compete on an equal basis and to pursue those opportunities for which our free society is justifiably famous, and costs the United States billions of dollars in unnecessary expenses resulting from dependency and nonproductivity" (42 U.S.C.A. sec. 12101(a)(9)). As Congress accurately observed, the end result of employment discrimination against the disabled not only costs the victims of the discrimination a chance to earn an equitable livelihood, it creates sizable expenses that the nation bears only because the employment discrimination occurs.

In public accommodations, individuals with disabilities have faced the twin problems of possibly not being able to get into or use the location and of not being allowed to use the location in the manner all other patrons are. Before the ADA, few new buildings were constructed with access for all as a priority. Even after the passage of the ADA, many older buildings remain completely inaccessible for those with mobility impairments. In establishments that are accessible, the disabled have had to deal with not being served, with being served in an isolated area away from other customers, or being served in a manner different from the way other customers are served. Any individual with an obvious impairment has experienced establishments refusing them entrance or providing service only in a limited manner. The disabled often are served in restaurants away from the other customers or given inferior service. The same historically has been true for stores and theaters.

Mrs. Donatello was planning a field trip for her tenth grade history classes. Three of her 80 students needed special assistance to participate in the visit to a traveling museum collection. She contacted the special education teacher, asking her to assist her during the museum's program, arranged for extra parents to chaperone the trip, and confirmed that the district school bus was accessible. A week before the trip, Mrs. Donatello personally contacted museum personnel to discuss the accommodations necessary for her students. The director agreed, in writing, to facilitate all planning.

As the students eagerly departed from school grounds, Mrs. Donatello was confident that every student would enjoy, and benefit from, this learning experience. Unfortunately, when the history classes arrived at the museum, the three students with special needs were told they would have to remain in the main lobby with a chaperone as the artifacts were displayed in cubicle areas too small for anyone with mobility or sensory impairments.

In local government, participation has been the major issue. Areas of discrimination have been in voting, transportation, and participation in government and court functions. Access to Bar membership, jury service, voting, and public offices have been areas of discrimination against the disabled that have only been addressed since the passage of the ADA. For example, in *Petition of Rubenstein* (1994), the court held that the Delaware Bar, as an instrument of the court, could not discriminate against disabled individuals who were seeking membership. A court is a "public entity" as defined by the ADA, and is legally required to comply with the ADA (*Galloway v. Superior Court of District of Columbia*, 1993, pp. 18–19). As a result, a policy excluding visually impaired jurors from jury duty was an obvious violation of the ADA, as the jurors were qualified to serve on juries with or without accommodation. The court stated that the only issue was whether the individual is otherwise qualified to serve on a jury, and a blind individual was certainly qualified to be a juror (p. 16).

The ADA was designed to reduce discrimination against the disabled in all aspects of society by two methods. First, the ADA was designed to "provide a clear and comprehensive national mandate for the elimination of discrimination against individuals with disabilities" (42 U.S.C.A. sec. 12101(b)(1)). Second, the ADA was intended to "provide clear, strong, consistent, enforceable standards addressing discrimination against individuals with disabilities" (42 U.S.C.A. sec 12101(b)(2)). The Department of Justice summarized the problem by stating: "The provision of goods and services in an integrated manner is a fundamental tenet of nondiscrimination on the basis of disability. Providing segregated accommodations and services relegates persons with disabilities to the status of second-class citizens" (56 Fed. Reg. 35544 (July 26, 1991)).

The historical lack of integration has been a major source for discrimination and isolation for the disabled in all areas of society, especially education. The disabled at first were simply not educated in this nation. Then the disabled for many years could only attend separate institutional schools. Once public schools were opened to the disabled, many students with disabilities who should have been integrated into general classrooms or schools were not. In schools, as well as many other parts of society, lack of integration of the disabled continues to be a significant issue. Section 504 of the Rehabilitation Act, which specifically prohibits "discrimination under any program or activity receiving Federal financial assistance," prohibits public schools from engaging in discriminatory practices (29 U.S.C.A sec. 794). Since all public schools, local educational agencies, and state educational agencies receive federal funding, they are all subject to the regulations of the Rehabilitation Act. The Rehabilitation Act protects the fundamental rights of disabled students and disabled teachers in public schools, but discrimination remains a tremendous problem in public schools.

Overall, the ADA and the Rehabilitation Act have served to reduce discrimination and improve integration, but deeply ingrained discriminatory views in society against a group of people cannot simply be legislated away. Even with the ADA prohibiting businesses, places of public accommodation, and governments from engaging in impermissible discrimination against the disabled and the Rehabilitation Act and IDEA prohibiting discrimination in public schools, discrimination continues to occur. Prevalent forms of discrimination against the disabled, such as resistance to making accommodations in the workplace, are so much a part of this culture that they can seem to result not from prejudice, but from "ordinary common sense" (Perlin, 1992, p. 375). Often times, the discrimination is on an interpersonal level not covered by the law or results from someone choosing to actively violate the law. The persistence of discrimination against the disabled is a result of accepted social beliefs that tend to create a gulf between those persons with disabilities and those persons without disabilities.

Addressing discrimination is further complicated by the fact that different forms of discrimination are directed against persons with different disabilities. Persons with physical disabilities face discrimination that differs from the discrimination which persons with mental disabilities face. People with physical disabilities must confront discriminatory attitudes that hold them incapable of many things beyond what is limited by their physical impairment.

> Jenna was a brilliant honor roll student at Hamilton High School. In addition to her academic achievements, she served as photographer for the yearbook and could always be found maneuvering her wheelchair on the football sidelines, around the track, and wherever stories

were taking place. One afternoon, Jenna and Marcy, a yearbook writer, took film to be developed. The store manager ignored Jenna, asking Marcy how he could help them. Marcy looked over at Jenna who was removing film from her camera case. In a loud and patronizing voice, the store manager said, "WHAT—CAN—I—DO—FOR—YOU?"

When Jenna told him she needed the rolls of film developed by Friday, the store manager looked at Marcy and asked how she, nodding at Jenna, was going to pay. When Jenna gave him a credit card, the store manager asked Marcy if Jenna could sign her name on the ticket.

On the surface level, uncountable numbers of people react to any obvious physical impairment by speaking slowly in a loud voice. On a more serious level, people with physical disabilities often suffer from discriminatory beliefs that the disability is a greater limitation than it actually is or that a physical disability also indicates mental impairment. As a result of discrimination, persons with mental disabilities are frequently deprived of the many fundamental rights, such as the making of basic decisions about their own health care, sexuality, child rearing, or finances. Striking comparisons have even been made between the medieval Inquisition and modern society's opposition to the movement toward more rights for those with mental disabilities (Szasz, 1971).

Discrimination against the disabled derives from many sources, such as stigmatization, awkwardness, and stereotyping. Of these three sources of discrimination, stereotyping is probably the most complex, since there are a number of major stereotypes, such as pity, patronization, hero worship, and projection. Most individuals with obvious disabilities have experienced all of these biases.

CROSS-EXAMINATIONS AND REBUTTALS

Have you ever felt as though you were experiencing discrimination?

• Why?
• When?
• By whom?

What types of discrimination might you expect to observe in your classroom?

How would you address the issue of discrimination with your students if a situation arises? With your colleagues? Administrators?

What types of discrimination, if any, do you see in the following situation?

One young woman from the Midwest had been confined to a wheelchair since the age of 15 after being hit by a drunk driver. She had more self-confidence and strength of character than most college students and did not perceive the wheelchair as an obstacle. As a young girl, Jaime knew she wanted to teach, gathering her friends together to play school. Even after her accident, she saw no reason why her dream could not become reality. Accepted to a state university, Jaime enjoyed the social aspects of college while maintaining a 3.0 grade point average. She began her English methods courses her junior year and created challenging and engaging lesson plans for her internship experiences. The middle school students were curious and receptive and she learned to navigate the classroom and use her voice for classroom management. At her high school placement, the students were uneasy and unresponsive until she pulled them into a group for an open discussion. She exhibited such skill and passion in all of her teaching experiences, including her student teaching experience. The principal gave her a key to the elevator and a phone to the office—that was all she needed for accommodations. After a Back-to-School Night, some parents contacted the principal and cooperating teacher questioning Jaime's credentials. Every time a position opened in the district, her application was overlooked.

Explain the difference between permissible and legally impermissible discrimination.

What legislation was passed to prohibit discrimination?

Chapter 4

IDEA, Part I: The Concepts of IDEA

The Individuals with Disabilities Education Act (IDEA) is of immense importance to all educators. It is "a fascinating law and a difficult federal mandate that touches on a contemporary American problem—the successful integration of historically excluded and disparate groups" (Siegel, 1994, p. 134). The vast majority of students with disabilities are protected by IDEA. With the degree of integration of disabled students into general education classrooms, many public school classes now have at least one student who is covered by IDEA, including, for example, students labeled mentally educable/trainable; students with learning disabilities, mobility impairments, visual impairments, hearing impairments; and students with emotional disorders, autism, and traumatic brain injury. Six million fifty-five thousand students with reported disabilities attend K–12 public schools in the United States. Two million seven hundred and eighty-nine thousand students have learning disabilities, 462,000 have severe emotional disabilities, 69,000 students are in wheelchairs, and 96,000 students possess dual sensory impairments (NCES Fact Sheet, 2000). As a result, every teacher and administrator in a public school needs to understand the rights and procedures of IDEA. However, many educators are still not familiar with IDEA.

A part of the reason for this lack of awareness comes from the fact that IDEA and the federal regulations for enforcement of IDEA are hardly the most reader-friendly documents ever created. Someone unfamiliar with the legal complexities will be further flummoxed by the legal terms of art, such as related services, special education, and the stay-put provision, as well as by the array of acronyms, such as IEP, LEA, SEA, FAPE, and LRE, standing for key concepts in the legislation. Further compounding the problem is that reference guides about the complexities of IDEA are usually designed for the legal specialist, not the educator looking to understand the law as an interested party who lacks legal training. Often times, educators and those who teach educators, unable to easily penetrate the language of IDEA and all the relevant federal regulations, give up due to the lack of available help. One legal commentator described the problem of IDEA and its regulations by noting how very few teachers "can unravel the Gordian knot federal agencies create in promulgating regulatory guidelines. For the most part, the average teacher or administrator may feel the need to ask a colleague or legal counselor for an opinion" (Greenwood, 1992, pp. 60–61).

Historically, however, many education programs have simply not done enough to educate future general education teachers about the laws. Though IDEA and its regulations may prove difficult reading, professional educators cannot ignore these laws. Unfortunately, in many education departments, it is still possible for general education majors to graduate without being exposed to IDEA at all. Many teachers don't understand IDEA due, at least in part, to "a failure of pre-service and in-service training rather than the legalese of the rules" (Huefner, 1993, p. 175). This situation is wholly unacceptable because IDEA is of preeminent importance to educators.

Some consolation for educators may be found in the fact that many trained lawyers are also ignorant of the details of IDEA. One of the authors of this text had the disturbing experience of addressing a group of approximately two dozen individuals with a legal education who knew virtually nothing about IDEA. Just as it is possible to receive an education degree and be ignorant of IDEA, it is possible to graduate from law school and be ignorant of IDEA.

IDEA is the primary means of protection for students with disabilities in public schools, guaranteeing a "free appropriate public education" to all disabled students. The act, which was passed in 1990, was an expansion and improvement of the Education for All Handicapped Children Act (EAHCA) of 1975. IDEA was substantially modified again in 1997. Through its various permutations, the purpose of the act has always been to ensure that children with disabilities receive:

A free appropriate public education that emphasizes special education and related services designed to meet their unique needs and prepare them for employment and living; to ensure the rights of children with disabilities and parents of such children are protected; and to assist States, localities, educational service agencies, and Federal agencies to provide for education of all children with disabilities; to assist States in the implementation of a statewide, comprehensive, coordinated, multidisciplinary, interagency system of early intervention services for infants and toddlers with disabilities and their families; to ensure that educators and parents have the necessary tools to improve educational results for children with disabilities by supporting systemic-change activities; coordinated technical assistance, dissemination, and support; and technology development and media services; and to assess, and ensure the effectiveness of, efforts to educate children with disabilities. (20 U.S.C.A. sec. 1400(d)(1–4))

In order to accomplish these highly ambitious and very necessary goals, IDEA is broken into numerous concepts, each with a particular function in accomplishing these goals. In order to be able to receive the benefits of IDEA, a child with a disability does not have to demonstrate that he or she will benefit from the public education in order to participate in public schools (*Timothy W. v. Rochester, New Hampshire School District*, 1989). In *Timothy W.*, the court held that all disabled children should be included in public schools, underlined by a "zero-reject policy" that no child should be deprived of a public education "regardless of the severity of their handicap" (p. 960). In the case where the court made this policy statement, the student at issue was profoundly disabled, heightening the poignancy of the holding. The boy in the case had multiple physical disabilities, including cerebral palsy, seizure disorder, quadriplegia, and complex developmental disabilities, and was so profoundly mentally impaired that he had almost no function in his cerebral cortex. In spite of these drastic impairments, the court held that the boy had the right to a free appropriate public education.

IDEA is for students who have "Mental retardation, hearing impairments including deafness, speech or language impairments, visual impairments including blindness, serious emotional disturbance, orthopedic impairments, autism, traumatic brain injury, other health impairments, or specific learning disabilities." (20 U.S.C.A. sec. 1401(3)(A). Students with these various conditions are all protected by IDEA, and they must receive "a free appropriate public education that emphasizes special education and related services" which addresses their educational needs according to their individualized education program (20 U.S.C.A. sec. 1400(d)(1)). To understand the implications of this requirement, we must discuss the meanings of the terms "special education," "related services," "individualized education program," "least restrictive environment," "free appropriate public education," "stay-put provision," "local educational agency," and "state educational agency."

Special education is "specially designed instruction" which meets "the unique needs of a child with a disability" (20 U.S.C.A. sec. 1401(25)). The combination of these two factors makes for special education. It is specially designed for the unique needs of one particular disabled child. Beyond that, it is difficult to more precisely define special education, since it is child-specific to the student for whom it is designed. The scope of what special education includes is rather broad, encompassing far more than traditional classroom academic instruction. Special education can include settings of physical education, vocational instruction, and home-based education, as well as education in a hospital or other institution if necessary. Special education can provide instruction on daily-living skills, community inter-action skills, job training, and other skills intended to prepare the disabled student to be self-supporting upon completion of public education. IDEA requires the placement of students with disabilities in general classrooms to the maximum extent possible.

Primarily, special education is related to supporting general academic instruction. For some students, special education means part-time or full-time placement in a classroom environment specifically for students with special education needs. In rare cases, special education means placement of the student in a residential facility for special education purposes. For most disabled students, however, special education means receiving some special learning services in a general education classroom, as historically the majority of disabled students who receive services are either learning disabled or speech impaired. For a learning disabled student, the special education might include special testing formats. For a student with a visual impairment, the special education would include big print or Braille ma-terials. For the seriously emotionally disturbed child, the special education could include a special curriculum to address the emotional problems.

Related services, as defined by IDEA, are support services such as trans-portation, corrective services, developmental services, and other functions that help the disabled student benefit from special education. Related serv-ices include, but are certainly not limited to, social work services, assistive technology, physical therapy, occupational therapy, recreation therapy, au-diology, speech pathology, psychological services, counseling services, ori-entation and mobility services, and medical services specifically for diagnostic or evaluative purposes (20 U.S.C.A. sec. 1401(22)). Medical services not expressly for diagnostic or evaluative purposes are not related services under IDEA and therefore not the responsibility of the school. The scope of certain related services merit further explanation. "Counseling services" are "services provided by qualified social workers, psychologists, guidance counselors, or other qualified personnel" (34 C.F.R. sec. 300.24(b)(2)). "Psychological services" include "planning and managing a program of psychological services, including psychological counseling for children and parents" (34 C.F.R. sec. 300.24(b)(9)).

A student's individualized education program (IEP) is the document that details the academic, educational, and placement needs of that particular student based on the student's abilities, as well as levels of performance and goals to accomplish. It is, in short, the heart of the application of IDEA. The IEP describes the appropriate coursework, learning environments, and other services for the child, as well as other related academic and educa-tional goals. An IEP can only be developed following a multidisciplinary evaluation of the student's needs and abilities, including assessment of the nature and extent of the suspected disability. A school district must use multiple non-discriminatory tests or evaluations in the student's native or dominant language (20 U.S.C.A. sec. 1412(a)(6) and 1414(a)(1)(A)). An IEP must be reevaluated at least once a year.

Created in collaboration between the student's teachers, counselors, other school personnel, and the parents of the student, the IEP is a cooperative effort intended to customize the educational process to maximize the learning potential of the student. Parents are mandatory participants in the IEP process, with procedural safeguards and appeals in place for disagreements between the parents and school officials regarding the provisions of the IEP. The IEP must specify the student's current level of performance, measurable educational goals and objectives for the student, and the special education and related services required for the student to achieve these goals (20 U.S.C.A. sec. 1414). The IEP should detail the starting point and duration of special programs, the extent to which the student will be integrated into general education classrooms, and the ways that will be used to measure the student's progress (20 U.S.C.A. sec. 1414). For students 16 years and older, the IEP must explain the transition services that will be provided for the student to facilitate movement to post-secondary education, vocational training, employment, or adult services by the time the student reaches the age of 21 (20 U.S.C.A. sec. 1414). The process of creating and implementing an IEP is dictated by very detailed legal procedures (34 C.F.R. sec. 300.340–300.349).

Under the requirements of IDEA, a student with a disability must be placed in the least restrictive environment (LRE) possible that still meets the academic and educational needs of the student. The presumption of LRE is for integration, with segregation of the disabled student only permitted when the child cannot be successfully educated in the general education classroom. IDEA mandates that, "to the maximum extent appropriate," disabled students are to be "educated with children who are nondisabled" (34 C.F.R. sec. 300.550(b)(1)). A disabled student is to be removed from the general educational environment only when "the nature or severity of the disability is such that education in regular classes with the use of supplementary aids and services cannot be satisfactorily achieved" (34 C.F.R. sec. 300.550(b)(2)). The LRE for a particular child can be placement for all of the day in a general classroom, for part of the day in a general classroom, or for none of the day in a general classroom based on the needs of the child. The least restrictive environment possible is a general education classroom, while the most restrictive environment possible is a hospital or residential facility. The placement setting has to allow the most time feasible in the general education environment. For a disabled student who can perform normally in all classes except mathematics, the LRE would be all general education classes except for the student's math class. If that student were placed in any non-math special education classes, the student would not be placed in the least restrictive environment possible.

The concept behind LRE is not to be confused with "mainstreaming" or "inclusion," two educational buzzwords that have become popular without having a formal basis in disability law. Academics, school officials, and parents have mistakenly taken to using one or both of these terms (primarily inclusion) as synonyms for LRE. These terms have assumed accepted meanings as educational jargon, but they are not legal terms of art and are not defined in IDEA (20 U.S.C.A. sec. 1401). Though some people use the terms interchangeably, mainstreaming and inclusion do not really indicate the same concept. Mainstreaming is commonly thought of as the placement of a disabled child in a general education classroom for some classes. Inclusion is generally accepted to mean the placement of a disabled child primarily in a general education classroom. Some courts have been guilty of misusing these terms, but some other courts have actually written about the inappropriate terminology in opinions (*Oberti v. Board of Education of the Borough of Clementon School District*, 1993; *Mavis v. Sobol*, 1993).

Many education scholars currently employ the term inclusion to try to describe the LRE requirement of IDEA, speaking of "full inclusion" and "partial inclusion." Such terms are profoundly inaccurate from a legal standpoint. The grammatical stupidity of these two terms is obvious—full inclusion is redundant and partial inclusion is an oxymoron. However, more distressingly, they both miss the point of IDEA. The term full inclusion implies integration without individualization. The implication of the term partial inclusion is selective integration, which also means selective segregation. IDEA is designed to ensure that students with disabilities are integrated to the maximum extent feasible based upon the individual needs and abilities of each student. This means that each student with a disability is integrated as much as possible, into the least restrictive environment, based on an evaluation of the situation of that particular student. IDEA mandates integration to the fullest extent, taking into account the individual.

Despite the differences in terminology, the essential concept of LRE is the integration of disabled and non-disabled students. LRE ensures that most disabled students have the right to be integrated into classrooms with non-disabled students. When disabled students are segregated, they suffer from being unable to interact with most other children and become targets of prejudice, discrimination, and pity by many of the other students, as well as many teachers (Hill, 1986). The historical practice of segregation of all disabled students resulted in students with disabilities being undereducated, socially stigmatized, and emotionally traumatized (Stick, 1976). For disabled students, the psychological benefits of being integrated are enormous. "The biggest benefit will come when disabled students feel they 'belong' with the regular education children, rather than being segregated in separate classes or separate schools" (Arnold & Dodge, 1994, p. 26).

Even the earliest studies of the effect of integration on disabled students demonstrated a clear positive impact, especially in areas of social skills, peer interaction, and increased personal expectations (Wang, Reynolds, & Walberg, 1986).

A free appropriate public education (FAPE) is the category including all the services and requirements for the education of the disabled child. An FAPE encompasses the special education, related services, and the requirements of the individualized education program of the disabled child. According to IDEA, an FAPE is defined as special education and related services that "have been provided at public expense, under public supervision and direction, and without charge," and that "meet the standards of the State educational agency, include an appropriate preschool, elementary, or secondary school education in the State involved, and are provided in conformity with the individualized education program" (20 U.S.C.A. sec. 1401(8)). The free public education is easy enough to understand; public schools cannot charge for the education of a disabled student. Each disabled child has an affirmative right to be educated in a public school at no cost, just as every other child does. The difficulty comes in assigning a logical standard for what constitutes appropriate education.

The Supreme Court attempted to provide guidance as to what constitutes appropriate education. In *Board of Education of the Hendrick Hudson Central School District v. Rowley* (1982), the Court held that appropriate education does not mean that a disabled student must receive all assistance that might conceivably improve the student's level of education. Instead, the Court held that schools must provide some acceptable educational assistance to make the educational environment more conducive to learning for the disabled student. The Court also noted that courts should avoid imposing their views of preferable educational methods upon state and local governments.

The plaintiff in the case, Amy Rowley, was deaf and virtually without residual hearing. An excellent lip reader, Amy was provided only an FM hearing aid, which did her little good when placed in a general education classroom. In spite of these limitations, Amy was in the upper half of her class and passing from grade to grade at a normal progression. Amy's parents were concerned that, with lip reading as her only real means for understanding what was going on in the classroom, Amy was missing too much in her classes. Her parents requested the school district supply a qualified sign-language interpreter for all Amy's academic classes. The school district argued that since Amy was still achieving educationally, academically, and socially, she was getting an appropriate education. With the interpreter, she would have had greater success in all those areas, but the school district claimed that she evidenced some success; it was providing an FAPE. The Supreme Court agreed. The Court put great weight on the fact that Amy was a successful student in determining she had an FAPE;

passing marks and advancement from grade to grade were held to be important measures of educational benefit. The Court found it "sufficient to confer some educational benefit upon the handicapped child" (p. 200).

In the *Rowley* opinion, the Supreme Court established a two-part test for evaluating if a free public education is appropriate for a disabled student. First, the state must comply with the procedures detailed in IDEA; second, the IEP must be reasonably calculated to provide some educational benefits to the child. The first part of the test is based upon the procedural requirements of IDEA. The second part of the test is based on an assessment of the individual child's educational needs. But if the child is progressing from grade to grade, the Court's implication is that the child is receiving some educational benefit. If these two requirements are met, then the state has complied with the act and courts can impose no further duty, as "questions of methodology are for resolution by the States" (p. 208). The Court summarized: "Certainly the language of the statute contains no requirement . . . that States maximize the potential of handicapped children commensurate with the opportunity provided to other children" (p. 189).

The unfortunate result of this holding is that a disabled child need only receive some educational benefit for the free public education to be appropriate. The student does not have to be achieving to full potential or even to the same level of potential as other students for a program to qualify as appropriate. Though this standard might not automatically seem too upsetting, consider if the context were voting. What if the Supreme Court had held disabled voters had a right to vote but did not have the right to vote in every election? So long as they got to vote sometimes, disabled voters would have no claim of a violation of their rights. The holding in *Rowley* is not very different. Disabled students have a right to learn but not the right to learn to their full potential or to the same potential as students without disabilities. Following *Rowley*, some schools inevitably tried to provide the most minimal accommodations possible to comply with the law.

Satisfying the procedural requirement for an FAPE is relatively logical, since complying with the specified procedures of IDEA will result in compliance with the procedural requirement. If a school district convenes an IEP meeting without the student's parent(s), the student's teacher(s), or any other individual required by IDEA to be present, the IEP will be held invalid as denying an FAPE to the student (*W. G. v. Board of Trustees of Target Range School District*, 1992). If a school district creates or changes an IEP without a hearing, the IEP will be held invalid as denying an FAPE to the student (*Jackson v. Franklin County School Board*, 1986). If a school district creates or changes an IEP without providing prior notice to the student or the student's parent(s), the IEP will be held invalid as denying an FAPE to the student (*Jackson v. Franklin County School Board*, 1986). In a fairly unique case, an IEP with no written performance levels or goals has been held to be a valid FAPE, only because all procedural requirements had been followed and the members of the IEP team had understood what the unrecorded performance levels and goals were (*Doe v. Defendant I*, 1990). Complying with the specified procedures is a very literal process that must be done completely and with as little deviation as possible.

Compliance with the procedural requirements is useless, however, if the substantive requirements are not also met. Courts have held that the substantive requirement necessitates more than minimal benefit to the disabled student to be a valid FAPE. When a student was not advancing from grade to grade and was not achieving any measurable academic success, a court held that the student was not receiving an FAPE, since he was getting no meaningful educational benefit (*Polk v. Central Susquehanna Intermediate Unit 16*, 1988). The basic point of the substantive requirement is that the disabled student must receive some measurable or meaningful educational benefit to qualify as an FAPE. A student can be held to have a substantially valid FAPE even if the education plan is one of a number of possible educational alternatives. An FAPE can be substantially valid so long as it is reasonably calculated to provide meaningful educational benefits (*G. D. v. Westmoreland School District*, 1991). An FAPE will meet this substantive requirement so long as the student receives measurable benefits, even if the plan is not the first choice of the parents or the student or even if it is not the choice that will produce the most educational benefits for the student (*G. D. v. Westmoreland School District*, 1991).

Once an IEP has been validly created for a disabled student, IDEA has a mandated stay-put provision to protect the student. When a disagreement arises between parties involved in the creation of the IEP, most likely between the parents and the school district, the stay-put provision keeps the student "in the then-current educational placement" until the dispute is decided (20 U.S.C.A. sec. 1415(j)). The stay-put provision prevents the child from being bounced between educational programs or settings every time a change is proposed. If all parties involved in the student's IEP agree with a proposed change, then there is no need for the stay-put provision. However, in circumstances where the parents feel the student needs one situation and the school district asserts a different position, the stay-put provision prevents the student from being moved until the issue is settled to avoid undue stress and upset. Stay-put provisions have become a source of controversy, with some critics claiming that stay-put provisions can negatively affect classroom safety or the teacher's ability to teach in certain circumstances.

Finally, under IDEA, the local educational agency (LEA) is the administrative authority that controls and directs a public school system. A public board of education, or another type of public authority that is a political subdivision, is responsible as the LEA to ensure that all disabled students residing within its geographic boundaries receive an FAPE. Each state government, through its state educational agency (SEA), also has a role in special education, including the monitoring of each LEA within the state and ensuring distribution of funding for special education within the state.

Having addressed the major terms, and all the various acronyms, that are essential to an understanding of IDEA, we will next examine the procedural requirements of IDEA and how they impact the implementation of the law in the classroom.

CROSS-EXAMINATIONS AND REBUTTALS

Define and explain the following:

- IDEA
- IEP
- LRE
- FAPE
- LEA
- SEA
- Stay-put provision
- Zero-reject policy

Pick one of the requirements of IDEA and discuss how it affects your teaching responsibilities.

Chapter 5

IDEA, Part II: Procedures and Implementations

A letter in Susan's file from her elementary school principal read: "Susan will need some special educational programming to help her overcome academic deficits. I also feel she will require support from school staff to enable her to adjust to the high school environment. She will also need encouragement from teachers to help maintain self-esteem. Susan is a good kid deserving of a chance in the school of her choice."

IDEA has specific procedural mandates that must be followed. These procedural mandates are designed to ensure that IDEA is implemented correctly and with the best interests of the student in mind. Any student who is covered by IDEA receives the same procedural protections. IDEA applies to any student needing special education and related services as a result of having "mental retardation, hearing impairments including deafness, speech or language impairments, visual impairments including blindness, serious emotional disturbance, orthopedic impairments, autism, traumatic brain injury, other health impairments, or specific learning disabilities" (20 U.S.C.A. sec. 1401(3)(A)). Under IDEA, the conditions of ADD and ADHD (attention deficit hyperactivity disorder) might be considered as "other health impairments," so long as the condition results in "limited strength or vitality or alertness." Each student who is protected by IDEA has the legal right to an FAPE, regardless of the nature or severity of his or her disability. Students with multiple disabilities have the same rights as students with a single disability.

IDEA and its supporting documents are located at 20 U.S.C.A. sec. 1400 *et seq.* and 34 C.F.R. sec. 300 *et seq.* (Note: To avoid being redundant and overwhelming to most readers, the specific citations to these IDEA or IDEA regulations are provided only for direct quotations from these sources in this chapter. Otherwise, most sentences would end with a citation to one or both sources.)

It is the intent of IDEA that the law should be implemented by the cooperative efforts of the student, the parents, and the school. As Senator Jim Jeffords stated during the floor debate about the 1997 Amendments to IDEA, the law is designed "to encourage educators and parents at the school building level to work together to set goals to help children, with and without known disabilities, succeed" (143 Cong. Rec. S4295 (May 12, 1997)). The collaborative process under IDEA is meant to create the best possible plan to provide the disabled student an FAPE.

Once a student is suspected to have a disability, the LEA has an affirmative duty to evaluate or seek evaluation of the student to test for the suspected impairment. The LEA must provide detailed notice of the situation to the student's parents and seek approval for the evaluation. Under IDEA, the term "parents" can include biological parents, legal guardians, and any other caretakers. IDEA views other relatives raising the child in place of parents, guardians, surrogates, or anyone else legally responsible for the child's welfare to be able to act in the role of the parent. The only instance where the legal guardian of the child cannot act in the role of parent is when the child is a ward of the state. In that case, a surrogate parent must be appointed to represent the best interests of the child in the IEP process.

Before an LEA can initiate or alter an IEP, the LEA must first provide written notice to the parents of the student. The parents should be notified a reasonable amount of time in advance, which is usually taken to mean at least 10 days prior to the event. The notice must contain information describing the proposed action by the LEA and an elaboration of the procedural safeguards in language that is easily understood in the mode of communication used by the parent (in the native or preferred language of the parents and, if necessary, in an alternate format). This description of the procedures must specify all methods and procedures available for resolving conflicts and making appeals, as well as clearly stating that all hearings will be impartial. Any subsequent changes to the IEP of the student must also be delivered to the parents in a similar format. Parental consent is needed for the initial evaluation and placement. If the parents refuse consent, then state law can provide a process to still have the student evaluated and placed. If no state law exists, a public agency can proceed without the approval of the parents under pressing circumstances, especially if the student is in desperate need of special services.

Once the evaluation is completed, an initial meeting is held to determine whether the student has a disability and, if so, what placement or services might be available to provide an FAPE for the student. The placement decision must be made so that placement anywhere other than a general education classroom occurs only after a determination is made that placement in general education classes will be unsuccessful (*Board of Education v. Holland*, 1992). All of the information creates the backbone of the IEP document. A school district that makes a placement decision without following the IEP is actively violating the law. Containing information regarding identification, evaluation, and educational placement of the individual student, the IEP is the keystone to safeguarding equal educational opportunities for disabled students.

THE IMPORTANCE OF THE IEP

The individualized education program (IEP) is a rather profound concept. It is flexible and can be designed in many different ways to meet the needs of children with many different types of impairments. It also has specific structural and procedural guidelines that must be followed to ensure the best for the student. If done well, an IEP can dramatically improve the education of a student with a disability. Perhaps the best description of the potential of the IEP states that the IEP

avoids attempting to mandate specific services; it recognizes the rights of recipients, empowers them, and involves them in the process; it avoids treading on the professional discretion of teachers and potentially enhances their influence over placement decisions; it provides a means of holding local administrators accountable while paying some deference to the belief that the federal government should not interfere too much with local autonomy in education; and it appeals to local school officials by fixing the upper limit of the liabilities with respect to the child. (Neal & Kirp, 1986, pp. 349–350)

This is only fully accomplished, however, when an IEP is created within the accepted procedural manner and designed with great care to accommodate the specific needs of the child for whom it is written. An IEP must be designed to meet the special needs of the student as an individual, not as a member of a group. The special education and related services detailed in the IEP should be based on educational need, not the type of disability the student has.

I met Billy while attending an IEP review. A five foot eight inch young man with curly dark hair and beautiful complexion, Billy seemed to have cerebral palsy or a similar type of condition. His involuntary motor control seemed more apparent when he was nervous, and his movements were much more deliberate than the other students. Nonetheless, Billy always seemed to have a smile on his face and was very enthusiastic about attending school. As I began to respond to his questioning look about the physical challenges I experience, he put his hand on my arm and said, "That's okay. I have a handicap too."

He then began: "Did you know I am a quadruplet? Well, I have three sisters and when I was born, the oxygen was cut off to my brain and I learn slow and I have some problems. I have always been in only special education classes until now and this is my first normal school. My sisters are okay. They don't have any problems. Just me. I was the last one born."

His openness and candor were endearing and I was touched by his optimistic nature and positive outlook. I told his parents about my conversation with Billy and when I mentioned how much I enjoyed him, they proudly said, "Everyone says that about Billy." His mother's biggest concern was one of social adjustment and acceptance for Billy, while his father was interested in the improvement in their son's grades over the first semester.

A later evaluation revealed:

"He has more confidence in himself and a much higher self-esteem. He participates more and is willing to take chances. He also likes the respect he has received from his peers from working on the stage crew. During a preview of the play, every time Billy put his head out from behind the curtain, all the students cheered."

"Billy uses language as a way of improving. He looks forward to vocabulary exercises and writes excellent sentences."

"Billy is a student with obvious physical limitations. He works hard and is enthusiastic about his work and is enthusiastic in his dealings with teachers and students. Billy won two awards at the school's awards ceremony which really helped his self-esteem."

An IEP is created by an "IEP team," comprised of knowledgeable individuals, familiar with the educational needs of the student at issue. The IEP team is also sometimes called the multidisciplinary team. At a minimum, the team must include the student's parents, the student's general education teacher (at least one of the student's teachers if there are multiple), a special education teacher, a school administrator, someone who can interpret the tests and evaluations (often a school psychologist), and "the LEA rep." The LEA rep, a representative of the agency qualified to implement and supervise special education services, will evaluate the school district's ability to assist the student in terms of curriculum and funding. The LEA representative should be familiar with LEA resources and have the authorization to commit them. The team can also include any other experts or education professionals at the discretion of the parents or the special education agency, such as related services personnel or transition services personnel. IDEA regulations encourage keeping the IEP team relatively small to facilitate communication and efficiency. If the team determines it is appropriate to include the student, then the individual for whom the IEP is written can take part in planning the IEP as well.

The LEA has the responsibility to schedule the IEP meeting at a mutually agreed upon time and place when at least one of the student's parents can attend. The notice to the parents must be sufficient to allow them the ability to arrange their schedules to attend. If no other options are available, parents may participate in the meeting by telephone in a conference call format. If the parents do not opt to attend and the LEA proceeds with the IEP planning, the LEA must document multiple attempts to arrange a mutually agreed upon time and place for the meeting. The LEA must document the phone calls made or attempted, copies of all correspondence, visits made to parents at home or at work, and the results of each call and visit. If parents simply refuse to participate, the school district still has the affirmative duty to design and implement an FAPE for the disabled student. Once an IEP team reaches a decision, it cannot be vetoed by administrators, by the superintendent, or by the school board.

The IEP, once implemented, must be reevaluated at least once every year by the IEP team. Reviews of existing IEPs often occur during the summer, since an IEP is supposed to be in place at the beginning of the school year. The IEP team has the discretion to alter the plan upon review, focusing on whether the needs of the student have changed and whether changes in services would improve the student's ability to meet the goals of the IEP. The IEP team can request further testing of the student at review to make these determinations. In unusual circumstances, it is possible for an IEP team to determine upon review that the student no longer has a disability and no longer needs special education services. The IEP team can decide to review or alter the plan at any time before the year if the members of the team deem it necessary. If the parents of a student with an IEP elect to move that student into private school, the parents must provide at least 10 business days prior notice of their intent. Parents always are to be officially notified of all decisions of the IEP team.

The IEP is supposed to be a cooperative process among the team members; the law requires the participation of the parents of the student. Parents are supposed to be involved from the beginning of the process, participating in the initial decision to determine if the student is eligible for special education services. IDEA, in fact, specifies that parents are to receive training and counseling to help them acquire the skills necessary for them to support the implementation of their child's IEP. However, educators too often simply treat the parents as bystanders. The National Council on Disability, an advisory committee, reported to then-President Clinton that "in spite of provisions mandating parent participation in decision making, parents in many parts of the country still feel largely left out of the process. Many parents reported that they arrived at IEP planning meetings only to be presented with a completed plan," (National Council on Disability, 1995, p. 11). Such a situation is completely unacceptable, as it utterly misses the intent of IDEA. The team is intended to work cooperatively for the benefit of the student, with all members of the team aware of the reason for a meeting before the meeting occurs. Congress intended parents to be an integral part of IDEA. Involving parents ensures family input into and support for the IEP, and provides unique insights from the parents as to what is most appropriate for the child. Parents have "a critical role in assuring that their children are placed in a program that meets their needs" (Bruser, 1998, p. 82).

One study has identified four important considerations for educators to bear in mind when planning IEPs and working on IEP teams to avoid alienating the students and their parents:

1. The potential contributions of the parents in decision making;
2. The effect of the labeling on both the student and the parents;
3. The reliance on process and procedure to minimize the input of the parents; and
4. The conveyance of an us/them mentality identifying the teachers with the schools and not the family. (Harry, Allen, & McLaughlin, 1995)

The parents must be allowed to play an important part in devising the IEP for their child. If the parents feel excluded from the IEP planning process or are dissatisfied with the outcome of the IEP process, they have the right to appeal for a due process hearing and a review by the LEA or SEA. If the parents are still dissatisfied with the decision of the LEA or SEA, then they have the right to appeal that decision to state court or federal court.

The IEP document must contain a number of very specific items. It must take into account the student's strengths and weaknesses based on recent evaluations and input from teachers and parents. At a minimum, an IEP must detail:

1. The present level of educational performance of the student;
2. The measurable annual goals for the student, such as instructional objects and performance levels, as well as short term benchmark goals between the annual goals;
3. The special education, related services, assistive technology, and supplementary aids and services to be provided for the student;
4. The extent to which, if any, the student will be educated outside the general education classroom;
5. The modifications, if any, to student assessment procedures;
6. The dates for initiation of services;
7. The location, duration, and frequency of services; and
8. The means for measuring the student's progress toward goals and a schedule for sending information to the student's parents regarding progress.

For certain types of disabilities, there are further requirements regarding the content of an IEP. For a visually impaired or blind student, the IEP should provide for instruction in the use of Braille, unless the team determines it is not appropriate for the student. For a student with a hearing impairment or profound deafness, the IEP should provide for development of the student's language and communication needs by planning for direct communication with peers and education personnel, including instruction. For a disabled student with limited language proficiency in English, the IEP should address the language needs as they relate to the IEP. For a student whose disability includes behavior that impedes the learning of the student or others, the IEP should detail positive intervention strategies and supports to address the behavioral issues. The IEP should also address any necessary testing accommodations or modifications the student will need in order to participate in state and national standardized achievement tests. If the team decides these types of tests cannot accurately assess the student, a detailed explanation must be included in the IEP. When an IEP is completed, it should be implemented without delay.

When students reach certain ages, the IEP must contain further provisions. Starting at age 14 and continuing each year subsequently, the IEP should discuss the educational needs of the student to effectively make the transition to life after secondary school. The educational program should be designed to tailor studies to post-secondary needs. At age 16, the IEP should include any necessary transitional services beyond school, including statements regarding the responsibilities of agencies to provide such services.

Failure to include any required element of the IEP can result in the invalidation of the entire document. All requirements must be discussed at the IEP meeting and written into the document. Failure to write at least one measurable goal for each identified area of need can also result in invalidation of the IEP. Not every flaw, however, is necessarily fatal to an IEP. Some courts have been willing to ignore minuscule inadequacies in the IEP process, so long as the school district substantially complied with the requirements under IDEA. One court, while noting, "the school system did not technically comply with a number of IDEA provisions," stated the errors "were not done in bad faith, still allowed [the student] to benefit educationally, and still allowed [the student's] parents to participate fully and effectively" (*Myles S. v. Montgomery County Board of Education*, 1993, p. 1561). In that case, the court held that the minor flaws had to be corrected but did not invalidate the IEP or render inadequate the past education and services provided for the student.

The IEP should be written as an integrated document, intended to systematize the student's educational program. The IEP should be written with a clear understanding of the skills and behaviors at issue and how they are to be addressed. The annual goals should detail the expected levels of performance for a year's progress. All objectives should be measurable, as should the steps needed to reach the objectives. The objectives should be based on the student's current level of performance and build logically to the long-term goals. The IEP should be very specific about how much time the student will spend in general education settings and how much in special education settings. The type and amount of general education should be detailed in the same way the special education and related services are. These precise objectives and goals of the IEP "significantly reduce the discretion heretofore left to the education agency as to instructional methods" (Huefner, 1998, p. 1113). There is no requirement in IDEA that the document created by the IEP team must be signed. However, it is good practice to have all members of the team sign and date the document to avoid future problems.

For students who attend charter schools, this process is the same as if the student were in a typical public school. An IEP, in rare circumstances, can be developed to place a student in a private school or a private residential facility. Private placements occur if the LEA cannot meet the needs of the disabled student within the school district or at a nearby public facility. The two likeliest needs for a private placement are when a student requires the consistent, structured environment of a 24-hour program to learn or when a student can encode and generalize learning only in a single environment. When a student receives a private placement for medical reasons, such as psychiatric problems, the LEA is responsible solely for meeting the student's educational needs (See, e.g, *Clovis Unified School District v. California Office of Administrative Hearings*, 1990). However, if a student receives private placement for an interrelated set of needs (educational, medical, social, and emotional) which cannot be separated, then the LEA will be responsible for the entire cost of the placement (See, e.g, *Kruelle v. New Castle County School District*, 1981). When an LEA places a student in a private school or institution, the LEA retains responsibility to assure that the IEP is complied with and must work with representatives of the private facility to do so.

If a private placement is to occur, the LEA is responsible for developing the initial IEP and for ensuring compliance with the IEP after the placement is made. The LEA remains responsible for ensuring that the student receives the special education and related services guaranteed by the IEP. The LEA must also make sure the parents are allowed to participate at the appropriate level after the student has been placed in a private school or facility. When the IEP is created or modified so that a private placement is to occur, a representative from the private school or facility must be a part of the IEP team.

If parents choose to unilaterally place their child in a private school or facility, even though a public school can meet the educational needs of the child, the LEA will still have responsibilities. Though it will not have to pay for the private education costs, the LEA will be responsible to assure that the disabled student still receives special education and related services, including proper evaluation and the implementation of an IEP. The SEA has a duty to monitor each LEA for compliance with these requirements. If the parents unilaterally move their child into a private setting following denial of their procedural rights, the LEA may be responsible for reimbursing the costs of the private education (*Florence County School District Four v. Carter*, 1993; *School Committee, Town of Burlington v. Department of Education of Massachusetts*, 1985). However, if parents move their child for unusual reasons, the LEA will not be responsible for the costs the parents incur. For example, when parents who feared their deaf daughter would learn sign language in a public school moved her to a private school, the court refused to order reimbursement of private education expenses, as the move had no valid educational basis (*Bonnie Ann F. v. Calallen Independent School District*, 1993).

DUE PROCESS REQUIREMENTS

In creating IDEA, Congress allotted "a generous bill of rights for parents, guardians, and surrogates of handicapped children who might wish to contest the evaluation and placement policies of educational authorities" (*Stemple v. Board of Education*, 1980, p. 898). When the parents or the LEA disagree regarding any of the matters addressed in the IEP process, including identification, evaluation, placement, or provision of an FAPE, either party may initiate a due process hearing. Parents can initiate a due process hearing if they do not agree with the identification or non-identification of a disability or the classification of the disability or the placement decisions. If parents disagree with the evaluation, they can seek to get an independent evaluation of the student. Parents also can initiate a due process hearing if the LEA fails to follow the proper procedures during the identification and placement process. When parents refuse to consent to evaluation or placement, the LEA can initiate a due process hearing or, if state law allows, seek judicial intervention. The majority of IDEA disputes arise from placement decisions, such as whether a student should be in a general education classroom, a special education classroom, or a residential facility. Other long-term areas of contention have included appropriateness of the IEP (*Burke County Board of Education v. Denton*, 1990), appropriateness of the related services (*Irving Independent School District v. Tatro*, 1984), special needs for transportation (*Hurry v. Jones*, 1984), and the need for year-round schooling (*Battle v. Pennsylvania*, 1980). If a disagreement between parents and the LEA is entirely methodological, such as which type of speech development program is used to work on the student's speech impediment, IDEA gives discretion to the schools. The LEA, however, does not receive discretion for any disagreement that involves a mixture of methodology and another kind of issue. Courts have been very careful, however, to not let school districts claim non-methodological issues as methodology to assure an outcome in the school district's favor (*Lachman v. Illinois State Board of Education*, 1988). Otherwise, parents have the right to use the due process hearing and appeals process to challenge the opinions of the school officials.

This hearing is designed to be impartial, no matter which party requests it. Depending on state law, the hearing will be conducted either by the LEA or the SEA. The parents have the right to have the hearing conducted by an individual who is not employed by the LEA or the SEA and who does not have any other conflict of interest relating to the hearing. The hearing must be scheduled to accommodate the parents, the student, and the representatives of the LEA. There is no established time limit on how long the parents have the right to appeal a placement decision. Both sides in the hearing have the right to counsel, as well as the due process rights to present evidence, obtain a verbatim transcript of the hearing, compel attendance by witnesses, and confront and cross-examine those witnesses. Before the hearing, parents should be informed of the availability, if any, of free or low-cost legal assistance. Somewhat surprisingly, fewer than half of parents involved in due process hearings hire legal counsel (Shemberg, 1997). If the parents have counsel, the school district is not responsible for paying the attorney's fees, but the parents can request reimbursement if they prevail in the proceedings. IDEA also allows parents to bring in individuals with expertise relevant to the case. Evidence must be disclosed to the opposing party five days prior to the hearing. If it is not, such evidence will only be admissible if the opposing party does not object to it being used.

The hearing officer will decide the issue as presented by the parties; hearing officers generally will not suggest creative solutions of their own devising. When the hearing officer reaches a decision, it must be in writing and have detailed findings of fact. The decision must be made no later than 45 days after the request for the hearing. Some state laws may have additional deadlines within the 45-day period. Once this decision is made, the losing party may appeal to the SEA in states where the LEA makes the initial decision. In such states, the SEA must make the ruling on the merits of the appeal within 30 days of the request of the appeal. Upon review, the SEA is required to examine the record in its entirety, verify all due process requirements were met, gather any additional evidence that is necessary, allow further argument if necessary, and make an independent decision regarding the appeal. The parties must receive a written copy of the findings and the decision.

After the SEA has reached a decision, an appeal can be made as a civil action in state court or federal court. The case cannot, however, be simultaneously litigated in both state and federal court. In states where there is no hearing at the LEA and the SEA makes the first decision about the case, the first appeal is directly to the state court or the federal court. When the case enters state court or federal court, additional evidence may be introduced. The court will rule on the case based on the standard of a preponderance of the evidence, which means the winning party need only be slightly more persuasive. Under a standard of a preponderance of the evidence, the court will find for the party whose correctness is more probable than not. The court will give due weight to the conclusions of the administrative hearing, but will not hesitate to use their significant power to protect the rights of children under IDEA. If the parents prevail in the appeals process and the LEA still does not implement the decision, the parents can seek to have the court enforce the decision.

Since 1997, IDEA has been written to encourage the use of mediation to resolve disputes regarding placement decisions. Mediation is a type of dispute resolution that is informal, with the mediator being a neutral third party. The most unique feature of mediation is that it is non-binding. The mediator cannot force the parties to accept a decision. The goal of mediation is to have the neutral mediator act as a facilitator for the two opposing parties to reach a compromise or a consensus. What is discussed in the mediation remains entirely confidential, as both parties must sign confidentiality agreements beforehand, and cannot be used in subsequent due process hearings or court proceedings.

Mediation has been encouraged for a number of reasons. First, the appeals process can vary wildly in duration, as short as few weeks or as long as years. Second, it can be a costly process for school districts and for parents who elect to employ an attorney for the proceedings. Even if the parents ultimately prevail and receive reimbursement for their expenses, the initial outlay of money can be quite taxing. Third, many families face great emotional stress while going through a series of due process hearings and appeals. Also, due process hearings tend to be confrontational, which is not conducive to the parties working together in the best interests of the student. Congress decided the mediation option might make the process less taxing and less confrontational.

Each state maintains a list of qualified, impartial mediators for IDEA disputes. If the parties agree to mediation, the mediator is selected randomly from the list and serves only if both parties accept that selection. State law dictates whether attorneys are allowed to attend the mediation proceedings, but the state is responsible for the cost of the entire mediation. One commentator has insightfully suggested that states should tighten the requirements for mediators further, employing only mediators who are certified in sophisticated mediation techniques, knowledgeable about special education law, employed by an independent organization, and ready to take an active role in problem solving (Beyer, 1999). Participation in the mediation process is entirely voluntary; if parents choose not to participate, their rights to a due process hearing cannot be delayed or denied.

While the appeals process is ongoing, the stay-put provision applies. Until a final decision is reached regarding the placement of the student, the student will remain in the then-current placement prior to the beginning of the disagreement regarding the student's placement. Stay-put does not mean that every minor detail of a placement must be kept the same. However, any significant or substantial change in the education or special services provided to the student would constitute a violation of the stay-put provision. School districts also cannot use subterfuge to circumvent the stay-put provision. A school district cannot discontinue or stop funding a program that is the center of a dispute.

The stay-put provision does not affect the decisions of the parents, just the decisions of the school board. The parents and the school board can agree to a change to a mutually agreeable interim placement while the dispute is occurring, but such an agreement does not constitute an admission by either party that the other is correct. This action allows both parties to act on the best interests of the student in the situation without creating legal ramifications to the case. Whether the student stays in the then current placement or is moved to a mutually agreeable interim placement, the stay-put provision applies so long as hearings and appeals continue. The court can intercede and change a placement during the appeals process if the court finds immediate intervention necessary for the health of the student. Courts will only do this on the rare occasions when one side clearly has a stronger argument and the student is in danger of suffering some form of irreparable injury unless the court takes immediate action.

The federal government, through the Department of Education, provides the ultimate safeguard that the due process rights of students with disabilities are protected. The Department of Education audits the states to ensure proper conduct under IDEA and appropriate use of IDEA funds. If the Department of Education is displeased with the activities of a state, it can withhold funding, issue a cease-and-desist order, or negotiate a compliance agreement with the state. These are not idle threats, as there was concern that the state of New York would lose its IDEA funding in 2000 (Fleischer & Zames, 2001). The federal government even has some standing to sue states to force compliance with IDEA in some areas. A district court held that the federal government, under the Civil Rights of Institutionalized Persons Act of 1980, has standing to sue a state that is not providing an FAPE to the students in state-run residential facilities (*United States v. Tennessee*, 1992). The state governments are also responsible to monitor the activities of each LEA and can withhold funding until the LEA is in compliance in the same way the federal government can force compliance by state governments. The individual school, in turn, must monitor all teachers for compliance with each student's IEP. Willful disregard of an IEP by a school or by an individual teacher can result in liability to suit. In one case, a student's social studies teacher disregarded the testing accommodations in the student's IEP, of which he was fully aware, and failed the student who was unable to take the tests in the format presented by the teacher (*Doe v. Withers*, 1993). The parents sued the teacher and received a jury award of $15,000.

INFANTS, TODDLERS, TRANSITIONS

Children with disabilities also have rights before they begin school and when they are making the transition after graduating from high school. IDEA contains what is known as the Infants and Toddlers with Disabilities Act (ITDA). For children from birth to school age, ITDA is designed to prevent young children with disabilities from suffering developmental delays that would put them behind once they began school. These early intervention services are for children with diagnosed physical or mental disabilities. Under ITDA, definition of disabilities is more flexible than under the regular part of IDEA.

These publicly funded and publicly supervised services are intended to meet the special needs of the child, such as physical, cognitive, communicative, social, emotional, or adaptive needs. These services can include counseling, family training, therapy, home visits, psychological services, case management services, social work services, transportation, or assistive technology. To the maximum extent feasible, these services are to be provided in natural environments, such as the child's home and other local community settings. Unlike the main part of IDEA, coordination and supervision of ITDA services are not the direct responsibility of the SEA. Instead, most states use an interagency panel to direct the activities between education, welfare, health, and other state departments. ITDA is more oriented toward working with the whole family and with diverse agencies than the regular part of IDEA.

As the IEP is the keystone of normal IDEA services, an Individualized Family Services Plan (IFSP) is the keystone of services under ITDA. The IFSP is developed by a team, which includes the parents and other family members, an interagency case manager, representatives of all agencies involved, and persons conducting the evaluations of the child. The IFSP team must meet at least every six months to review, update, and evaluate the IFSP. The IFSP must state the following:

1. The objective level of physical, cognitive, communicative, social, emotional, and adaptive development;
2. The family resources, concerns, and goals relating to the child with a disability;
3. The expected outcomes of the plan, including timelines, objectives, procedures, and evaluation criteria;
4. The thresholds when modification or revision of the plan will be necessary;

5. The specific services to meet the special needs of the child, including frequency, intensity, and method by which services will be delivered;

6. The natural environments in which the child can feasibly receive services;

7. The projected start of services and the anticipated duration of the services;

8. The names and positions of individuals responsible for managing and coordinating the planned services; and

9. The transition steps necessary to prepare the child for special education.

States also have the option of making children age 3 to 5 eligible for special education services before they start school.

IDEA also has special provisions for students with disabilities once they complete high school. Transition services, based on the individual needs of the student, can include development of employment and adult living skills, daily functional skills training, community experience, and vocational evaluation. These transition services, which can be special education or related services, can prepare students with disabilities for post-secondary education, vocational training, employment, and other post-school objectives. The course schedule of the student should reflect the goals of the transition planning. When the IEP team begins to address transition services, which must begin at age 14, the student should be allowed to participate so that the transition services can match the interests and personal goals of the student.

Transition services are important for creating a long-view perspective in the IEP planning. Such considerations will, it is hoped, help the student reach full potential as an adult. The transition plan, which must be updated annually, should address instruction, community services, employment, and other adult-living objectives in terms of measurable goals and criteria. The transition services should be designed to adequately prepare students for the time when they can no longer receive services under IDEA.

CONFIDENTIALITY

The Family Educational Rights and Privacy Act (FERPA), which is designed to protect the privacy of all students, applies to students with disabilities (20 U.S.C.A. sec. 1232g). However, IDEA provides more specific protections of the privacy of students with disabilities than are provided by FERPA. IDEA protects the confidentiality of students and their records. This protection extends to several areas: parental access and amendment, protection from disclosure, and destruction of records. Parents have the right to access all records. The school district is obliged to comply with requests from the parents to inspect or review the records in a timely manner. Parents can also request a copy of all the records. If parents find that information in the records is incomplete or inaccurate, the parents can request the records be amended. If the school does not comply with this request, the parents can request a due process hearing. If the parents prevail in the hearing, the school must alter the records. If the school prevails in the hearing, the parents still have a right to place a challenge in the records.

The records must be kept confidential, with access provided only to school personnel with a legitimate need to know what is in the records, such as the student's teachers and principal. Third parties who have no legitimate need to know the content of the records can only get access to the records if parents give consent. Schools must maintain a list of those who inspect the records other than parents and relevant school personnel, as well as the time, date, and purpose of each inspection. The records should be kept and maintained by a single employee, with appropriate training for the task. If a school fails to ensure the confidentiality of the records, such as by releasing the records without parental authorization, it is liable to suit for damages (*Sean R. v. Town of Woodbridge Board of Education*, 1992).

When the records are no longer necessary for provision of education and related services, parents must be informed by the school district that they have the right to request that the records be destroyed. If the parents do not make such a request, the school may keep the records indefinitely. This right to request destruction of records only involves personal information about the student needed for special education or special services. This right does not include permanent records kept by the school on all students. Further, the notification of the right to destruction of records must also include a statement describing whether any information in the special education records might otherwise be needed, such as for social security benefits.

REMEDIES AND DAMAGE AWARDS

To enforce IDEA, parents are able to seek several kinds of remedies in the courts. These remedies are available so that parents can be compensated completely for expenses or difficulties created by school districts which were not in compliance with the requirements of IDEA. Parents may seek injunctive relief, compensatory education, tuition reimbursement, and attorney's fees. It may be possible, though highly unlikely, that parents might be able to receive punitive damages as well. Most of these remedies must be sought through the courts, and each remedy has a different function. Depending on the particulars of the case, parents may be able to receive a number of different remedies against a school district for one action. In a case of very egregious behavior by a school, the parents who prevailed in that action could conceivably receive injunctive relief, compensatory education, tuition reimbursement, and attorney's fees.

Injunctive relief comes in the form of an injunction, which is a court order to temporarily or permanently cease a particular action or practice. An injunction does nothing for past practices; it only serves to prevent future harms. A preliminary injunction is temporary and is issued before a trial if the party requesting the injunction can prove that some harm would occur if the injunction were not issued. A permanent injunction, awarded by a court after a case is heard, is a ruling by the court to permanently end a certain practice. The ruling in the famous *Mills v. Board of Education of the District of Columbia* (1972) is an example of a permanent injunction. In *Mills*, the court issued a permanent injunction preventing the school district from excluding disabled students from public schools or otherwise denying them the right to receive a public education.

Compensatory education is awarded to students whose educational progress has been negatively affected by denial of an FAPE. An award of compensatory education consists of education beyond what would otherwise be required under law to try to undo the past harm. Compensatory education can be provided in after-school programs, tutoring, summer school, extended school year services, extra related services, or provision for future services (*Jefferson County Board of Education v. Breen*, 1987). Compensatory education can even extend eligibility for services beyond the standard cutoff age of 21. As one court explained, "imposing liability for compensatory educational services on the defendants 'merely requires [them] to belatedly pay expenses that [they] should have paid all along' " (*Miener v. Missouri*, 1986, p. 753). Compensatory education can be awarded by a hearing officer, by the SEA, or by a court.

Tuition reimbursement is an award to parents to cover the expenses the parents incurred by making a unilateral placement of their child in a private institution when the public school failed to provide an FAPE. Such an award is not considered a traditional monetary award, but simply a repayment for expenses that the parents only faced due to an error on the part of the public school. The award can cover both educational expenses and related services. The Supreme Court has held that tuition reimbursement is available to parents when the public school proposes an inappropriate IEP or fails to implement an IEP and, as a result, the parents unilaterally move the student to a private school where the educational needs of the student are met (*School Committee, Town of Burlington v. Department of Education of Massachusetts*, 1985). Parents can receive tuition reimbursement even if they place their child in a school that is not on the state's list of approved special education schools (*Florence County School District Four v. Carter*, 1993). However, if a public school has proposed an appropriate IEP and the parents move the student regardless, tuition reimbursement is not an option (*Florence County School District Four v. Carter*, 1993). Aside from tuition expenses, courts have allowed reimbursement for transportation (*Taylor v. Board of Education*, 1986), psychotherapy (*Max M. v. Illinois State Board of Education*, 1986), lost earnings for parents while they were defending the rights of their child (*Board of Education of the County of Cabell v. Dienelt*, 1988), interest on tuition loans (*Board of Education of the County of Cabell v. Dienelt*, 1988), insurance costs (*Shook v. Gaston County Board of Education*, 1989), expenses in locating related services (*Rapid City School District v. Vahle*, 1990), and costs of residential placement (*Babb v. Knox County School System*, 1992).

Parents, if they prevail in their dispute, can request reimbursement for reasonable attorney's fees. If parents do not prevail on a major or central issue in their suit, attorney's fees are not available. The parents don't have to prevail on every issue, or most issues, they simply must prevail on a significant issue they raise. If the ruling in the case is similar to a settlement offer that was rejected by the parents, they cannot be reimbursed for attorney's fees. For an award of attorney's fees to be considered by a court, the action must be completely settled. The fee scale is based on the standard rates in the community for the type of services provided. An award cannot include a bonus or any other special fees. The fee award may include work in preparation for and during due process hearings and court actions, as well as the costs of evaluations, tests, travel, expert witnesses, monitoring to ensure enforcement, and administrative and secretarial tasks. If the court finds that the parents protracted or delayed the resolution of the case, attorney's fees can be reduced or waived. The award may also be reduced if the attorney failed to provide the LEA with information essential to the specific nature of the case. Schools are protected from paying attorney's fees when the parents try to undermine the resolution of the case or when the parents are unnecessarily litigious. Attorney's fees are not available for mediation sessions or for IEP meetings.

All of the remedies listed above are definitely available for parents to seek in IDEA disputes. However, there is another remedy that might be available: punitive damages. Unlike the remedies that are definitely available, Congress has never clearly made punitive damages available under law. Courts are generally unwilling to provide a remedy which is not clearly stated in the relevant law. Punitive damages are an award of monetary damages above and beyond the actual harm as a punishment against the wrongdoer. Punitive damages in any situation are fairly unusual, requiring completely egregious and wrongful behavior. It is hard to imagine a situation where a school could go so far afoul of the requirements of IDEA that punitive damages would become a real option. However, the punitive damages against schools under IDEA may be at least theoretically possible.

THE IEP MATTERS TO EVERYONE

General education teachers need to have a basic understanding of the processes involved in identifying and accommodating students with disabilities. The first step is to recognize that a child possibly needs special education and related services. A school professional may ask that a child be evaluated to see if he or she has a disability. Parents may also contact the child's teacher or other school professional to ask that their child be evaluated. The second step is to have the child evaluated in all areas related to the child's suspected disability. The evaluation results will be used to decide the child's eligibility for special education and related services and to make decisions about an appropriate educational program for the child. The third step is to determine if the child is eligible for special services. If the child is found to be a "child with a disability," as defined by IDEA, he or she is eligible for special education and related services. An IEP meeting is scheduled and the IEP is written. The school then makes sure that the child's IEP is being carried out as it was written. Progress is measured and reported to the parents. The IEP team at least once a year, or more, reviews the child's IEP. Clearly, the IEP is a very important document for children with disabilities and for those who are involved in educating them. Done correctly, the IEP should improve teaching, learning, and achievement. Each child's IEP is different. The document is prepared for that child only and describes the program designed to meet that child's needs.

As the general education teacher on an IEP team, it would be helpful to know the following acronyms.

- EMH—Educable Mentally Handicapped
- TMH—Trainable Mentally Handicapped
- OI—Orthopedically Impaired
- SI—Speech Impaired
- LI—Language Impaired
- VI—Visually Impaired
- EH—Emotionally Handicapped
- SLD—Specific Learning Disabled
- HH—Hospital/Homebound
- PMH—Profoundly Mentally Handicapped
- DSI—Dual Sensory Impaired
- SED—Severely Emotionally Disturbed
- TBI—Traumatic Brain Injury
- DD—Developmentally Delayed
- OHI—Other Health Impaired

This is just a sample of the acronyms used for exceptional students in school systems across the country. A special education teacher can provide you with a more extensive list.

Teachers are vital participants in the IEP meeting as well. At least one of the child's general education teachers must be on the IEP team if the child is (or may be) participating in the general education environment. The general education teacher has a great deal to share with the team. For example, he or she might talk about the specific curriculum in the general classroom; the aids, services, or changes to the educational program that would help the child learn and achieve; and strategies to help the child with behavior, if behavior is an issue. The general education teacher may also discuss with the IEP team the supports for school staff that are needed so that the child can advance toward his or her annual goals, be involved and progress in the general curriculum, participate in extracurricular and other activities, and be educated with other children.

Supports for school staff may include professional development or more training, important for teachers, administrators, bus drivers, cafeteria workers, and others who provide services for children with disabilities. The child's special education teacher contributes important information and experience about how to educate children with disabilities. Because of his or her training in special education, this teacher can talk about such issues as how to modify the general curriculum to help the child learn; the supplementary aids and services that the child may need to be successful in the regular classroom and elsewhere; how to modify testing so that the student can show what he or she has learned; and other aspects of individualizing instruction to meet the student's unique needs. Beyond helping to write the IEP, the special educator has the responsibility for working with the student to carry out the IEP. He or she may work with the student in a resource room or special class devoted to students receiving special education services; team teach with the general education teacher; and work with other school staff, particularly the general education teachers, to provide expertise about addressing the child's unique needs. Depending on the child's individual needs, some related service professionals attending the IEP meeting or otherwise helping to develop the IEP might include occupational or physical therapists, adaptive physical education providers, psychologists, or speech-language pathologists. A child may require any of the following related services in order to benefit from special education. Related services, as listed under IDEA, include, but are not limited to, audiology services, counseling services, medical services, occupational therapy, orientation and mobility services, parent counseling and training, physical therapy, psychological services, recreation, rehabilitation counseling services, school health services, social work services in schools, speech-language pathology services, and transportation.

Kelly and Keyboarding

The IEP goal says that Kelly will learn keyboarding skills. The IEP may say, "By the end of the first semester, Kelly will touch-type a passage of text 15 words per minute with not more than 5 errors on a 5 minute test. By the end of this academic year, Kelly will touch-type a passage of text for 5 minutes at 35 words per minute with not more than 5 errors."

Randi and Reading

Randi is in the fifth grade. According to educational achievement tests, her reading decoding skills are at the second grade level. Randi's parents request special education services to remediate their daughter's reading problems. How will her parents know if Randi is benefiting from the special education program? If Randi is being appropriately educated, her test scores in reading will begin to improve as she goes through the process of remediation. An appropriately written IEP should indicate that after a year of remediation, Randi will make progress in her reading ability and that her educational progress will be measured with educational achievement tests. The ultimate goal is closing the gap between Randi's ability and her reading skills.

An IEP for each child must include:

- A statement of the child's present levels of educational performance
- A statement of annual goals, including short-term instructional objectives
- A statement of the specific special education and related services to be provided to the child and the extent that the child will be able to participate in regular educational programs
- The projected dates for initiation of services and the anticipated duration of the services
- Appropriate objective criteria and evaluation procedures and schedules for determining, on at least an annual basis, whether the short-term instructional objectives are being achieved.

An IEP for each student, beginning no later than age 16 (and at a younger age, if determined appropriate), must include a statement of the needed transition services including a statement of each public agency's and each participating agency's responsibilities or linkages, or both, before the student leaves the school setting.

If a child in your class shows a deficit of several years below the grade level of the rest of the class, then your goal should be more than one year's growth for one year of instruction and to get the child up to grade level. Being behind in a general class can lead to teasing by other students in the class and that must be addressed as well. The IEP is a critical document for a child with special needs and must be prepared with care and high expectations.

A goal should have five components:

- The direction you want to take
- The problem you are specifically addressing
- The present level of achievement
- The amount of change expected by the end of the school year
- The methodology required to achieve the goal.

For example, Marty will increase in-seat, on-task behavior from 0 percent of the time presently to 50 percent of the time by the end of this year by training the teacher in positive behavior interventions that give reinforcement to in-seat, on-task behavior. In another example, Karen will increase self-control from overreacting emotionally to stimuli that are normal in the classroom to the ability to function with limited supervision in classroom settings through individual counseling and reinforcement of positive behaviors in the classroom. Figure 1 is an example of an IEP that begins to provide clear objectives to address the needs of the child.

Any related service must be based on evaluation. The evaluation report must be made available to the parent prior to the IEP meeting. The evaluation report should indicate, if the diagnostician believes the student needs the related service, what the baseline of need is, what should be attained in that area by the end of the year, and what the nature, duration, frequency, and location of the service should be. Related services must be discussed at the IEP meeting and must be written on the IEP. Since the IEP is the agreement by which the school allocates resources, the IEP has to be specific about the related service.

QUESTIONS FOR PARENTS TO CONSIDER

- Did you receive your procedural safeguards prior to the IEP meeting as required by law?
- Did you receive prior written notice as required by law?
- Did the school consider Extended School Year for your child?
- Is your child's IEP in accordance with IDEA?
- Do you have quarterly objectives that will be reported to you in writing?
- Were all the required personnel at the IEP meeting for your child?
- If your child has a behavior that impedes his/her learning or that of others, did the school do a positive behavior plan as part of the IEP?
- Did your child have the required evaluations for the basis of the IEP?
- How was assistive technology handled at your IEP meeting?

Figure 1
Individualized Education Program Example for Erin Roberts

Fill in the following information to construct an Individualized Education Program:

Date of Meeting:

Presenting Problem 1:
Erin has trouble with short-term memory. She forgets homework, especially Math, and she forgets to turn in homework she has completed.

Objectives
(Who, What, When, How)

Objective 1:
Erin's mother will get a daily planner for her. For the next month, her Math teacher will initial Erin's entry in her planner at the end of each class involving an assignment or a turn in. Each day Erin's mother will check for the initials to ensure that homework is not forgotten.

Objective 2:

Objective 3:

Presenting Problem 2:

CROSS-EXAMINATIONS AND REBUTTALS

Peter was a 9-year old boy with diagnosed ADHD, learning disabilities, and emotional problems. He was provided special education services in the general education classroom. His classroom behaviors often upset his new, first-year teacher. He would often ask that directions be repeated and he needed extended time on most assignments. He would also become agitated and frustrated when he could not follow the teacher's instructions. One day Peter was trying to figure out how to cut out and paste a picture onto his class assignment. He was using blunt end plastic school scissors. When a classmate pulled his work away from him, Peter picked up the scissors he was using in a threatening manner to the student and told him he had better watch out.

Write an IEP for Peter.

Explain the role of the LEA and SEA in the IEP process.

Why is parental involvement important on an IEP team?

What are the minimum requirements of an IEP?

How often must an IEP be reevaluated?

When may a due process hearing be initiated?

Explain the purpose and features of mediation.

Define and explain the following:

- ITDA
- FERPA
- IFSP
- Transition Services
- Injunctive Relief
- Compensatory Education

Chapter 6

IDEA, Part III: Applying IDEA

Now that you are acquainted with the terms and concepts of IDEA as well as all of the procedural requirements relating to IDEA, this chapter will illustrate some of the major areas of application of IDEA in the classroom. These areas are the most likely to be encountered by general education teachers when teaching students with disabilities. As with the preceding chapter, general citations of IDEA and the enforcement guidelines of IDEA are not made for each statement. Unless otherwise noted, all information in this chapter about the requirements of IDEA is from the IDEA statute or IDEA enforcement regulations and guidelines.

> It's the beginning of a new school year and Jeremy is in your class. During pre-planning you were informed that he has an emotional/behavioral problem and an IEP was on file. The IEP recommends two periods a day in special education classes and the remainder of the day in general education classes. He runs into the room, sliding down the rows as he proudly takes the last seat in the far left corner of the room. What are your thoughts for goals and objectives for Jeremy?

LRE, PART I: THE IMPORTANCE OF THE LEAST RESTRICTIVE ENVIRONMENT

It has been observed, rather accurately, "regular education teachers, however, are not trained to provide diversified instructional methods or to cope with the needs of diverse learners" (Roberts & Mather, 1995, p. 50). Confounding the situation further, "[m]ost educational theories have been formulated with little, if any, regard for disability; and most teachers are not disabled themselves" (Hahn, 1997, p. 323). Most teachers feel unprepared to handle students with disabilities and must face many other pressures that reduce the ability to individualize instruction. In fact, to most teachers, disability is a strange and unfamiliar concept that both their personal experiences and their general education degrees have left them unprepared to face. Further, with an increase of external pressures on teachers, such as incessant achievement testing and a proliferation of dictated curricular goals, the inherent flexibility of IDEA is significantly constrained. Teachers in general education classrooms feel unprepared to meet the needs of students with disabilities and, even if they felt prepared, the external pressures on the classroom would still inhibit the ability to teach to the best of their ability.

The concept of least restrictive environment has brought many students with disabilities, who would otherwise be segregated, into general education classrooms. The application of LRE has, without question, complicated the job of the educator. But in no way should the concept of least restrictive environment be considered a problem. The concept underlying LRE is that a student with a disability will benefit, academically and non-academically, from being integrated into a general education classroom, so long as such integration is appropriate for the student and does not impair the education of other students. There can be sizable academic benefits for the student with a disability who is educated in a general classroom. The LRE, by forcing schools to place students with disabilities in the most integrated setting possible, enforces a very basic type of equality: the ability to share the same space while doing the same thing. Being in the general education classroom, the same classroom as other students, brings many benefits beyond academics. Disabled students get a chance to be among their peers, to feel like "normal people," to feel like they have a chance to be a part of the real world, and, most importantly, to feel like they have a future in society. These considerations are not minor. Creating an appropriate LRE is of utmost importance to the IEP team; making sure the LRE is properly implemented is of utmost importance to the classroom teacher. Effective integration can change the world for a student with a disability.

> The third of four children in a middle-class family, Andrew James (A.J.) began high school as a five-foot, 100 pound, awkward and insecure freshman. Although the smallest in size in the class of 30, A.J. did not go unnoticed. From the moment he entered each class, he was picking fights with his classmates, taking books from the other boys, pushing students out of their seats, and continually asking to go to the bathroom. When the teachers said no, he would walk to the garbage can, throw away miniscule scraps of paper, and stand by the teacher claiming he was going to have an accident. If he were able to persuade the teacher, the moment he was released from the confines of the class-

room, he would run out the door, down the hallway, banging on the lockers and yelling into classrooms. When he returned to class as though nothing out of the ordinary had occurred, he began talking to his neighbors and asking the teacher what he missed. His grades were poor, he didn't do his homework, and he was continually in detention.

A.J. attended an elementary school where his grade reports included mostly D's and F's. He was retained one year for failures and another year he was assigned to the next grade although his records indicate he did not meet the requirements for promotion. On one standardized test after another, he scored between the 50th and 80th percentiles, yet in the fifth grade he was labeled LD and placed in special education classes several times a day. Notes from previous teachers indicate an ability to do the work but severe attitude and behavior problems. In addition to his poor academic performance, he was regularly in detention for disruptive behavior. His parents transferred him to a different school in the seventh grade, hoping to improve his behavior; they had given up on his academic achievement. The next two years kept his parents in conferences with teachers and administrators and they changed schools one more time.

There was a steady evolution during A.J.'s freshman year. For the first semester he was the chief irritant of the teachers and administration, but his IEP team remained confident. His grades were improving, but he constantly had to be reminded to go to tutoring and complete his homework. The most dramatic change came when A.J. became the manager for the basketball team, as outlined in the IEP. With this responsibility and involvement came a new attention to what was going on in school. When he tried out for the crew team, his classroom behavior calmed down and he wasn't as anxious to start fights. He became interested in keeping his grades up with his fellow crew team members. His mother was really proud of him for trying out for crew as he couldn't swim and was deathly afraid of water. Crew was definitely significant in his growth as his circle of friends grew and he belonged on a team.

LRE, PART II: CREATING AND IMPLEMENTING A LEAST RESTRICTIVE ENVIRONMENT

The least restrictive environment is determined by balancing the requirements of a student's free appropriate public education with the need for the student to be in the most inclusive and least restrictive environment possible. The IEP team must ascertain what environment will allow the student to receive the appropriate education with the highest degree of integration. The IEP must carefully explain the extent to which the disabled student will participate and will not participate with non-disabled students in academic, non-academic, and extracurricular activities. According to the U.S. Department of Education, the goal of the IEP is to "weave in an emphasis upon student involvement in the general curriculum" (United States Department of Education, 1997). There is great flexibility in devising the LRE for an IEP. However, there are certain significant guidelines that must be followed when creating a least restrictive environment.

The least restrictive environment should be in a school as close to the student's home as possible. Unless the student is being sent to a special school or institution that can better serve individual needs, the student should attend the school that a similarly situated non-disabled student would attend. There is no absolute right to attend the closest school. If the closest school cannot provide an FAPE, the student must be sent to another school (*Flour Bluff Independent School District v. Katherine M.*, 1996; *Murray v. Montrose County School District*, 1995; *DeVries v. Fairfax County School Board*, 1989). Further, if the district has a special program at a particular school, it will not be required to replicate the program in other schools simply for the convenience of some students in the program (*Schuldt v. Mankato Independent School District No. 77*, 1991; *Barnett v. Fairfax County School Board*, 1991; *A. W. v. Northwest R-1 School District*, 1987). At the school in which the child is placed, the LRE should be designed to account for all the activities in a student's day, including academic classes, recess, physical education, breaks, and lunch. In each of these activities, the student should be placed with non-disabled students for the "maximum extent appropriate" (34 C.F.R. sec. 300.550(b)(1)). The IEP team should determine a separate least restrictive environment for each of these activities. If a student can only attend special education classes, these other times of the school day provide at least some opportunity for the student to participate in the most integrated, truly least restrictive, environment.

The least restrictive environment can be chosen from a continuum of placement options. The options, from least restrictive to most restrictive, are a general education classroom, special education classes, special education schools, instruction in the home, and instruction in a hospital or a residential institution. A student with a disability is often times placed in a general education classroom for some parts of the day and in a special education classroom for other parts of the day. In that case, the LRE is either the general or special classroom depending on the content or the subject matter or some other reason. If a general education classroom is determined to be the LRE, the school must provide any necessary supplementary services. If the public school district cannot provide the required placement, the student can be placed in a public school in a nearby district, in a private school or institution, or even in an out-of-state facility. In each case, the placement should be in the least restrictive environment that can provide appropriate education and services for that individual student. Though being placed in an out-of-state residential facility may not sound like a least restrictive environment, it may be the least restrictive environment in which a particular student could receive a proper FAPE.

When determining the least restrictive environment, the IEP team has the affirmative duty to consider what placement will give the most benefit, but also what potential harmful effects may come from a particular placement. The LRE must be the least restrictive environment that can provide the appropriate education and services for the student. What is truly least restrictive is an individual matter, determined by the needs of the individual student. The most appropriate LRE can only be decided on a case-by-case basis. Since a school district has the right to determine how to most efficiently allocate its resources, the reasonableness of the cost of a particular placement can be used as a factor in determining the LRE (*A. W. v. Northwest R-1 School District*, 1987; *Roncker v. Walter*, 1983). However, if the IEP team determines a more restrictive placement is necessary, the school district may not refuse to implement the restrictive placement. A school district also may not refuse to permit students with certain types of disabilities from participating in general education classes.

A least restrictive environment cannot be created in a general education classroom if the student is so disruptive in a general education classroom that the education of the other students is significantly impaired (34 C.F.R. sec. 300.552. See, e.g., *Clyde K. and Sheila K. ex re. Ryan D. v. Puyallup School District*, 1994). A teacher should not spend the vast majorit of time working with one student simply to create an LRE for one student (*Daniel R. R. v. Texas Board of Education*, 1989). The general education curriculum should not be modified beyond recognition in attempting to create an LRE (*Daniel R. R. v. Texas Board of Education*, 1989). Further, if a student has a condition that is contagious and poses a health risk to other students, such as HIV, AIDS, or Hepatitis B, the LRE may be the situation where the health risk is best minimized, which would mos likely not be a general education classroom. However, if the disable student is not disruptive and does not pose a significant health risk, but simply requires significant amounts of time and attention, the LRE can be created in a general education classroom by the addition of a teaching assistant or a teacher's aide (*Daniel R. R. v. Texas Board of Education*, 1989).

The case of one particular student is illustrative of how a student's disruptive behavior and difficulty in learning can create a situation where a general education classroom simply cannot be a least restrictive environment. Kari H. suffered from a very rare form of severe mental impairment known as Cri du Chat syndrome, which resulted in her having an I.Q. of 21 (*Kari H. v. Franklin Special School District*, 1999; *Kari H. v. Franklin Special School District*, 1997). The syndrome is characterized by a constant cat-like mewing by the sufferer and further punctuated by hand clapping, noise making, and other types of listlessness. Kari H. manifested all of these symptoms. The court supported the school district's decision to not put Kari H. in any general education classes for the reasons that Kari H. would not get any academic benefit from general education and her behaviors were so disruptive as to significantly curtail the ability of other students to learn.

Courts have identified several important factors for IEP teams and school districts to consider in determining if a general education classroom will provide a least restrictive environment. The benefits, both academic and non-academic, should be considered for the student with a disability in deciding whether the appropriate LRE is in a general education classroom or a special education classroom (*Greer v. Rome City School District*, 1991). Academic factors include ability to keep up with peers, ability to learn most effectively, and ability to progress. Non-academic factors can include self-concept, language skills, and interactions with peers. Courts will generally assume that any meaningful time spent in a general education classroom will also produce non-academic benefits (*Sacramento City Unified School District v. Rachel H.*, 1994).

Courts will also carefully examine the proper use of supplementary aids and services in creating a least restrictive environment (*Oberti v. Board of Education of the Borough of Clementon School District*, 1993). The provision of the correct supplementary aids and services, such as resource rooms, aids, assistants, interventions, and behavior management plans, can allow a student with a disability to participate in a less restrictive, more integrated learning environment. If a school district fails to make appropriate use of or application of supplementary aids and services, or completely fails to provide supplementary aids and services, courts will find that an LRE has not been created for the student (*Oberti v. Board of Education of the Borough of Clementon School District*, 1993; *Greer v. Rome City School District*, 1991; *Daniel R. R. v. Texas Board of Education*, 1989). A school district must consider all potential supplementary aids and services when creating an LRE (*Oberti v. Board of Education of the Borough of Clementon School District*, 1993; *Greer v. Rome City School District*, 1991; *Daniel R. R. v. Texas Board of Education*, 1989). However, if no supplementary aids or services could possibly allow a particular student to participate in a general education classroom, then the student does not have to fail in the general education classroom before a special education classroom will be considered the appropriate LRE (*Poolaw v. Bishop*, 1995).

EXTENDED SCHOOL YEAR PROGRAMS

An extended school year program is the provision of education and services by the school district to a particular disabled student for more than the typical 180 days in the traditional school year. This type of program allows students with disabilities, who might otherwise regress without constant instruction, to not fall below levels of progress they had previously attained. If the IEP team decides that a student's LRE includes an extended school year program to ensure the FAPE, then the school district must provide such a program, even if the district normally does not. An extended school year program is certainly not required, or even useful, for many students with disabilities. However, if the IEP team deems an extended school year program necessary, it must be provided for the student at no cost to the parents. Students with disabilities can only receive an extended school year program if the IEP determines the services are necessary, on an individual basis, for the student to have an FAPE (*Cordrey v. Euckert*, 1990; *Alamo Heights Independent School District v. State Board of Education*, 1986). Most students who receive extended school year instruction do so because they would otherwise regress in the time that school is not in session. An interruption in education and services would likely lead to the student being harmed academically.

A school district cannot prevent an IEP team from determining that extended school year services are necessary. The courts have routinely held against school districts that have had a policy prohibiting instruction beyond the traditional 180 days (*Cordrey v. Euckert*, 1990; *Johnson v. Independent School District Number 4*, 1990; *Crawford v. Pittman*, 1983). The factors that should be considered in relation to the necessity of an extended school year program include the type and degree of impairment, the student's skill level, the educational structure provided by parents in the home, the availability of resources, and the areas where the student needs ongoing instruction (*Johnson v. Independent School District Number 4*, 1990). Before including extended school year programs in an IEP, the IEP team should be sure such a program is truly necessary (*Johnson v. Independent School District Number 4*, 1990).

DISCIPLINE AND THE DISABLED STUDENT

Students with disabilities are not above or exempted from normal disciplinary procedures. In many occasions when a student with a disability is disciplined, though, IDEA becomes a relevant issue. First, a student with a disability cannot be punished for being disabled. Second, each student with a disability is protected from any disciplinary procedures that result in a unilateral change in placement. If the disabled student's educational placement is not changed by a disciplinary action, the school generally may use the same disciplinary measures on students with disabilities as on all other students (34 C.F.R. sec. 300.513, Comment; 20 U.S.C.A. sec. 1415(k)). The FAPE and the LRE, however, must be considered in any punishment of a student with a disability.

A student with a disability cannot be disciplined for reasons resulting from the disability. A deaf student cannot be punished for failing to comply with spoken instructions. A blind student cannot be punished for knocking over something in a walking path. A student with Tourette's syndrome cannot be punished for having an outburst during class. A student with a learning disability cannot be punished for being a poor speller. All this seems pretty straightforward. However, before IDEA, such absurd reasons for discipline were not uncommon. "Because the states had proven either unable or unwilling to provide students with the protection and education they needed, the federal government provided in IDEA a statutory remedy for those so wronged by school districts and administrators" (Jensen, 1996, p. 36). To prevent such injustices, IDEA created specific discipline procedures and requirements to protect students with disabilities from being punished for having disabilities.

Under IDEA, an FAPE must be provided to all students between the ages of 3 and of 21, even those who have been suspended for an extended period or expelled from school. For the first 10 days each school year that a student with a disability is suspended for disciplinary reasons, the school need not provide any educational services. After a cumulative total of 10 days of suspension for a school year, however, the school then becomes responsible to assure that education and services are provided to the extent necessary so that the student can continue to advance in order to approximate the IEP goals. School personnel, including the special education teacher, determine what constitutes necessary education and services for the individual student. The interim alternative educational setting must enable the student to continue receiving education and services as required by the IEP, as well as services and modifications to address the behavioral issues. Suspensions should not be used in a way that they function as change in placement for the disabled student (*Honig v. Doe*, 1988). The Supreme Court did allow for temporary suspensions for up to 10 school days for students posing an immediate threat to others' safety (*Honig v. Doe*, 1988). However, any out-of-school suspension of a disabled student for more than 10 days constitutes a change in placement (*Honig v. Doe*, 1988). An in-school suspension can be longer than 10 days, so long as it does not constitute a change in placement under the IEP (*Hayes v. Unified School District No. 377*, 1989). A student with a disability cannot get a permanent injunction against being suspended (*Christopher W. v. Portsmouth School Committee*, 1989).

Less drastic punishments are, of course, allowable. The Supreme Court has endorsed the use of "study carrels, timeouts, detentions, or the restriction of privileges," among other disciplinary options, for students with disabilities (*Honig v. Doe*, 1988, p. 325). Further, IDEA does not "limit the equitable powers of district courts such that they cannot, in appropriate cases, temporarily enjoin a dangerous disabled child from attending school" (*Honig v. Doe*, 1988, p. 327). The real question in each punishment for a student with a disability is whether the misbehavior is related to the disability or a manifestation of the disability. This relatedness test partly results from "the traditional principle in Anglo-American law" that "punishment should attach to the notion of fault" (Dagley, McGuire, & Evans, 1994, p. 14). If a student's misbehavior stems from a disability, then the behavioral problem is not the fault of the student. The student cannot be faulted for being unable to hear, unable to walk, or unable to control certain emotional outbursts.

When reviewing major disciplinary actions taken against disabled students, courts will examine whether the discipline was related to the disability. If a serious disciplinary action is taken as a result of the student's disability or is related to the disability, the proper response is a change in placement rather than suspension or expulsion (*Doe v. Koger*, 1979). However, if a suspension or expulsion of a disabled student is not related to or resulting from the student's disability, courts accept such disciplinary actions as proper, so long as the student is not denied the education or related services necessary under the IEP (*S-1 v. Turlington*, 1981). If there is no finding of a relationship between the disability and the misbehavior, the disabled student faces the same punishment as any other student.

In most cases, it is fairly clear if a disability has caused a certain discipline problem. For example, throwing spitballs, carrying a knife, and drinking on school property are not likely to be caused by being deaf or being mobility-impaired. The difficulties with the relatedness of discipline to disability can become difficult in extraordinary circumstances where the disability may have a very attenuated relationship to the misbehavior. A small number of cases have received quite a bit of attention for how courts found a relationship between a discipline problem and a disability. In one such case, a court held that a student's learning disabilities prevented him from understanding the implications of what his peers had asked him to do; his peers had convinced the student to become involved in drug trafficking (*School Board of Prince William County v. Malone*, 1985). In another case, a court curiously held that children with orthopedic disabilities were more likely to get involved in fights to cope with the stress and vulnerability (*S-1 v. Turlington*, 1981).

The results of both of these cases are unusual for two reasons. First, few courts would even consider such tenuous relationships between discipline and disability. Most courts have held that attenuated relationships between misbehavior and disability were not distinguishable from the relationships between the problems of non-disabled students, such as hunger or low self-esteem, and their discipline problems (*Doe by Gonzales v. Maher*, 1986). Second, such holdings are deeply insulting to individuals with disabilities. The assertion is that a person with a learning disability has no ability to tell right from wrong and a person with a physical disability has no control over their emotions. Such holdings demonstrate a profound bias against disabled individuals, treating them as helpless and unable to think for themselves.

If a student with a disability misbehaves in a way that is not rationally connected to the disability, the student should be punished like any other student, so long as the IEP does not specify precise punishments. Such a policy is only fair to both students with disabilities and everyone else in the school environment. There is one significant exception to this statement, however. If you work in a school district that still adheres to the practice of corporal punishment, do not employ it on students with disabilities. A school that uses corporal punishment on a student with a disability may quickly be in federal court answering to serious charges of violating the due process rights of the student (*Waechter v. School District No. 14-030*, 1991).

When a disabled student is facing disciplinary action, the following steps should be taken to avoid problems under IDEA. Members of the IEP team should determine if the behavior is related to the student's disability. Such a determination is known as a manifest determination review, as in the misbehavior was a manifestation of the disability. A behavior isn't a manifestation of the disability only if the IEP and placement were appropriate, the education and services provided were consistent with the IEP, the disability did not impair understanding the consequences of the behavior, and the disability did not impair ability to control the behavior. The team should consider the student's IEP and placement, evaluations, diagnostic results, and the nature of the behavior and subsequent disciplinary action. If the review finds the behavior was related to the disability or that the IEP was inappropriate, the student cannot be suspended for more than 10 days or expelled.

If there is no reasonable relationship between the misbehavior and the disability, normal disciplinary actions may be taken so long as they don't conflict with the IEP and so long as the FAPE is provided. A school that wants to suspend a disabled student for more than 10 days must begin proceedings to have a change in placement made before the suspension can begin. The parents, however, can agree to the suspension as a change in placement. For a truly dangerous disabled student, the school may seek a preliminary injunction keeping the student out of school until an administrative hearing can make a determination regarding the change in placement. One federal circuit court created a very useful test for removing a dangerous student with a disability. The *Light v. Parkway* test allows schools to remove a potentially dangerous disabled student if keeping the student in the current placement is likely to result in injury to the student or others and the school has made reasonable attempts to minimize the risk of injuries (*Light v. Parkway School District*, 1994). If a student is kept out of school for being a danger, an alternative placement must be available for the student within 45 days. If a disabled student brings a weapon or drugs on to school property, in violation of the Gun-Free Schools Act of the Goals 2000: Educate America Act, school officials can unilaterally place the student in an interim alternative setting for up to 45 days (20 U.S.C.A. sec. 7151).

The following interview is from a student who successfully finished high school as a result of a caring general education teacher and the requirements of IDEA.

I had trouble when I was younger because I didn't fit in. I seemed older than everyone. I didn't act crazy or do drugs. I want to be a cop. My dad was a cop. Now he is a security guard. I had trouble with kids on my block. I wasn't a fighter. I always tried to talk my way out of it. I had a lot of problems with kids. I didn't fit in. In school I got in fights all the time. I tried not to fight back but I'd end up a bloody mess. I had a very bad temper. I suppressed all my anger and let it out on the teachers. I was suspended a number of times. I didn't want to stay in school. I was asked to leave a few schools. I had a bad attitude. When I came here everyone was so different. My dad taught me to watch my back. Schoolwork was boring but I read all the time. I collect antiques so I would read everything I could find about antique watches, clocks, victrolas. I was kicked out of six schools and held back two grades. I argued with the teachers and didn't have any friends. I've been through psychiatric counseling because when my grandfather died I couldn't take it. I was paranoid. I was in counseling for five years and I've been labeled as unstable. My mother was put in an institution and when they recommended I be put in one, she said no way. They put me on three medications and a strict diet. I joined the track team but practice was in the park and my dad told me to never go to the park because there were muggers and rapists and drug dealers so I bought two starter pistols I carried around. One fell out when I was running and I was expelled. Then I went to another school. I was so scared. I got in tons of fights and I was afraid of the kids. I thought I was going to die. I finally made a few friends but I got in with the wrong group. I started smoking at 12, still do. In eighth grade I started failing everything. I failed summer school. I was ready to drop out. If I hadn't come here, I would have. But I was scared and my reputation proceeded me. Mr. Starkey helped me the most. He put his neck on the chopping block for me and bailed me out of fights a couple of times. He is the person who has made the biggest impact on my life. I didn't like being bossed around by a 16-year old senior when I was a 17-year old freshman so I didn't get involved in too many activities. Mr. Starkey talked me into staying in school when I thought about dropping out. This will be the first time I have completed school somewhere.

When a student with a disability begins to have significant or continuing problems with discipline, the IEP team must consider whether the student's placement is appropriate. A student with a disability who is in an inappropriate placement will often times display feelings of discomfort or helplessness through behavior. In any case where a disabled student is evidencing consistent discipline problems, the classroom teacher and the other members of the IEP team should seriously consider reviewing the specifics of the IEP.

Regardless of whether or not the school seeks to take a serious disciplinary action, an IEP meeting must be held for any significant or continuing disciplinary issue to discuss if a change in placement or another part of the IEP would address the educational problem. This meeting must occur within 10 days of the disciplinary decision. If the parents and the other members of the IEP team agree, the placement can be changed to hopefully improve the behavior of the student. If the parents and the school do not agree on the appropriate actions to improve the student's behavior, then the two sides may pursue the administrative and legal processes. In disciplinary matters, the parents have the right to an expedited hearing.

If a student with a disability is disciplined for actions as a result of a disability that the school has not recognized, the procedural protections under IDEA will protect the student prior to formal classification, so long as the LEA had some warning that the student might be disabled. For these purposes, warning can be construed from parental concern about a need for special education, a parental request for an evaluation, performance or behavior of the student that suggests the need for special education, or concern expressed by a teacher about the need for special education. If the LEA has had warning that the student might be disabled and the student is identified after a disciplinary action related to the disability has been taken, the protections of IDEA regarding discipline will attach to the student for the disciplinary action taken prior to identification. Also, inappropriate punishments for actions related to a student's disability can be expunged from the student's permanent record at the parents' request in some situations.

Several steps can be taken to avoid problems with discipline under IDEA. The best place for the preemptive steps is in the IEP. When creating the IEP, the parents and other team members can set behavioral goals and standards, as well as detail acceptable disciplinary procedures. The discipline in the IEP then can directly match the student's level of understanding and the anticipated areas in which the student might cause problems. An IEP, of course, cannot anticipate all potential disciplinary problems of any given student, but it can address many potential problems and create a frame of reference for unexpected behavioral issues, ultimately allowing the student to receive specific, productive discipline when necessary.

EXTRACURRICULAR ACTIVITIES

Under IDEA, students with disabilities have the right to "an equal opportunity for participation" in non-academic and extracurricular activities as well as academic activities (34 C.F.R. sec. 300.306(a)). These activities "may include counseling services, athletics, transportation, health services, recreational activities, special interest groups or clubs," as well as "referrals" and "employment" (34 C.F.R. sec. 300.306(b)). This requirement is of equal opportunity and does not dictate the participation of disabled students in the extracurricular activities of their choosing. However, if the activity is written into the IEP, then the student has the right to participate in the activity.

CROSS-EXAMINATIONS AND REBUTTALS

Explain the benefits of the LRE for a student with a disability.

When would an extended year program be written into an IEP?

As the general education teacher on a student's IEP team, what steps should you follow when the student is facing disciplinary action? Why?

When may a student with a disability not be disciplined?

What factors would you propose to include in an IEP for a student diagnosed with ADHD in your class?

What might you encourage the IEP team to consider in planning an IEP for a student with a severe emotional disorder who possesses low-self esteem, feelings of alienation which result in anger and violent outbursts?

Chapter 7

IDEA, Part IV: Much Ado

The first outspoken proponent of universal education was Jan Amos Komensky, who wrote using the name Comenius. Comenius proclaimed: "The slower and weaker the disposition of any man, the more he needs assistance" (Comenius, 1910, p. 66). Comenius, in the middle of the seventeenth century, was already recognizing the need for special education at a time when the vast majority of children were not educated at all. (For a study of Komensky and his ideas about education, see Sadler, 1966.) This insight, however, remains misunderstood by many people who comment on the education of students with disabilities.

IDEA and the advances in the educational rights of the disabled have not been universally praised. Some critics claim IDEA costs too much. Other critics assert that IDEA endangers the safety of the non-disabled students. A further group of critics believes that IDEA robs general education students of their rights to an appropriate education by placing disabled students into traditional classrooms. Many interesting attempts have been made by various schools, districts, and even one state to avoid complying with the requirements of IDEA. Though these actions are not accompanied by a critical theory to justify them, attempts to avoid complying with the law certainly also constitute criticisms of IDEA. Obviously, IDEA is not perfect. No law ever is. However, attacks on the essential principles of IDEA are hardly warranted.

The previous chapters present the benefits of IDEA and the good it accomplishes; the existence of numerous criticisms of the statute should also be recognized. Rather than attacking a large number of the provisions of IDEA, critics have focused on a relatively limited number of points about the law. So why, you ask, would there be a small, but particularly bellicose, chorus of voices singing, "How Do You Solve a Problem like IDEA?" The answer is undoubtedly multifaceted, but the likeliest reasons are painful ones, such as misunderstanding and bias. For an individual who has not been in school, either as a student or a teacher, for many years, it may be difficult to conceive of an integrated classroom. Such individuals may be so used to, and comfortable with, the outdated notion that the disabled students belong separated from the other students, they will have difficulty understanding how an integrated classroom can function properly. One court actually had to hold a district in violation of IDEA for a policy (that the district asserted was central to its educational philosophy) preventing integration of disabled students (*Roncker v. Walter*, 1983). Other critics misunderstand IDEA and what it means for students and schools. The more sinister reason for attacking IDEA derives from social bias against the disabled. Someone who is uncomfortable around the disabled or holds prejudiced ideas about people with disabilities will not want equal educational opportunities for students with disabilities. The same critics will certainly not want disabled students educated in the same classrooms as other students. It is not fair to assume everyone who criticizes IDEA is prejudiced against the disabled; however, it is important to remember that such people do exist.

In the popular media, much of the discussion about the education of the disabled has revolved around the costs of educating disabled students and whether these expenditures are worthwhile. Depressingly, arguments are still made today that educating some or all disabled students is a waste of public funds. Some critics seem to believe that educating students with disabilities has, by itself, created the federal deficit. Complaints about the costs of educating disabled students have been appearing in the popular media for years (Allis, 1996; Gubernick & Conlin, 1997). One article labels IDEA as "an unmonitored mess," "a costly failure," and "a scandalous waste of money" (Gubernick & Conlin, 1997, p. 66). Though educating disabled students can be expensive in some cases, the costs do not justify any reactionary arguments that educating disabled students is too expensive. Each school district faces very real costs to educate disabled students, but those costs are necessary to provide free appropriate public educations to students with disabilities.

IDEA applies to many public school students; the number annually tends to be approximately 10 percent (Hallenbeck & Kauffman, 1994). Usually, more than 5 million children with disabilities are receiving some form of special education at any time (Vanderwood, McGrew, & Ysseldyke 1998). Under IDEA, the cost of educating one profoundly disabled public school student can be over $100,000 annually (McCarthy, 1993). If the child is also in a residential care facility, that cost can increase substantially (Bartlett, 1993). Cases like these, however, are extremely unusual. The extraordinary cases, however, are often cited by critics of IDEA as somehow typical of spending on disabled students. In one extremely unique case, a school district paid for the education of one "autistic and severely mentally retarded" student at a special Japanese institution (*Drew P. v. Clarke County School District*, 1989). In another unique case, a South Dakota school district paid for the education of a severely autistic student in a special private school in the Boston area, as well as eight trips a year for the student's family to visit (Allis, 1996). These cases were noteworthy for the fact that they were very unusual, but critics of IDEA try to use these cases as an indictment of the law itself.

A sampling of court decisions from the past few years in which parents have sued under IDEA demonstrates just how expensive the education of disabled students can be in the most extreme circumstances. A school district was ordered to provide continuous one-on-one nursing for a ventilator dependent student so that student could participate in special education classes (*Cedar Rapids Community School District v. Garrett F.*, 1999). For the same reason, another school district was ordered to provide continuous one-on-one nursing for monitoring and adjusting a tracheotomy tube and applying ointment to a student (*Morton Community School District No. 709 v. J. M.*, 1998). If no appropriate learning environment is available in a public school, then the school district must pay for the costs of a private education to meet the needs of the child (*Borough of Palmyra Board of Education v. Hurley*, 1998). If a school fails to provide an IEP for a student who merits one, the school district and the state board of education must pay the private school expenses of the student who sought appropriate education at a private school (*Gadsby v. Grasmick*, 1997; *Shanahan v. Board of Education of the Jamesville-Dewitt School District*, 1997). If the legal efforts of the parents led to the creation of a new IEP or the modification of an existing IEP, the school district and state board of education can be liable for the costs and fees of the parents in the court actions required to alter the IEP (*Mr. X v. New York State Education Department*, 1998; *Tatum v. Andalusia City School*, 1997).

Courts can even order a district or a state to spend more money on special education in general under IDEA (*Corey H. v. Board of Education*, 1998). These costs are certainly substantial enough to get the attention of any state that has to pay them. In some states, the spending on special education, even with the federal funds and local contributions, is very high. State governments on average pay 56 percent of special education expenditures (Lankford & Wycoff, 1999). However, Alabama pays a stunning 85 percent of special education costs in the state, while Oregon contributes a mere 17 percent (Lankford & Wycoff, 1999).

All of these examples and arguments, however, do not demonstrate that the education of disabled students is too expensive a task for public schools. Using the numbers supplied in the mid-1990s in one discussion of the cost of IDEA, special education costs average roughly $30 billion annually for

5 million disabled students (Shapiro, Loeb, & Bowermaster, 1993). Though $30 billion dollars is quite a bit of money, 5 million is a significant number of students. Based on that estimate, the average expenditure is only $6,000 per student. This is hardly inordinate. However, there is a lack of comprehensive data on the exact level of total special education expenditures by state, local, and federal governments, making it "difficult to provide current estimates of the national cost of special education" (Parrish & Wolman, 1999, pp. 214–215). A 1999 study found that only 24 states were able to accurately report statewide special education costs, and only 13 of those states indicated a high degree of confidence about their data (Parrish & Wolman, 1999).

Too often, though, critics of IDEA point to the exceptionally expensive cases. In one notorious case, a federal district court judge actually stepped in to prevent the implementation of an IEP, agreed upon by the school district and the parents, because the judge decided it was against public policy on the grounds of being too expensive (*In re Smith*, 1991). The plan called for placing a severely disabled student in a residential facility, with total education costs being approximately $160,000 a year. Though a large expenditure for one child, it was the method agreed upon by all interested parties to provide an FAPE to this particular student. Instead, the judge held that taxpayers had the right to be protected from paying the education costs of severely disabled students, especially the costs of educating "drug abuse children who are going to be infused into the school system" (p. 1029). Not surprisingly, the judge was swiftly overruled by a higher court (p. 1030). However, the actions of this one particular judge typify the hostility some people feel toward spending a large amount of money on the education of a single student.

The other side of the cost argument is based on the concept that "all children are exceptional, special, and remarkably unique" (Macht, 1998, p. 1). If disabled students receive special education, the argument goes, then all students should receive special education. This kind of argument derives from the different meanings of the word special. In one way, all children are special, but in the context of educational terminology, only disabled children are special. Disabled students became known as "special" or "exceptional" students as euphemisms; educators found it more appealing to speak of "special education" than "disabled education" or "handicapped education" or many other more offensive possibilities. Special education is only called that because, in this context, special means disabled. Students with disabilities do not get treatment anyone else would deem special in the sense most people use the term. There is no private, disabled-only club with saunas, hot tubs, and unlimited private tutors hidden away in each school. In fact, most students who receive special education likely would readily trade in their special education programs if it meant also being rid of their disabilities.

One popular critic of IDEA waxes: "How wonderful it would be if we could spend up to $200,000 annually on all girls and boys to maximize their potential" (Howard, 1994, pp. 147–148). Based on the notion that if a larger sum is spent to educate a disabled student than a student without a disability, then the higher amount should be spent on each student, this argument is nonsensical and demonstrates complete incomprehension of the goals of IDEA. The goal of IDEA is to provide equal education, not equal funding. As an example, consider the following two classmates. Brandy has a disability and Julie does not. The goal of the school year is to teach the same set of skills to each person in the class. It costs $5,000 per student to teach the set of skills to Julie and all her classmates who do not have disabilities, while it costs $10,000 to teach the same set of skills to Brandy because she requires some special learning aids. The purpose of IDEA is to ensure that the extra $5,000 is spent toward Brandy's education so that she will learn the set of skills for that grade. The extra $5,000 allows her to equal the achievement of her classmates; it does not give her double the education of her classmates.

Much of the non-compliance by schools, districts, or states is an unstated variation on the argument that IDEA is too expensive. In order to save money on students with disabilities, "school districts often request parental contributions or may eliminate programs citing lack of funds" (Bates, 1994, p. 220). Courts will often intercede when a school or district attempts such actions. The most interesting situation of this sort occurred when an entire state tried to get out of complying with IDEA. New Mexico tried to bow out of IDEA and was not allowed out of the requirements (*New Mexico Association for Retarded Citizens v. The State of New Mexico*, 1982). New Mexico had "elected to not participate in the Handicapped Act's funding program for primary and secondary school-age handicapped children" and meet only the state law requirements (p. 14, n. 6). The federal courts did not look upon this innovative cost-cutting measure favorably, noting, "[t]he state is, of course, obligated by both federal and New Mexico law to provide all its pre-college age children with appropriate educations" (p. 20).

The circuit court held that New Mexico was still bound by the requirements of the federal law in providing a free appropriate education to its disabled students by still receiving Rehabilitation Act funds. The implication of this holding is that a state which refuses to accept IDEA funding will still have to comply with the requirements of IDEA by virtue of the fact that the state is bound to the requirements of disability laws. The court determined that an entity that refuses to accept IDEA funds from the federal government is still bound by all the requirements of IDEA. To refuse to comply with IDEA would mean losing IDEA funding, Rehabilitation Act funding, and other federal education dollars. For example, in 2000, there was concern that the federal government would withhold a sizable portion of New York State's federal education funding for failure to comply with the requirements of IDEA; had the federal government done so, New York State would have lost $335 million (Fleischer & Zames, 2001). This policy of the courts and the federal government means that any entity directly or indirectly receiving federal education funds, which includes all public schools, school districts, and state education agencies, is going to be bound to the requirements of IDEA without exception.

Ultimately, what is a costly accommodation is entirely relative. One scholar who uses a wheelchair has asserted that chairs are simply a costly accommodation for people who can walk, and by providing chairs, schools spend quite a lot of money accommodating the basic needs of students who don't use wheelchairs (Hahn, 1997). Many pieces of school equipment can be viewed in this manner. Projectors and other visual equipment are accommodations for students who can see. Audio equipment is an accommodation for students who can hear. No one criticizes schools for providing for the basic educational needs of non-disabled students, yet it can be controversial for the federal government to require schools to provide for the basic educational needs of disabled students. Any critic of the costs of IDEA would likely be mortified if a school decreed that chairs and audio/visual equipment were accommodations too costly to provide. However, what constitutes a costly accommodation simply depends on the situation. The year IDEA was first enacted as many as 4 million disabled children were in state-run institutions that were not schools, in which the children would likely spend all of their lives (Kirp, Buss, & Kuriloff, 1974). Considering overall social and economic costs of such treatment, the system under IDEA certainly should seem not only much more humane, but also much less expensive.

Aside from costs, critics of IDEA tend to focus on the impact of the law on the students who are not disabled. One line of this criticism claims that the presence of disabled students in a general education classroom can endanger the safety and sense of security of the non-disabled students. The second line of this criticism asserts that the presence of disabled students in a general education classroom inhibits the learning potential of the other students. Basically, this second argument asserts disabled students will always slow down and detract from the learning process for other students. The first argument is an overreaction to a potential problem; the second is profoundly offensive and unfair.

In a 1996 article entitled "Special Ed," the television program *60 Minutes* presented the implementation of IDEA as a battle between students with disabilities and students without disabilities, with funding as the prize (Special Ed, 1996). The piece showed some parents of general education students expressing anxiety that funding special education takes away from the educational rights of their children (Special Ed, 1996). Such fears are not uncommon. As the disabled have gained legal rights, many non-disabled individuals have felt threatened. In education, the fear expressed by many parents of general education students, as well as by a number of critics of IDEA, is that the presence of disabled students in a classroom will reduce the ability of the other students to feel secure and to learn.

Much of the criticism of IDEA has focused on the stay-put provision. The stay-put provision, according to the arguments of critics, severely limits the ability of teachers and other school officials to take disciplinary action against disabled students or remove disruptive disabled students from classrooms. The stay-put provision mandates that when a change in educational placement is pending for a disabled student, unless the parents agree to the change, the student must remain in the current placement until a final decision is made (20 U.S.C.A. sec. 1415). If discipline problems are related to a student's disability, then the discipline problems must be adequately addressed through the procedures of IDEA. The disabled student will remain in the current educational situation until a final decision is reached regarding a change in placement. The stay-put provision applies even if the student in question is disruptive, as the behavior may be related to or caused by the disability. This policy clearly and unambiguously prevents school officials from having unilateral authority to make education decisions that result in exclusion of disabled students (*Honig v. Doe*, 1988). It also keeps disabled students from being unfairly removed from general education classrooms and prevents disabled students from being bounced around between settings each time a school official decides to alter a placement. Some critics of IDEA incorrectly believe this stay-put provision, by protecting the rights of disabled students to remain in their current educational placements, endangers the safety of other students.

The Supreme Court, addressing this issue in *Honig v. Doe*, gave schools several alternatives for disciplining a disruptive or potentially dangerous student with a disability. The Court decided that indefinite suspensions and expulsions are changes in placement under IDEA and therefore would be a violation of the stay-put provision. However, the presumption in favor of the student's current placement can be overcome by a showing from school officials that the placement endangers the student or others. Further, the Court gave schools the right to suspend disabled students for up to 10 days without it being considered a change in placement. Schools also have the right to use carrels, detentions, timeouts, restriction of privileges, and other alternate disciplinary methods for disruptive disabled students. The Supreme Court, though limiting suspensions and expulsions of disruptive disabled students, provided numerous avenues for disciplining students with disabilities. The Court, however, did clearly state that IDEA was intended "to strip schools of the unilateral authority they had traditionally employed to exclude disabled students, particularly emotionally disturbed students, from school" (p. 306).

IDEA also provides a procedure for changing the placement of a disruptive or potentially dangerous disabled student (20 U.S.C.A. sec. 1415(k)).

Schools have the right to seek a court order compelling the removal of a disabled student who poses the threat of injury (20 U.S.C.A. sec. 1415(k)). Another federal law also provides a method for removing a dangerous student with a disability (20 U.S.C.A. sec. 7151). If a student with a disability is determined to have brought a weapon to school, the child may be placed in an interim alternate education setting for up to 45 days while a permanent change in placement is determined (20 U.S.C.A. sec. 1415(k)). Finally, there is the obvious route to changing the placement of a disruptive or potentially dangerous disabled student. In most cases, the parents of the student are more likely to be concerned about providing the environment that is safest and most conducive to learning for their child than keeping the child in the current placement. If a disabled student is being disruptive or posing a danger, the parents will usually be quite anxious to work with school officials to change the placement. Clearly, schools have numerous alternatives for dealing with a disruptive or potentially dangerous student with a disability.

Critics of IDEA, however, view these methods for addressing disciplinary problems as insufficient. The criticisms of the stay-put provision seem to ignore the reasons for creating the stay-put provision and the available avenues of discipline discussed above. One commentator labels the stay-put provision as part of "the Congressional rush for inclusion at all costs" (Bunch, 1998, p. 321). Another commentator frets about not disciplining disabled students for actions related to their disabilities, since schools are supposed to be instilling "a solid foundation of society's values in our children" (Nelson, 1997, p. 61). A further assertion is that the stay-put provision gives students with disabilities rights that are superior to all other students (Ramsingh, 1995). Perhaps the most sweeping and preposterous attack on the stay-put provision claims that students, "whether disabled or not, can assault their classmates, threaten to kill their teachers, or possess a weapon in school without fear of being expelled. . . . A student merely must make an unverifiable, possibly even unsubstantiated, claim to be disabled in order to be protected by the IDEA" (Rachelson, 1997, p. 127).

Perhaps a bit of perspective regarding the actual nature of the issue would address such peculiar concerns about IDEA and remind critics why IDEA has a stay-put provision in the first place. The stay-put provision was not the result of a congressional conspiracy to limit the power of school officials without reason, nor are all disabled students accidents waiting to happen, desperately anxious to use disability as an excuse for offending social values. The essential reason for the stay-put provision is to prevent school officials from punishing or expelling a disabled student for actions or behaviors that result from the student's disability, which is exactly what used to happen on a consistent basis. Would you discipline a profoundly deaf student for failure to accurately follow verbal instructions? Would you fail a student who was a wheelchair user for being unable to successfully complete a long jump? Would you remove a visually impaired student from your class for being unable to accurately describe how the ocean looks? Would you punish a student with Tourette's syndrome for having an episode during school hours? Hopefully, your answer to these questions would be negative. However, the stay-put provision was created because historically it was not uncommon for school officials to answer questions like those above in the affirmative. The stay-put provision is an essential guarantee of the rights of disabled students in public schools.

Other opponents of IDEA focus criticism on what is commonly called inclusion. As previously noted, the term inclusion is not a legal term defined in IDEA (20 U.S.C.A. sec. 1401). It is a term that has come to have the accepted meaning of placing as many disabled students as possible in general education classrooms. The underlying principle, based on findings of research, is that disabled students will fare better academically, socially, and personally when mixed into classrooms with non-disabled students. In many cases, the least restrictive environment for a disabled student is a general education classroom, and the IEP is written accordingly, requiring that the student spend most or all of the school day in a classroom with non-disabled students. IDEA dictates the removal of a disabled student from the general education environment only when "the nature or severity of the disability of a child is such that education in regular classes with the use of supplementary aids and services cannot be achieved satisfactorily" (20 U.S.C.A. sec. 1412(a)(5)(A)). So integration, from a legal standpoint, has to be considered as an element of the least restrictive environment requirement. Some commentators, whether labeling it inclusion or least restrictive environment, are quite unhappy with the practice. The concern centers on what the presence of students with disabilities will do to the others in the classroom. Unlike criticisms of the stay-put provision, focusing on the ability to discipline, the criticisms of least restrictive environment stem from a fear that disabled students will impair or inhibit the learning of all other students in the classroom.

Prior to the passage of IDEA, a "substantial minority" of teachers felt "students with disabilities would be disruptive to their classes or demand too much attention" (Scruggs & Mastropieri, 1996, p. 71). Most of the concerned teachers, both before and after the passage of IDEA, felt they didn't have "sufficient time, training, or material/personnel resources to implement mainstreaming/inclusion successfully" (Scruggs & Mastropieri, 1996, p. 71). Teachers surveyed also expressed a preference for working with children with mild disabilities (Scruggs & Mastropieri, 1996).

The first issue these data demonstrate is that some teachers, who haven't taught disabled students, have apprehension about working with disabled students. It would be interesting to find out how many of those apprehensive teachers had ever been exposed to, had been familiar with, or had a personal relationship with an individual with a disability. Unfamiliarity breeds apprehension. The second concern these data reveal is that teachers feel they may not get the proper level of support (time, training, and resources) for their disabled students. This concern is not related to the presence of disabled students, but to external factors of support services. IDEA provides for the time and the resources, but the training is a real concern. Schools of education typically do a scandalously insufficient job of preparing general education majors to work with disabled students in their classrooms. The third concern evidenced by these data is really quite self-evident, as most teachers will want to work with students who are easiest to teach. Most teachers may prefer teaching students with mild disabilities, but they also undoubtedly prefer teaching students who are well behaved, well fed, happy, from stable homes, intelligent, and glad to be in school. Students with mild disabilities are generally easier to teach than students with severe disabilities. Students who had breakfast are generally easier to teach than those who go hungry. Students who enjoy attending school are generally easier to teach than those who hate school with a passion. In public schools, teachers get some students who are harder to teach for all kinds of reasons. That teachers would prefer to work with students with mild disabilities is really no surprise.

However, critics of the LRE requirement see the situation differently. The presence of disabled students can create disruptions, and "[d]istraction and breaks in concentration for individual students, as well as distraction and breaks in self-discipline within the classroom community, make it more difficult to create an environment where serious learning can and will take place" (Dupre, 1997, p. 847). True enough, but any student, with or without disabilities, can create distractions. The implication is that disabled students are unusually disruptive, a very unfair assumption. This same critic further asserts that disabled students may require individualized lesson plans and alternate materials, and "[i]ncreasing the demands on a teacher's time can decrease the quality of education for all students" (Dupre, 1997, pp. 848–849). The implication is once again that disabled students are the only students in a typical classroom where the teacher may have to individualize the learning process. In fact, many disabled students do not require the teacher to dramatically individualize lessons and materials, while many students without disabilities will require highly individualized lessons and materials.

The criticisms of integration of disabled students into general education classrooms suffer from singling out the disabled as if they were the only students who might require individual attention or have special needs. It is certainly true teachers must adapt instructional strategies, materials, and environments to meet the needs of many disabled students (Scruggs & Mastropieri, 1995). It is also true that "teachers attempting to accommodate a wide diversity of students must orchestrate a greater number of activities and materials, substantially complicating their job" (Fuchs & Fuchs, 1994,

p. 302). However, it is simply not reasonable to assert that the drive toward full integration inhibits the elevation of "academic achievement over academic setting" and leads to "failure to allow the public school to fulfill its mission as a community of learning" (Dupre, 1997, p. 858). These claims seem exceptionally peculiar in light of a mid-1990s Department of Education report revealing that nearly two-thirds of the states were not in compliance with the integration requirements of IDEA (cited in *Oberti v. Board of Education of the Borough of Clementon School District*, 1993, p. 1214). This study also noted only 26 percent of students with mental impairments nationally spent at least of 40 percent of the school day in general education classrooms, while only 2.35 percent of mentally impaired students in New Jersey (the most segregated state) spent any time in a general education classroom (cited in *Oberti v. Board of the Borough of Education of Clementon School District*, 1993, p. 1214). If states are having so much difficulty placing students with disabilities in general education classrooms, how can they be causing such enormous problems in general education classrooms?

Schools in the United States today serve a population that is multicultural in many ways. Most general education classrooms now include students of diverse racial, ethnic, social, economic, religious, and familial backgrounds. A modern classroom is a mosaic of uniqueness, with students from a plethora of different backgrounds, cultural or otherwise. Disability is a part of this mosaic. A teacher has to be aware of these important differences and teach accordingly. "Everyone's heritage is due respect, and differences should be regarded as strengths on which to build rather than deficits to be stigmatized or overcome" (Gallimore & Goldenberg, 1996, p. 16). Ultimately, the teacher must offer the opportunity for each student "to understand and respect his or her own cultural heritage and to develop the knowledge, skills, and attitudes to become functional within other ethnic cultures as well as the mainstream culture" (Smith, 1999, p. 51). As with differences in family structure, economic background, national origin, or religious heritage, the teacher must consider students with disabilities when preparing and when teaching.

The presence of disabled students in a classroom should be no greater challenge than the other challenges posed by the innumerable differences among students. For example, you have assigned an essay that requires students to write about their relationships with their respective fathers. Hopefully, you would not consider it a great hindrance on your ability to teach the other members of the class if you modified the assignment for a student who had never met his/her father and for another student who lived in foster care and had no relationship with his/her parents. Simplistic example, possibly, but the principle is the important part. You will be the teacher of all your students. However different they may be, it is your responsibility to teach them, every one of them, whoever and whatever they happen to be.

You may find preparing and teaching to be most time consuming with a disabled student. You may find your most time-consuming student to be the one who lives in a mansion and is envied by all the other students for her wealth but is an absolute wreck because her parents are too busy working and socializing with colleagues to notice that she exists. Some disabled students create extra work for their teachers, but so do some students from wealthy homes. However, no one suggests segregating neglected students of financial privilege in special classes to prevent them from disrupting the other students. Whoever your most time-consuming students are, they all deserve to be in a classroom with their peers. IDEA mandates that disabled students have the right to be educated in a general education classroom. Just because teaching some disabled students is costly and time consuming doesn't mean their presence detracts from the learning of other students or the ability of teachers to teach. Students can be disruptive or time consuming for many reasons; focusing on disabled students as somehow more disruptive and time consuming is simply wrong.

IDEA, with its costs and stay-put provisions and LRE requirements, has been a tremendous advancement for the disabled in this nation. Our public schools are supposed to be a meeting ground for all constituents of society, and the disabled finally have a place there along with everyone else. IDEA may not be perfect, but no law ever is. The rights guaranteed by IDEA and methods for ensuring those rights are essential to providing equality in education to individuals with disabilities. Being educated in an integrated environment increases opportunities for individuals to become fully-functioning, equal members of society (*Oberti v. Board of Education of the Borough of Clementon School District*, 1993). It's a brilliant IDEA; don't believe anyone who tells you otherwise.

CROSS-EXAMINATIONS AND REBUTTALS

Prepare a speech advocating IDEA and its many provisions and requirements. Make sure you address every potential criticism you may encounter.

What thoughts come to your mind as you consider teaching students with disabilities?

Chapter 8

Section 504 of the Rehabilitation Act

Section 504 of the Rehabilitation Act is another federal law that provides protection for individuals with disabilities. In fact, the Rehabilitation Act, originally passed in 1973, was the first federal law expressly asserting guaranteed rights for the disabled citizens of the United States. It is "the first major civil rights legislation for disabled people" (Scotch, 2001, p. 3). The Rehabilitation Act is codified at 29 U.S.C.A. sec. 701 *et seq.*; the regulations for implementation and enforcement of Section 504 of the Rehabilitation Act are codified at 34 C.F.R. sec. 104 *et seq.* Section 504 of the Rehabilitation Act is intended to prevent discrimination against the disabled in education, employment, social services, and other areas. Unlike IDEA, which only applies to elementary and secondary students, Section 504 can have ramifications for preschool, elementary, secondary, and postsecondary students. First, it protects all students with disabilities from discrimination. Second, it provides procedural and substantive protections for students with disabilities who do not receive protection under IDEA.

As surprising as it may seem, some students with disabilities have impairments that are not covered by IDEA. Section 504 of the Rehabilitation Act can provide protections for those students whose disabilities do not qualify for protection under IDEA, as it is broader and less specific than IDEA. This difference in specificity "indicates that Congress intended the IDEA to be the main vehicle for enforcing the right to a free appropriate education" (Wenkart, 1993, p. 301), while intending Section 504, as well as the ADA, would be the primary mechanisms for preventing broader forms of discrimination. In the contemporary classroom, the great majority of students with disabilities will be covered by IDEA. However, students protected by Section 504 are common enough to merit discussing the differences between an IEP under IDEA and the requirements for a Section 504 plan.

THE STRANGE BUT TRUE HISTORY OF SECTION 504 OF THE REHABILITATION ACT

> It is a tremendously tragic commentary upon the United States of America that it was only in 1977 that disabled people came to have enough hope to protest. It took two hundred years after this country was formed—*two hundred years*—for these people to begin to have hope. This is what happened. A law had been passed in 1973, the Rehabilitation Act of 1973, and included in it was Section 504, which many people realized was going to become the cornerstone of the civil rights of disabled Americans. . . . In 1977, four years after the passage of that law, there was still nothing happening on it. . . . For four years we had fought behind the scenes to try to get the law implemented and enforced. And at the beginning of 1977, for the first time, we had some reason to hope that the law was at last going to become effective. (Bowe, 1979, pp. 88–89)

To be completely thorough, Section 504 of the Rehabilitation Act was not the first federal law to address the presence of the disabled in education. In 1958, the federal government allotted funds for the training of special education teachers (The Expansion of Teaching in the Education of Mentally Retarded Children Act of 1958). The Elementary and Secondary Education Act of 1965 (ESEA) included extremely vague language about the need to end all kinds of discrimination, presumably including disability discrimination. Though the act was aimed primarily at addressing inequality of educational opportunities for economically underprivileged students, some federal grants under ESEA became the first federal funds used to specifically provide educational opportunities for students with disabilities. These funds, however, were primarily for placing students with disabilities in segregated, state-run institutions. In 1966, Congress began providing annual grants to states for fairly basic special education initiatives, such as creating special education programs.

These laws did not do all that much good for disabled students, however, as schools still did not have to contend with any law requiring students with disabilities to receive public education, much less an appropriate education in an integrated setting. After these two laws were passed, discrimination and outright exclusion of students with disabilities was still commonplace, if not the norm, in public education. In 1969, only seven states educated half or more of children with disabilities in the state (Zettel & Ballard, 1982). At the beginning of the 1970s, public schools enjoyed the support of most state legislatures and courts in the exclusion of students with disabilities (Zettel & Ballard, 1982). In 1958, the same year federal funds first went toward special education, the Illinois Supreme Court held that the state compulsory education statute did not apply to students with mental disabilities (*Department of Public Welfare v. Haas*, 1958). The Illinois Supreme Court wrote: "Existing legislation does not require the State to provide a free educational program, as a part of the common school system, for the feeble minded or mentally deficient children who, because of limited intelligence, are unable to receive a good common school education" (*Department of Public Welfare v. Haas*, 1958, p. 270). A North Carolina statute passed in 1965 made it a crime for parents of a disabled child to push for the right for their child to attend school if the school had determined the child would not "profit from instruction" (1965 N.C. Sess. Laws, Ch. 584, amending N.C. Gen. Stat. sec. 115–165, 1963). In Ohio, the superintendent of a school district could refuse to educate a child whose "bodily or mental condition does not permit his attendance at school" (Ohio Rev. Code Ann. Sec. 3321.04). Even in states where the legislature or courts mandated education for students with disabilities, flagrant violations of the mandates went unacknowledged and uncorrected, such as the public school system of Boston openly violating Massachusetts law by refusing to allow physically disabled children to attend school (Handel, 1975). It would take the *PARC* case in 1971 and the *Mills* case in 1972 to finally start the long, painful process of ending the exclusion, the segregation, and the non-education of students with disabilities.

Against this backdrop, Congress made the first meaningful attempt to address disability discrimination in education. The Rehabilitation Act prohibited disability discrimination by any entity receiving any federal funds, obviously including all public schools. This law should have been a major step forward for the disabled in the United States; it didn't really work out that way. Though the Rehabilitation Act came before the original version of IDEA, it is IDEA that has been canonized as the "Bill of Rights of the Handicapped" (Meyen, 1995). The reason for this state of affairs has as much to do with the pathetic, yet darkly comic, story of the passage, implementation, and enforcement of Section 504 as it does with the differences in the substance of the Rehabilitation Act and IDEA. The story of Section 504 is a perfect sketch of this society's historical mistreatment of and biases against individuals with disabilities.

Initiating the patently odd pattern of disability rights statutes being signed into law by notably conservative presidents, the Rehabilitation Act was signed into law by President Nixon in 1973, but only after he had vetoed stronger versions of it on two previous occasions (October 26, 1972 and March 27, 1973). It is a curious fact that Nixon, Ford, and the elder Bush are the presidents who have signed the three major laws protecting disability rights. President Bush, in signing the ADA, however, was the only one of the three who did not evidence hesitation while increasing the legal rights of individuals with disabilities. It is worth noting, however, that the

ADA had seemingly countless opponents tripping over each other to encourage Bush not to sign the bill into law. This ignominious list includes: the U.S. Chamber of Commerce, the National Federation of Independent Businesses, the Restaurant Association, the *New York Times*, the *Wall Street Journal*, Greyhound Bus and most public transportation companies, Pat Buchanan, and a number of conservative members of Congress, including former House Majority Whip Dick Armey (R-Tex.) (Fleischer & Zames, 2001, p. 88).

President Nixon approved the Rehabilitation Act after the third time it was passed by Congress. President Ford criticized the original version of IDEA at the moment he was signing it into law. During the same time period, no major disability rights laws came about during the administrations of President Carter and President Clinton, more liberal presidents who seemed to be more likely candidates for lobbying for and enacting civil rights laws. This peculiar dichotomy seems an appropriate way to introduce the strange but true history of the creation of Section 504 of the Rehabilitation Act.

Perhaps inevitably, as the Rehabilitation Act was the first major federal attempt to grant rights to the disabled, the statute was so imprecisely written and so flawed in conception that it was spectacularly useless at the time it became a law. The rampant flaws and holes in the text of law evidenced uncertain attitudes toward the status of the disabled and their legal standing, reflecting "a complex mixture of stereotyping and sympathy, apprehension and accommodation" (Rebell, 1986, p. 1438). Not surprisingly, there was tremendous initial confusion over the meaning of the entire Rehabilitation Act, and Section 504 in particular, as Congress had somehow neglected to provide a means for preventing disability discrimination, a system for enforcing the law, or any civil or criminal remedies for victims of disability discrimination. These omissions made Section 504 the legislative equivalent of a car with neither an engine nor wheels. Without mechanisms for implementation, enforcement, or remedies, Section 504 was not going anywhere. It was passed as little more than a gesture, sounding valiant but being profoundly useless in application. Amendments passed in 1974 began to make Section 504 theoretically more meaningful, but the actual situation did not improve. The federal government under the Nixon and Ford administrations did absolutely nothing to implement the law, actually working to prevent the law from being implemented or enforced. Health, Education, and Welfare Secretary David Matthews simply refused to take actions that might make the act effective (Fleischer & Zames, 2001).

The emptiness of the original version of the law was evidenced by the fact that the federal government made no steps to promulgate guidelines for enacting or enforcing Section 504 once the law was passed. After Section 504 was passed, law reviews were actually still publishing articles that legitimately spoke of a lack of federal government protections of students with disabilities to receive even a minimal education (Handel, 1975; McClung, 1974). It took a 1976 lawsuit against the government to force the creation of rules and guidelines for Section 504 (*Cherry v. Matthews*, 1976). In the *Cherry* opinion, the court noted, not without considerable sarcasm, that Section 504 was not likely to implement or enforce itself. Even a court order, however, did not get the Ford administration to start work on guidelines for enacting and enforcing Section 504. On the day the court order was issued, Matthews immediately tried to send the matter back to Congress (Fleischer & Zames, 2001). The matter was left for the Carter administration to address. The officials of the Carter administration, primarily Secretary of Health, Education, and Welfare Joseph Califano, simply continued to avoid the issue after taking office. These further delays spurred a festive series of protests by disability rights activists, including wheelchair blockades of certain government offices and Joseph Califano's driveway.

Some of the stories that arose from these demonstrations are simply astounding. Califano reportedly ordered that the demonstrators should receive no food and not be allowed communication outside the offices (Shapiro, 1993). The protest in the San Francisco office of Health, Education, and Welfare lasted the longest, with 60 individuals with numerous types of disabilities staying 25 days, leaving only after the Section 504 regulations had been signed (Shapiro, 1993). During the demonstration, encouragement, food, and supplies came from sources as divergent as McDonald's, the California Department of Health Services, Safeway markets, unions, the Black Panthers and San Francisco mayor George Moscone (Shapiro, 1993). On the down side, the Health, Education, and Welfare officials treated the demonstrators as obstreperous children, offering punch and cookies as a bribe to leave (Heumann, 1979; Shapiro, 1993). The demonstrators in New York faced much more ridiculous and demeaning treatment, including having a registered nurse stay with them to make sure the demonstrators could look after themselves (Fleischer & Zames, 2001).

The first guidelines for Section 504 finally were signed on April 28, 1977 and formally issued on May 4, 1977, a mere four years and three presidents after President Nixon had originally signed the law. The regulations were signed the same day as the regulations for the original version of IDEA, which had been passed two years later than the Rehabilitation Act. It took four years of legal maneuvering and political action, culminating in the first major disability rights protests this nation had ever seen, to get Section 504 implemented, a job the government should have done immediately without encouragement. Ultimately, amendments to Section 504 as part of the Rehabilitation, Comprehensive Services, and Developmental Disabilities Act of 1978 finally began to make it clear that civil rights remedies and procedures were being extended to individuals with disabilities (Schoenfeld, 1980).

Since the Rehabilitation Act was greeted with unbelievable bigotry and initially implemented with the kind of governmental sloth and incompetence that makes the conversion to the metric system seem like an overwhelming success, Section 504 has never been given enough attention. It often seems to be the forgotten one of the three major disability laws. While part of this neglect of Section 504 is due to the ridiculous legislative and legal history of the act, Section 504 is also procedurally and substantively different from IDEA. Until recently, Section 504 has played a very minor role in protecting elementary and secondary students with disabilities. A federal case in 1993 was "perhaps the first case to address the substantive standard [for a free appropriate public education] for a student eligible solely under Section 504" (Zirkel, 1996, p. 475). A school is obliged to provide special education to a student who is disabled under the Rehabilitation Act but not under IDEA when the student's educational needs cannot be adequately met without special education (*Lyons by Alexander v. Smith*, 1993). Recently, the implementation and enforcement of Section 504 has begun to receive considerably more attention from the federal government and the courts. For example, the 1997 report by the United States Commission on Civil Rights on the implementation of Section 504 in public elementary and secondary schools is the size of a phone book and runs in excess of 400 dense pages (United States Commission on Civil Rights, 1997). This type of attention is considerable progress from the time when the federal government pretended that Section 504 did not even exist.

THE SUBSTANCE OF SECTION 504

Section 504 states that no individual with a disability can, as a result of the disability, "be excluded from the participation in, be denied the benefits of, or be subjected to discrimination under any program or activity receiving Federal financial assistance" (29 U.S.C.A. sec. 794(a)). As with other disability rights laws, the protections are designed for any "otherwise qualified individual with a disability," which means any person who is qualified for a position or an opportunity in spite of having a disability. Students in elementary or secondary schools are otherwise qualified under Section 504 if they are of the age that children are required to attend school, the same age as non-disabled students, or provided a free appropriate education (34 C.F.R. sec. 104.3(l)). In schools that directly or indirectly receive federal funding, Section 504 protects students with disabilities, including those who do not receive protection under IDEA. Section 504 protections apply to the provision of education and related services, accessibility, and participation in extracurricular activities. The Department of Justice guidelines state that receipt of federal funds can be in the form of federal grants, loans, or contracts, as well as the use of such funds to provide services or personnel (28 C.F.R. sec. 41.3). Under this definition, most schools receive federal funding in some manner and, as a result, must comply with the requirements of Section 504.

In the schools, Section 504 protects a student who "has a physical or mental impairment which substantially limits one or more [of the person's] major life activities, has a record of such an impairment, or is regarded as having such an impairment" (34 C.F.R. sec. 104.3(j)). Under Section 504, a major life activity is a function "such as caring for one's self, performing manual tasks, walking, seeing, hearing, speaking, breathing, learning, and working" (34 C.F.R. sec. 104.3(j)(2)). In an educational environment, the major life activity at issue is learning. A student with any physical or mental impairment that substantially limits learning will have rights under Section 504. A person with a record of impairment is someone who once had a physical or mental impairment but no longer does. Section 504 prohibits discrimination against an individual for a disability that is no longer present. A person who is regarded as being disabled is someone who has a minor impairment that is not a disability or has no impairment but still is discriminated against by stereotypical, negative attitudes toward the perceived disability.

Unlike IDEA, Section 504 does not have a list of disabilities covered by the law. Section 504 is much broader than IDEA. Under Section 504, physical and mental impairments include:

any psychological disorder or condition, cosmetic disfigurement, or anatomical loss affecting one or more of the following body systems: neurological; musculoskeletal; special sense organs, respiratory, including speech organs; cardiovascular; reproductive, digestive, genito-urinary, hemic and lymphatic; skin and endocrine; or any mental or psychological disorder, such as mental retardation, organic brain syndrome, emotional or mental illness, and specific learning disabilities. (34 C.F.R. sec. 104.3(j))

This list is not even exhaustive. One federal district court has written that Section 504 protects individuals with any condition that substantially "weakens, diminishes, restricts, or otherwise damages an individual's health or physical or mental activity" (*E. E. Black Limited v. Marshall*, 1980, p. 1098).

Any student who is protected by IDEA will be protected by Section 504 by definition (34 C.F.R. sec. 104.3(l)). However, the reverse is not true, as Section 504 has a broader definition of disability than IDEA does. To receive protection under IDEA, a student must have a need for special education or related services due to the disability. To receive protection under Section 504, a student need only have a disability that impairs a major life activity, such as learning. For example, one court held that a student with Attention Deficient and Hyperactivity Disorder was not protected by IDEA, but was protected by Section 504 (*Lyons by Alexander v. Smith*, 1993).

Other students who may be covered by Section 504 but not IDEA include those suffering from diabetes, sickle-cell anemia, asymptomatic HIV, and temporary disabilities. Section 504 can even protect students with drug or alcohol addictions that impair learning (34 C.F.R. sec. 104, appendix A).

Section 504 covers physical conditions as diverse as cerebral palsy, diabetes, asthma, arthritis, deafness, blindness, epilepsy, chronic fatigue syndrome, and heart problems. However, Section 504, like other disability laws, does not apply to physical characteristics or conditions, such as height, weight, strength, handedness, and pregnancy. Mental conditions covered by Section 504 are those conditions that are recognized by medical professionals as mental impairments that limit a major life activity, such as learning disabilities, mental illness, and mental retardation. As with physical impairments, Section 504 has clear boundaries as to what mental impairments are covered by the act. The act specifies that impairments cannot include homosexuality, bisexuality, transvestitism, transsexuality, pedophilia, voyeurism, exhibitionism, kleptomania, compulsive gambling, pyromania, gender identity issues, and sexual behavior disorders (29 U.S.C.A. sec. 705(20)(E-F)). The act does not cover anyone who has "environmental, cultural, or economic disadvantages" unaccompanied by a physical or mental impairment (34 C.F.R. sec. 104, appendix A). Students, who are slow learners, of low intellectual caliber, or behind for their grade level but do not have a diagnosed mental impairment, are also not covered by Section 504 (United States Commission on Civil Rights, 1997, p. 95). Further, any negative personality traits, such as poor judgment, irresponsible behavior, and poor self-control, are not disabilities under Section 504 (*Daley v. Koch*, 1986).

The Supreme Court has established that Section 504, like IDEA, does not require more than reasonable accommodations for students with disabilities. The Court wrote that while a recipient of federal funds "need not be required to make 'fundamental' or 'substantial' modifications to accommodate the handicapped, it may be required to make 'reasonable' ones" (*Alexander v. Choate*, 1985, p. 300). Modifications will be considered substantial if they produce an undue burden for the school (*Alexander v. Choate*, 1985). A school can demonstrate an undue burden by "showing that funding was simply unavailable, or that the program requested by the plaintiff could not have been provided without great expense and detriment to the system" (*Sanders by Sanders v. Marquette Public Schools*, 1983, p. 1371). This standard means that schools need to provide accommodations to ensure fair educational opportunities for students with disabilities but are not compelled by law to provide the best possible education to disabled students. Appropriate means a program tailored to fit the student's individual needs (*Springdale School District v. Grace*, 1980). These programs, however, must be designed to meet the needs of the students and not the school district (*Gladys J. v. Pearland Independent School District*,

1981; *Campbell v. Talladega County Board of Education*, 1981). There is a difference in use of cost as a factor between IDEA and Section 504. Under IDEA, unavailability of resources cannot be used as a reason for not providing certain types of services or denying all services to a disabled student; cost can only be used as a factor when choosing between multiple service options (*Clevenger v. Oak Ridge School Board*, 1984).

Though Section 504 has no least restrictive environment language like that of IDEA, it does also favor integration of students with disabilities with non-disabled students. Section 504 mandates that students with disabilities should be integrated "to the maximum extent appropriate" into general education classrooms (34 C.F.R. sec. 104.34). The act presumes that a student with a disability will be placed in a general education classroom unless it is shown "that the education of the person in the regular environment with the use of supplementary aids and services cannot be achieved satisfactorily" (34 C.F.R. sec. 104.34(a)). Section 504 presumes that if a student with a disability is so disruptive in a general education classroom that the learning of other students is impaired, the needs of the disabled student cannot be met in that environment (34 C.F.R. sec. 104, appendix A, paragraph 24). Any separate classroom or other facility for students with disabilities must be "comparable to the other facilities" in the school or district (34 C.F.R. sec. 104.34(c); see, e.g., *Students of California School for the Blind v. Honig*, 1984). Section 504 also guarantees that students with disabilities should receive the same benefits as other students, such as the option of attending summer school classes (*Yaris v. Special School District of St. Louis County*, 1983).

Although Section 504 does not establish a specific timeline for the identification, evaluation, and placement of students under Section 504, a school district that is not acting in a diligent manner will find itself held in violation of Section 504. Waiting 61 days to perform an evaluation of an identified student has been held to be a violation of Section 504 (*Philadelphia (PA) School District*, 1992), as has waiting nine months to place a student following evaluation (*Dade (FL) County School District*, 1993). When a school decides to evaluate a student under Section 504, the parents must be notified, but, unlike IDEA, the parents do not have to consent for the evaluation and placement to be made.

APPLYING SECTION 504

The regulations for Section 504 have specific requirements that public elementary and secondary schools must follow. First, schools must identify, evaluate, and appropriately place students with disabilities (34 C.F.R. sec. 104.32–104.35). Second, schools must comply with the procedural safeguards with respect to these actions (34 C.F.R. sec. 104.36). Third, each student with a disability must receive a free appropriate public education

(34 C.F.R. sec. 104.33). Schools must be conscious of complying with all these requirements when working with students with disabilities.

Elementary and secondary schools have very specific procedural and administrative obligations under Section 504. Every school district with 15 or more employees (which is pretty much all school districts) are required to appoint a Section 504 coordinator, who is responsible to ensure that the school district is in compliance with the act. The coordinator is responsible for keeping the public and the school district personnel aware of the requirement that the school district not discriminate on the basis of disability. Teachers and other school personnel must be educated about Section 504 and other disability laws. The coordinator must also ensure that procedures for identification, evaluation, and placement of students with disabilities are established and properly used. The school district must also have procedural safeguards and administrative appeals procedures in place for students with disabilities and their parents, as well as for school district employees with disabilities. All interested parties should be made aware of the procedures. The regulations for Section 504 do not have specified procedures like those for IDEA. The process for appeal of a decision should involve the Section 504 coordinator, a written investigation and evaluation of the disputed decision, and an appeal within the school district prior to filing a civil rights complaint against the school district. The Department of Justice publishes a technical assistance guide for school districts for Section 504 procedures such as review and coordination.

Section 504 prohibits a school district that is receiving federal funding from discriminating against students with disabilities. Section 504 also requires that school districts provide any necessary reasonable accommodations for students with disabilities. Whether or not a student with a disability receives accommodations, the student cannot be discriminated against on the basis of that disability. If a student is identified with a disability under Section 504 and not under IDEA, a written plan similar to an IEP should be made to document the disability and the reasonable accommodations needed (34 C.F.R. sec. 104.33(b)(2); see also *Lunenberg School District*, 1994). Though a Section 504 plan does not have the mandated statutory requirements that an IEP does, a Section 504 plan should be created with the same level of care and precision as an IEP. If an IEP team decides that a student does not qualify for IDEA, it is good practice to automatically consider whether the student is protected by Section 504 and should have a plan under that act. A multidisciplinary team similar in composition to the IEP team, including the involvement of the student's parents, should design the Section 504 plan. The plan should address necessary general and special education accommodations, as well as any needed related services.

The Section 504 plan should be written to ensure an FAPE to the student. The regulations state that any recipient of federal funding "that operates a public elementary or secondary education program or activity shall provide a free appropriate public education to each qualified handicapped person who is in the recipient's jurisdiction regardless of the nature or severity of the person's handicap" (34 C.F.R. sec. 104.33(a)). Under Section 504, an FAPE is "provision of regular or special education and related aids and services that are designed to meet the individual educational needs of handicapped persons as adequately as the needs of non-handicapped persons are met" (34 C.F.R. sec. 104.33(b)). The concept of appropriate education in Section 504 is the creation of a comparable education for students with disabilities and non-disabled students. Section 504 defines free as one "without cost to the handicapped person or to his or her parents or guardian, except for those fees that are imposed on non-handicapped persons or their parents or guardians" (34 C.F.R. sec. 104.33(c)(1)).

As with IDEA, the multidisciplinary team must address the appropriate placement in the Section 504 plan. The placement options under Section 504 are the same as those under IDEA. The student should be educated in the most integrated environment, placed with non-disabled students to the maximum extent appropriate in academic and non-academic settings. An FAPE should be provided to students protected only by Section 504, as the non-discrimination mandate in Section 504 is met by the provision of an FAPE. If a student with a disability protected only by Section 504 is being discriminated against on the basis of that disability, the student is entitled to an FAPE to address the discrimination and the needs of the student. When both IDEA and Section 504 cover a student, compliance with the requirements of IDEA will be viewed as compliance with the requirements of Section 504. Provision of an FAPE under IDEA constitutes compliance with Section 504.

Section 504 places an affirmative duty on school districts to work to identify and evaluate students who may qualify for protection under Section 504. The school district must make sure that students with disabilities who do not qualify for IDEA still receive any needed benefits under Section 504. A school district that does not evaluate or place students with disabilities unless they qualify for IDEA is in violation of Section 504 (*Mesa (AZ) Unified School District No. 4*, 1988). Students can be referred for evaluation under Section 504 by parents, teachers, or other school personnel. School districts also must have procedures in place to establish evaluation and placement standards for students with disabilities. A school district that fails to establish such procedures or fails to properly conduct evaluations will be in violation of Section 504. A school district should not delay in making evaluations and placements for students with disabilities.

Any student who qualifies for protection under both IDEA and Section 504 must pursue administrative remedies under IDEA, while a student protected only by Section 504 must follow the administrative process under Section 504 (34 C.F.R. sec. 104.35). Although Section 504 does not have an explicit equivalent procedure to the stay-put provision of IDEA, the Office of Civil Rights has determined that a stay-put provision is implicit in Section 504 and school districts should apply a similar principle for students protected by Section 504 during administrative proceedings (Yell, 1998). If a significant change in the placement of a student is proposed, a reevaluation of the student should be conducted. The reevaluation should be similar to the initial evaluation of the student. If a student protected by Section 504 is facing a change in placement due to discipline problems, they should receive a manifest determination, just as under IDEA, to determine whether the discipline problems are resulting from or related to the disability (Dagely, McGuire, & Evans, 1994). Even if the school does not propose a change in placement, a student with a Section 504 plan should be reevaluated periodically to ensure that the placement remains appropriate.

The enforcement regulations for Section 504 provide suggestions for schools to avoid discrimination against students with disabilities. These suggestions include modifications to assignment of courses; provision of assistive technology; and use of teaching assistants, structural alterations, and modifications to class assignments, tests, and procedures (34 C.F.R. sec. 104.22). These suggested modifications are parallel to the types of accommodations required by IDEA. There are some areas, however, where Section 504 and IDEA differ greatly. The most prominent difference is in the area of the appeals process. Under IDEA, if parents are dissatisfied with the final decision of an LEA regarding the placement of their child, the parents can appeal to the SEA and then to the courts. Under Section 504, the process is quite different. If the parents are unhappy with the final decision of an LEA, they can file a complaint with the state Department of Education, but they also can file a complaint with the Office of Civil Rights of the federal Department of Education. A complaint must be filed with the Office of Civil Rights (OCR) within 180 days of the occurrence of discrimination. Once a complaint is filed with the OCR, a school district can avoid an investigation or assessment of a violation by resolving the issue to the satisfaction of the parents and the OCR. If the OCR does investigate the school district and finds a violation, the OCR will give the district a chance to correct the problem before making the findings public. If the school district persists in the violation, the OCR will publish the violations and will attempt to negotiate an agreement to correct the violations. A school district that still persists in violating civil rights law will then face sanctions by the OCR.

In conducting an investigation, the OCR may examine several elements of the behavior of the school or district. First, the OCR will examine to see if discrimination exists in the form of disparate treatment against a student with a disability (United States Commission on Civil Rights, 1997).

Disparate treatment occurs when the school is discriminating by unfairly treating a particular student with a disability. The OCR may also look for evidence of discrimination in the form of disparate impact against all students with disabilities or all students with a type of disability (United States Commission on Civil Rights, 1997). A disparate impact occurs when a facially neutral policy or procedure results in an adverse impact on a particular group. The OCR may also investigate to determine whether the school or district is providing an FAPE to all students with disabilities (United States Commission on Civil Rights, 1997). Depending on the circumstances of the complaint, the OCR may investigate one or all of these grounds to ascertain if discrimination has occurred (United States Commission on Civil Rights, 1997).

In a final difference from IDEA, Section 504 also provides rights in schools for disabled parents of students. As Section 504 prohibits discrimination against people with disabilities of all ages, a school will have to accommodate a parent with a disability in certain circumstances. For example, deaf parents of a student successfully sued for the right to sign-language interpreters for meetings with teachers and administrators (*Rothschild v. Grottenhaler*, 1990). The court held that schools must provide sign-language interpreters for deaf parents in any conferences or meetings regarding academic or disciplinary matters of their child (*Rothschild v. Grottenhaler*, 1990).

THE CORNERSTONE: A CLOSING NOTE ON THE REHABILITATION ACT

In the contemporary public school, IDEA plays a much greater role than Section 504. The vast majority of students with disabilities are protected under the provisions and requirements of IDEA. There are enough students protected by Section 504, however, that everyone involved in the contemporary public school must know the statute. Knowing the story of Section 504 is of immense importance as well. The story of the implementation of Section 504 encapsulates the historical prejudice and bias faced by individuals with disabilities, the true birth of the idea of legal rights for individuals with disabilities, and the time when the disabled first began to fight for their rights. No matter how flawed its original conception or how absurd the battle to get it implemented, Section 504 truly is the cornerstone of legal rights for individuals with disabilities, bringing forth a greater meaning of hope in many individuals with disabilities and leading to IDEA and the ADA. It is the story of how students with disabilities began to have the right to an education, the right to integration, and the right to an equal place in schools. It is a story that cannot go untold. It is a story that cannot be forgotten.

CROSS-EXAMINATIONS AND REBUTTALS

Whom does Section 504 of the Rehabilitation Act protect?

What does the history of federal legislation to protect students with disabilities reveal about our society? Cite specific examples.

When is a student protected under Section 504 and not IDEA?

What are the obligations of the LEA under Section 504?

Explain the role of the Office of Civil Rights.

How does Section 504 impact disabled parents of students in the schools?

Chapter 9

The Disabled College Student,
the Disabled Intern

The Rehabilitation Act and the ADA protect post-secondary students with disabilities; however, post-secondary students are not protected by IDEA. Services under IDEA, except in very rare circumstances, end at the age of 18 and graduation from high school. IDEA specifically covers students with disabilities between age 6 and age 17 (20 U.S.C.A. sec. 1412). Once a student with a disability graduates from high school or voluntarily drops out, then the protections under IDEA end (20 U.S.C.A. sec. 1412). The only exception to this rule is the unusual circumstance when a high school graduates a student with a disability simply to avoid providing services; in such a case, the school district would have to provide compensatory education to the student up to age 21 (*Helms v. Independent School District #3*, 1985). Any individual with a disability who attends a post-secondary school, such as a community college, a university, or a graduate program, will almost certainly be beyond any assistance IDEA might be able to provide. The Rehabilitation Act and the ADA, however, provide protection to post-secondary students with disabilities.

Professors, administrators, and other school officials, when working with their students who have disabilities, are dealing with individuals who are covered by section 504 of the Rehabilitation Act and the ADA, but not IDEA. This distinction is important for understanding what college students are considered to have a disability and for what accommodations they may be eligible. When college students with disabilities are placed in internships, such as teaching internships, Section 504 of the Rehabilitation Act and the ADA protect these students. This chapter will first outline the protections Section 504 of the Rehabilitation Act and the ADA provide to college students, and then the issues faced in placing disabled college students in internships will be addressed.

SECTION 504 OF THE REHABILITATION ACT

Originally enacted in 1973, the Rehabilitation Act provided the first federal legal protections for individuals with disabilities. Section 504, the part relevant to post-secondary education, decrees that no "otherwise qualified" individual with a disability "shall, solely by reason of his disability, be excluded from the participation in, be denied the benefits of, or subjected to discrimination under any program or activity receiving Federal financial assistance" (29 U.S.C.A. sec. 794). According to Department of Education regulations for enforcement of the Rehabilitation Act, an "otherwise qualified" student is one "who meets the academic and technical standards requisite to admission or participation in the recipient's education program or activity" (34 C.F.R. sec. 104.3(l)(3)). The Rehabilitation Act defines "program or activity" of a post-secondary institution to include all the operations of colleges, universities, and other post-secondary institutions (29 U.S.C.A. sec. 794(b)(2)(A)). The regulations specifically state that a disabled student shall not, on the basis of having a disability, "be subjected to discrimination" in any academic, research, training, physical education, athletic, or other post-secondary education program (34 C.F.R. sec. 104.43(a)). The regulations further prohibit discrimination in recruitment, admissions practices and decisions, housing, financial assistance, employment assistance, non-academic services, physical education, athletic events, counseling, placement decisions, and social activities and organizations (34 C.F.R. sec. 104.41-104.47). The regulations also specifically forbid discrimination in the general treatment of a student with a disability (34 C.F.R. sec. 104.43). Even without these specifications, nearly every post-secondary institution, public or private, would be covered by the act for receiving federal financial assistance in some form, like research grants, student loans, tuition grants, and tax breaks.

The Rehabilitation Act defines a person with a disability as having "a physical or mental impairment which substantially limits one or more major life activities," having "a record of an impairment," or being "regarded as having such an impairment" (34 C.F.R. sec. 104.3(j)). In post-secondary institutions, those students eligible for protection by the Rehabilitation Act qualify to receive accommodations, which the act labels "academic adjustments" (34 C.F.R. sec. 104.44). The academic adjustments can include modifications of academic requirements, course examinations, auxiliary aids, and other rules and policies (34 C.F.R. sec. 104.44). Post-secondary schools are supposed to accommodate students with disabilities by modifying academic requirements when it is "necessary to ensure that such requirements do not discriminate or have the effect of discriminating" on the basis of disability against a qualified student with a disability (34 C.F.R. sec. 104.44(a)). These modifications can include "changes in the length of time permitted for the completion of degree requirements, substitution of specific courses required for the completion of degree requirements, and adaptation of the manner in which specific courses are conducted" (34 C.F.R. sec. 104.44(a)). However, any academic requirements that the post-secondary institution can demonstrate to be "essential to [the program of] instruction being pursued by such student or to any directly related licensing requirement will not be regarded as discriminatory" (34 C.F.R. sec. 104.44(a)).

The requirements placed on post-secondary institutions by the Rehabilitation Act are similar in many ways to requirements placed on elementary and secondary schools by IDEA. Basically, a post-secondary school cannot act in a discriminatory manner in intent, function, or application. For example, an examination in a college course cannot discriminate in material or manner of testing. Students with sensory, manual, or language impairments should have testing accommodations when necessary (34 C.F.R. sec. 104.44(c)). Auxiliary aids, such as interpreters or note-takers, must be provided if "necessary to ensure" that the student is not "denied the benefits of, excluded from participation in, or otherwise subjected to discrimination [under the education program or activity] because of the absence of auxiliary educational aids" (34 C.F.R. sec. 104.44(d)(1)). Auxiliary aids can also include making materials available as audio texts, enlarged print texts, or Braille texts. The school cannot place the burden of paying for or acquiring auxiliary aids on the students. It is the responsibility of the school to acquire, provide, and pay for all necessary auxiliary aids for a student with a disability. Further, the school cannot make rules that would prevent the participation of students with disabilities, such as a rule prohibiting the use of sign language, a rule prohibiting guide dogs in classrooms, or a rule that forbids the construction of wheelchair ramps.

Section 504 of the Rehabilitation Act includes requirements that students with disabilities be educated alongside non-disabled students as much as possible. The Supreme Court has emphasized the parallel between Section 504 of the Rehabilitation Act and IDEA, noting that both statutes "begin with an equal protection premise" that students with disabilities must be given equal access to publicly funded education (*Smith v. Robinson*, 1984, p. 1018). The Rehabilitation Act specifies that individuals with disabilities should be educated "to the maximum extent appropriate to the needs of the handicapped person" (34 C.F.R. sec. 104.34). This language, which is very similar to the least restrictive environment language of IDEA, establishes the mandate that students with disabilities must be educated with their peers not only in elementary and secondary education, but in post-secondary education as well.

THE AMERICANS WITH DISABILITIES ACT

The Americans with Disabilities Act (ADA), passed in 1990, extended the protection of individuals with disabilities to entities that do not receive federal funding, including the areas of employment, public services, public accommodations, and transportation (42 U.S.C.A. sec. 12111–12189). In many ways, the ADA and the Rehabilitation Act impose fairly similar requirements on post-secondary institutions. As Section 504 protects students with disabilities in all post-secondary institutions that receive federal financial assistance (29 U.S.C.A. sec. 794), the ADA provides similar protections at all state supported post-secondary institutions (42 U.S.C.A. sec. 12131–12133) and at all post-secondary institutions that are not controlled by religious organizations (42 U.S.C.A. sec. 12181–12189). However, the ADA, when passed in 1990, did have at least one important impact on post-secondary students with disabilities. "Although the ADA did not add significantly to the substantive protections afforded college students with disabilities, the media attention surrounding its passage enhanced the visibility and awareness of this issue" (Rothstein, 1994, p. 426).

The ADA specifies that "no qualified individual with a disability shall, by reason of such disability, be excluded from participation in or denied the benefits of the services, programs or activities of a public entity, or be subjected to discrimination by any such entity" (42 U.S.C.A. sec. 12132). The ADA forbids discrimination against students with disabilities by any publicly operated post-secondary institutions (42 U.S.C.A. sec. 12132) or by "undergraduate, or postgraduate private schools or other places of education" (42 U.S.C.A. sec. 12181). The ADA definition of an individual with a disability is very similar to the Rehabilitation Act definition of an individual with a disability. Under the ADA, an otherwise qualified individual with a disability is someone "who, with or without reasonable modifications to rules, policies, or practices" or "the provision of auxiliary aids and services, meets the essential eligibility requirements" for participation in the programs and activities of a public entity (42 U.S.C.A. sec. 12131(2)). The ADA also requires that the level of protection required by the Rehabilitation Act is the minimum level of protection required by the ADA (42 U.S.C.A. sec. 12201(a)).

The ADA states that the place and manner of courses and examinations must be accessible and fair to individuals with disabilities (28 C.F.R. sec. 36.309(c)(1)). Some appropriate modifications to ensure fairness and accessibility include "changes in the length of time permitted for the completion of the course, substitution of specific requirements, or adaptation of the manner in which the course is conducted or course materials are distributed" (28 C.F.R. sec. 36.309(c)(2)). Under the ADA, examinations must reflect the aptitude and achievement of a student with a disability, rather than be biased against the individual's disability, by employing appropriate modifications such as extended time for testing, use of alternate formats, or adaptation of the manner of the examination (28 C.F.R. sec. 36.309(b)).

As with the Rehabilitation Act, the ADA requires post-secondary institutions to make reasonable accommodations for the needs of students with disabilities. The ADA requires post-secondary institutions to make "reasonable modifications in policies, practices, or procedures when the modifications are necessary to avoid discrimination on the basis of disability," except when the modification would fundamentally alter the program of education (28 C.F.R. sec. 35.130(b)(7)). Also similar to Rehabilitation Act requirements, the ADA requires provision of auxiliary aids and services to individuals with disabilities except when doing so would fundamentally alter the program of education (28 C.F.R. sec. 35.130(b)(1)). As with the Rehabilitation Act and IDEA, the ADA forbids segregation of students with disabilities, requiring post-secondary institutions to "administer services, programs, and activities in the most integrated setting appropriate to the needs of qualified individuals with disabilities" (28 C.F.R. sec. 35.130(b)(8)(d)). Overall, both public and private post-secondary institutions "are required to make reasonable program modifications short of a fundamental change in the nature of those programs" (Leonard, 1996, p. 47).

THE REHABILITATION ACT AND THE ADA GO TO COLLEGE

The protections provided by the Rehabilitation Act and the ADA apply to the entirety of the post-secondary educational experience. The Rehabilitation Act regulations summarize the protections provided to disabled students by stating that a post-secondary school "may not, on the basis of handicap, exclude any qualified handicapped student from any course, course of study, or other part of its education program or activity" (34 C.F.R. sec. 104.43(c)). Issues regarding the rights of students with disabilities have become more important as the number of disabled students attending college has begun to rise. In 1978, 2.6 percent of college students had a reported disability but by 1991, 8.8 percent of college students had a reported disability (Rothstein, 1994). There are, however, several particular areas that are consistently problematic for individuals with disabilities.

Admission and Academics

The first place in post-secondary education where disability discrimination can occur is the pre-admission period. Schools may not discriminate against students with disabilities in recruitment, application, testing, interviewing, or decision making (34 C.F.R. sec. 104.42). A school "may not make pre-admission inquiry as to whether an applicant for admission is a handicapped person but, after admission, may make inquiries on a confidential basis as to handicaps that may require accommodation" (34 C.F.R. sec. 104.42(b)(4)). This means that a school may not require a person with a disability to identify the disability as a requisite for admission. However, the bar on pre-admission inquiries into disability status does not apply to schools or special programs specifically designed for individuals with disabilities (*Halasz v. University of New England*, 1993). Also, any school may make a pre-admission inquiry as to disability if the reason is to redress past discrimination (34 C.F.R. sec. 104.42(c)).

Students with disabilities, of course, have the right to self-identify the disability. There are several reasons one may wish to do so. First, it will initiate discussions about appropriate accommodations at the earliest possible time. Second, many schools will consider a disability to be a relevant factor in admission decisions. Demonstrating academic success in spite of a known disability will likely make an applicant highly regarded. Third, many individuals with disabilities simply feel more comfortable when others are aware of their condition. If the student has not self-identified a disability during the admission process, the disabled student, upon acceptance, has the responsibility to notify the administration of the need of accommodations or services (34 C.F.R. sec. 104.44). The school has the right to ask the student to provide proper evidence of the disability (34 C.F.R. sec. 104.44).

Disability laws do not mean that programs have to lower their standards for admission just for students with disabilities. However, admissions committees may not hold standardized tests taken with accommodations to be of lesser value than standardized tests taken under normal circumstances (*SUNY Health Science Center at Brooklyn-College of Medicine (NY)*, 1993). To devalue or undervalue standardized tests taken with accommodations is a violation of the law (34 C.F.R. sec. 104.42). Tests and other criterion used for admissions must be inherently fair to individuals with disabilities. Testing services, as public accommodations under the ADA, must make reasonable accommodations in administrations of their tests, such as the Scholastic Aptitude Test (SAT), the Graduate Record Exam (GRE), and the Law School Aptitude Test (LSAT) (42 U.S.C.A. sec. 12189). A school "[m]ay not make use of any test or criterion for admission that has a disproportionate, adverse effect" on students with any type of disability (34 C.F.R. sec. 104.42(b)(2)). The only exception to this rule is for cases where the test or criterion has been demonstrated to be a valid predictor of success in that particular program and no alternate test or criterion with a lesser disproportionate, adverse effect exists (34 C.F.R. sec. 104.42(b)(2)). Another issue in admission involving disability occurs in readmission for a student who has experienced academic difficulties in postsecondary education prior to diagnosis of a disability. In cases of late diagnosis of a disability, admission decisions should account for the late diagnosis and time to adapt to treatment in making decisions regarding readmission (*DePaul University (IL)*, 1993).

In cases where a student with a disability is not otherwise qualified for admission to a program, the student can legally be denied admission as a result of the disability. The majority of these cases involve the lack of physical ability that is a qualification for successfully performing the goal of the program without causing unnecessary risk to others. For example, a blind student was legally denied admission to a medical surgery program for the rather obvious reason that a blind surgeon would not likely have a high success rate (*Ohio Civil Rights Commission v. Case Western Reserve University*, 1996). In another case, a deaf individual was legally denied admission to a tractor-trailer driving school for the reason that verbal communication was an essential part of the program and the job itself (*Breece v. Alliance Tractor-Trailer Training II, Inc.*, 1993). A dental school was allowed to deny the admission of a student with AIDS for the reason that a dentist with AIDS could create an unacceptable risk to patients (*Doe v. Washington University*, 1991). If a school denies admission on the grounds that the student with a disability is not otherwise qualified, courts demand the school's reason be meaningful and related to essential functions of the program. If the school claims a student is not otherwise qualified due to a disability that is unrelated to the functions or goals of the program, courts will not hesitate to find the school guilty of discrimination. In one case, a court found there was no rational reason that a university could deny admission to a psychiatric residency program to Dr. Pushkin, an M.D. who had multiple sclerosis (*Pushkin v. Regents of the University of Colorado*, 1981). The court noted that the admissions committee notes demonstrated clear bias against Dr. Pushkin, focusing on stereotypes rather than his individual capabilities. In another case, a court found diabetes was no reason to deny admission to a candidate for the United States Merchant Marine Academy, especially since more than 50 current merchant marines had the same condition (*Lane v. Pena*, 1996).

Once a student with a disability has been admitted to a post-secondary school, the student has the right to receive accommodations appropriate to the student's disability. After admission, a school may confidentially inquire whether a student has a disability (34 C.F.R. sec. 104.42(b)(4)). These inquiries must relate to a disability that may require accommodation (34 C.F.R. sec. 104.42(b)(4)). The law specifically suggests academic adjustments, modification of examinations, and provision of auxiliary aids as the best ways to make appropriate accommodations (34 C.F.R. sec. 104.44). In the area of modification of examinations, two types of modifications are possible. The first is modification of format, such as enlarged print, tactile print, extended testing time, or oral examinations. These modifications are very unlikely to be a source of contention. For example, a court granted extended time and large print accommodation to a severely visually impaired individual who was taking the state bar examination (*D'Amico v. New York State Board of Bar Examiners*, 1993). An individual with severe learning disabilities was granted double time, use of a computer, and enlarged print for the bar exam by another court (*Bartlett v. New York State Board of Law Examiners*, 1997).

However, in some cases where a student with a disability has requested a modification of the type of test, difficulties have arisen. In one case, a law school refused to grant the accommodation of allowing a student with a disability to take three-hour in-class examinations at home in as much time as he wanted (*McGregor v. Louisiana State University Board of Supervisors*, 1993). The court upheld the law school's denial of the request because the student was not seeking a reasonable accommodation but an entirely different set of standards for himself (*McGregor v. Louisiana State University Board of Supervisors*, 1993). In a similar case, another court permitted a medical program to refuse to give biochemistry tests in anything but a specific multiple choice format because many professors in the field believed that specific multiple choice format was the only correct format with which to test for mastery of biochemistry (*Wynne v. Tufts University School of Medicine*, 1992). The issue of what required classes may be eligible for course substitutions for a student with a disability has also become an area of contention, especially regarding students with learning disabilities. If a student with a disability requests a course substitution as an accommodation, it will only be considered a reasonable request if the disability leads to insurmountable difficulties in the course. For example, a quadriplegic student would have a legitimate claim to have required physical education courses waived as a reasonable accommodation. However, a student whose disability does not prevent the learning of mathematics cannot expect to have the required mathematics courses waived as a reasonable accommodation (*Guckenberger v. Boston University*, 974 F. Supp. 106, 1997).

Another academic issue for students with disabilities in post-secondary education has been receiving proper evaluation for necessary accommodations and other services. This problem has primarily affected students with learning disabilities. For individuals with physical disabilities, determining appropriate accommodations is usually a straightforward process. However, determining proper accommodations for individuals with learning disabilities can often be a much more complex process. Further, there has been considerable resistance to accommodating students with learning disabilities in some institutions of higher learning. For example, in 1997, Boston University Chancellor John Silber commented: "Some of the things that pass for learning disabilities used to be called stupidity" (Shapiro, 1997, p. 31). Not long after that statement was made, however, one court chastised Boston University for having an "internally contentious, multi-tiered evaluation process involving evaluators who were not only inexperienced but also biased," leading to "delay and denial of reasonable accommodations and much emotional distress for learning disabled students" (*Guckenberger v. Boston University*, 957 F. Supp. 306, 1997; *Guckenberger v. Boston University*, 974 F. Supp. 106, 1997). Not surprisingly, the court found Boston University to have made numerous violations of the Rehabilitation Act and the ADA.

Social Life and Living Spaces

The Rehabilitation Act and the ADA are meant to eliminate discriminatory practices in more than just the academic areas of post-secondary education. Disability discrimination is forbidden in physical education, athletics, housing, and transportation. School funded or sponsored social organizations and functions both on and off campus, including sororities and fraternities, must be accessible as well. Official off-campus events also must be accessible. Providence College was found guilty of violating both the Rehabilitation Act and the ADA for holding its graduation ceremonies in an off-campus facility that was not accessible to persons with disabilities (*Providence College (RI)*, 1994).

Any post-secondary school "that offers physical education courses or that operates or sponsors intercollegiate, club, or intramural athletics shall provide to qualified handicapped students an equal opportunity for participation in these activities" (34 C.F.R. sec. 104.47(a)). These programs and activities must be operated in "the most integrated setting appropriate" (34 C.F.R. sec. 104.43(d)). This requirement, of course, takes into account the impact of a student's disability on the ability to engage in a specific athletic activity. A blind student would have a difficult time arguing that he or she belongs on a football team and a quadriplegic student is not likely going to win a spot on a swim team. However, there is no reason that a deaf student or a student with a learning disability could not be on either of those teams.

With regard to physical facilities, consider all the different types of buildings a college student must use in the course of everyday campus life. Classrooms, libraries, dorms, student unions, and numerous other buildings are part of any college routine, as is campus transportation. All these physical facilities should be accessible to students with disabilities (42 U.S.C.A. sec. 12141–12150). Schools must remove barriers in existing facilities to an extent that is readily achievable and so that the program, as a whole, is accessible in its entirety (28 C.F.R. sec. 35.150, sec. 36.304). New buildings, when constructed, must comply with the detailed specifications to ensure accessibility (28 C.F.R. sec. 35.151). When schools contract with outside providers for services or locations, these providers must be in compliance with the requirements of the ADA (42 U.S.C.A. sec. 12141(4)). When a school acquires a new vehicle for campus usage, the vehicle must be accessible to individuals with disabilities (42 U.S.C.A. sec. 12142(a), (b)).

An area of considerable interest regarding physical facilities is the accessibility of dormitories. Many schools have created accessible rooms or facilities for housing that are separated from the housing options for non-disabled students. Such an arrangement is hardly integration. Another potential cause for difficulty arises when schools modify existing dorm rooms to be accessible. Though normally done with little trouble, one school conscientiously created a floor of wheelchair accessible rooms and somehow neglected to make the building itself wheelchair accessible. Such physical problems, like an inaccessible building filled with accessible rooms, can be rectified. However, disability discrimination in housing can occur even if the building and rooms are accessible. In one case, a school violated the ADA by not allowing a mobility-impaired student to have a roommate (*Coleman v. Zatechka*, 1993). Though the student had an attendant who visited three times a day to check on her, the court found that the school had no legitimate reason to prevent the student from having a roommate.

Academic Counseling, Placements, and Internships

A school must provide "personal, academic or vocational counseling, guidance, or placement services" at the same level to students with disabilities and to non-disabled students (34 C.F.R. sec. 104.47(b)). In counseling, the school must make sure "that qualified handicapped students are not counseled toward more restrictive career objectives than are non-handicapped students with similar interests and abilities" (34 C.F.R. sec. 104.47(b)). A school should not try to persuade a student with a disability not to pursue particular academic and career choices because of the disability. A school, for example, is violating the law if a student with a disability is told not to pursue a particular program of study or simply not allowed to take that program of study. Schools, however, should provide "factual information about licensing and certification requirements that may present obstacles to handicapped persons in their pursuit of particular careers" (34 C.F.R. sec. 104.47(b)). In short, schools cannot tell students with disabilities not to enter an academic program or career path but should make them aware of potential difficulties that may arise in such an academic program or career path as a result of the disability so that the students can make informed choices.

When recommending or placing students with potential employers, schools must be careful not to reveal private information about the student's disability. Schools, as well as individual professors, must not reveal information about a student's disability in letters of recommendation or other documents sent to outside organizations, like employers or professional licensing organizations (*Rothman v. Emory University*, 1993). Further, letters of recommendation cannot be negative, or even qualified, solely based on a student's disability (*Rothman v. Emory University*, 1993).

Internships have been an area of considerable difficulty for some students with disabilities who have had problems with getting accepted for an internship or with being accommodated during an internship. As with any academic program that is part of a school's curriculum, internship placements cannot reflect disability discrimination, and the school must ensure accommodations during the internship. Failure to provide academic adjustments and services to a student with a disability in an internship is a violation of the Rehabilitation Act and the ADA (*San Jose State University (CA)*, 1993). One court explained: "It is meaningless for an institution to make internship opportunities off-campus available to students without ensuring that those internships are, in fact, accessible through accommodations to qualified students who require special assistance" (*San Jose State University (CA)*, 1993, p. 1322).

Numerous problems with disability discrimination can occur in the course of an off-campus internship. Clearly, students with disabilities should receive accommodations during internships just as they would in standard academic courses. The failure by an internship supervisor to provide needed accommodations to interns with disabilities is a violation of the law (34 C.F.R. sec. 104.44(a), (d)). An internship supervisor who is aware of the student intern's disability and yet refuses to provide the needed accommodations is clearly in violation of the ADA and the Rehabilitation Act (*San Jose State University (CA)*, 1993). The failure by a school to inform an internship supervisor of a student's disability is a denial of the full opportunity to participate, a violation of the law (34 C.F.R. sec. 104.43(b)). Turning over the education of a student with a disability to an internship supervisor who is not adequately informed, prepared, or trained to assist the student also constitutes a violation of the law by the school (34 C.F.R. sec. 104.43(b)). Interns in a wide variety of academic fields have had problems during internships, from social work (*San Jose State University (CA)*, 1993) to the law (*University of California, San Diego*, 1993). Students with disabilities doing student teaching assignments have also faced serious problems with receiving needed accommodations during teaching internships (*National University (CA)*, 1993).

Susan was an incredibly gifted pre-service teacher. Her university coursework was stellar and she had completed every observation and practicum with depth, reflection, and maturity. The only reference to her disability on her application for student teaching was the necessity for an accessible building. Each time the university sent Susan's application to a different school, it was returned with the notation that no placements were available.

Students with disabilities cannot be denied admission to an academic program, such as an internship, unless they are not otherwise qualified for the program, like the blind student seeking admission to a surgery program. Many students with disabilities seeking acceptance into student teaching internships have faced discrimination. Sadly, it is not uncommon for an elementary or secondary school where an intern with a disability has been placed to inform the university that there is no place for the disabled student teacher. All students with disabilities who want to pursue a college degree should not be denied access. Additionally, people with disabilities who choose a career in education should not be immediately directed to special education programs. As a society, we have been forceful in recruiting African-American and Latino teachers in our programs to serve as role models for our students; we have looked for strong, positive male role models for our classrooms. It is time to prepare and hire qualified teachers with disabilities. Suggestions for teacher educators include:

- Communication between the teacher educator and the pre-service teacher with a disability must be open and honest.
- Together, the teacher educator and pre-service teacher should discuss/develop accommodations and/or adaptations to manage difficulties throughout the program.
- Teacher educators should be open to innovative ways to meet the responsibilities of teaching.
- Teacher educators should include the pre-service teacher with a disability in all clinical experience placement decisions and be an active proponent in conversations with school and district staff.
- Teacher educators should help cooperating teachers and administrators develop awareness and understand their responsibility towards qualified teachers with disabilities.
- Teacher educators, cooperating teachers, university supervisors, and administrators must be forthright in all evaluations.

When K–12 students have qualified, talented teachers with disabilities, we will come to a better understanding of all peoples.

John always knew he wanted to be a high school teacher. A brilliant student, an energetic young man, and a personable individual, John was visually impaired. He negotiated the large state university campus with assistance from Abbot, his guide dog, but his disability had no effect on his academic or social activities. He played intramural sports, participated in journalism events, and held several leadership positions in university government. His adviser had openly discussed the potential employment obstacles he might face due to discrimination, yet John persevered in his program of study. A visitor in any of John's classes would never know he had a disability and always notice his innate teaching ability. He graduated with honors, passed the state teaching exam, had glowing reports from his student teaching placement but was denied one teaching position after another for three years.

SEEKING AND MAKING ACCOMMODATIONS IN HIGHER EDUCATION

More than 440,000 students with disabilities are enrolled at two-year and four-year post-secondary education institutions. Learning disabilities is the most frequent disability, with almost half of the students with disabilities in this category. Institutions reported 62,500 students with mobility or orthopedic impairments, 51,570 students with health impairments or problems, and 36,260 students with mental illness or emotional disturbance. Institutions also reported 25,860 students with a hearing impairment, 18,650 students that are blind or visually impaired, and 4,020 students with a speech or language impairment (NCES Fact Sheet, 2000).

Any college/university student requiring an accommodation must request such services directly from the institution's Students with Disabilities Office. All accommodation requests must be consistent with documented needs of the student requesting such accommodations. Documentation must be current so that accommodations are based upon the impact of the student's disabilities on his or her academic performance upon entry to college.

Learning disability and attention deficit disorders assessment includes complete intellectual assessment with all subtests and standard scores reported, comprehensive academic achievement battery with all subtests and standard scores, specific areas of information processing (memory, auditory/visual perception, processing speed, executive functioning, motor ability), statement of specific diagnosis, and a profile of strengths and weaknesses. All other disabilities assessment includes a medical diagnosis report explaining the description of functional limitation, medical diagnosis, medical history of condition, and current medication regimen. Accommodations are made to the degree to which the disability impacts the individual in a learning context. Specific recommendations for accommodations appropriate at the college level are made with an explanation of how each accommodation is substantiated through the assessment.

Although most institutions have made considerable progress with accommodations for persons with disabilities under the Americans with Disabilities Act, we offer the following suggestions for improving facilities:

• Modify elevators, hallways, doors, entrances, counters, food service lines, telephones, and bathrooms throughout campus so they are accessible to persons with disabilities;
• Create accessible circulation paths to, among, and within university buildings and other facilities by repairing sidewalks and ramps;

- Modify shuttle bus route schedules to ensure that accessible buses run regularly and frequently on each route;
- Make dormitory rooms fully accessible upon enrollment of students with disabilities and enlarge doorways in at least half of the rooms on floors with accessible rooms, so students using wheelchairs can visit friends;
- Provide accessible seating in assembly areas, access to stages and backstage areas around campus, and assistive listening devices in assembly areas;
- Provide accessible parking throughout campus; and
- Replace signs throughout campus so people with vision impairment can read them and so that people with mobility impairments are properly directed to accessible routes and spaces.

CROSS-EXAMINATIONS AND REBUTTALS

What protections are provided under the law for post-secondary students with disabilities?

How are the requirements of IDEA and the Rehabilitation Act similar? Different?

When can a student with a disability be denied admission to a post-secondary program?

Explain the obligations of an internship supervisor of a student with a disability.

Chapter 10

Educators with Disabilities

Students are not the only members of a school community who have disabilities. In this chapter, we will examine how disability issues and disability laws relate to teachers in the school community. There are many special issues that must be considered when teachers have disabilities (or become disabled after entering the profession), including legal rights when seeking a teaching position, legal rights when working as a teacher, and the general dynamics of being a teacher with a disability. For teachers with disabilities, this chapter details your rights and will hopefully help you realize you are not alone. For non-disabled teachers, this chapter will provide some insight into any disabled colleagues you have, their rights, and what special challenges they face.

BEING DISABLED

Before discussing the legal specifics relating to disabled teachers, let us take time to discuss what it means to be a disabled adult. Having a disability shapes a person's psychological character and makes one a member of the disability culture. Both of these influences of disability have a significant impact on the disabled individual. Psychologists have identified the primary core values of the individuals who belong to the disability culture:

1. Acceptance of differences among people
2. Acceptance of human vulnerability and recognition of the need to help others
3. Ability to handle uncertainty and unpredictability
4. Ability to laugh at disabilities and the problems they cause

5. Ability to manage multiple tasks simultaneously

6. Advanced orientation toward future goals and possibilities

7. Carefully honed capacity for closure in personal communication

8. Flexibility, ability to adapt, creativity, and inspired in situations of limited resources or untraditional modes of operation (Gill, 1995, pp. 17–18)

Another common trait that may be found among the disabled is in linguistics. As the disabled have become more empowered, they have begun to develop unique slang and original sayings relevant to the particulars of life with a disability. If you heard someone referred to as an "inspiration station," would you have any notion what the term meant? If you saw someone wearing a shirt or displaying a bumper sticker that pronounces "CRIP IS HIP," would know what the phrase meant? These are examples of linguistic elements that are becoming a part of the disability community.

In case you're wondering, and you well should be, an inspiration station is a person with a disability who is viewed as inspiring by non-disabled people. The term refers to a disabled individual who is admired for being successful by non-disabled individuals. It derives from how often disabled individuals are told that they are inspiring, with or without merit, by people who don't have disabilities. "Crip is hip" is meant to be an affirming slogan, a sign of disability pride. It also neatly subverts one of the traditional slurs used against the disabled (i.e., cripple) and turns it around in the same manner some African Americans and members of the gay community have turned the hate words of others into personal affirmatives.

Clearly, not every individual with a disability fits into generalizations, such as the list of characteristics, about the culture. However, these characteristics, both positive and negative, are at least a part of most individuals with disabilities. A surprising number of disabled individuals see much of themselves or of their friends in this list of core values. Another interesting insight of this list is the number of these characteristics that are great traits for teachers to have. In fact, virtually every characteristic on the list is quite valuable in a classroom. You ought to be wondering why more individuals with disabilities are not teachers. It is a problem that this chapter will try to illuminate.

Being disabled means more than having a disability; it means the disability is a part of the person. It is not something that can be turned off or that suddenly will go away. It's always there, influencing how things are done and experienced. The individual with a disability, though, does not define the self by the disability; it is just one element of the whole person. However, far too often, other people view a person with a disability as nothing more than the disability. To many non-disabled people, the presence of a disability obscures or obliterates the rest of the person. It makes no more sense than if eye color and nothing more defined people with blue eyes. Most unfortunately, the tendency to define the individual with a disability by the disability often surfaces in job interviews, even though legally it should not.

Virtually anyone with an obvious disability can list numerous occasions where a job interview came to focus on the interviewer's prejudice rather than the qualifications and abilities of the disabled job candidate. As an amusing example, one of authors of this text had the bizarre experience of being told that he couldn't be considered for a position in a law firm because they wanted all their employees to be able to golf. The other author of this text endured a job interview where, with every step, the interviewer nodded and repeated, "Good." Although the position was for a university professor and she met all the qualifications and secured an interview, the first question asked was, "Can you write on the board?" Such discrimination is illegal under the ADA, but employers often try to get away with discrimination in hiring. Disability has an impact on the employment status of many, many individuals with disabilities. Statistically, individuals with disabilities "work less, earn less, and have lower levels of economic well-being than those without disabilities" (Burkhauser & Daly, 1996, p. 164). Unfortunately, and disappointingly, some principals and school districts are not above discrimination against the disabled in hiring decisions.

In the hiring process, this discrimination is not overt. As one study found, "[p]rincipals are indeed aware of ADA regulations, and are sensitive to the legal liability the ADA imposes, and offer interviews defensively" (Young & Prince, 1999, p. 529). Because of the legal requirements, those who make hiring decisions for schools seem to interview disabled candidates for teaching positions to avoid being accused of discrimination. Obviously, as teachers with disabilities are not common in schools, the interviewing defensively does not lead to extension of employment opportunities. The reasons are not very clear. Some likely contributors to the paucity of disabled teachers are base discrimination, unvoiced anxiety that an individual with a disability will be a detriment in the classroom, and simple economics.

The primary reason for failure to hire otherwise qualified teachers with disabilities may be economic. It has been theorized that hiring decisions for schools are often made with a focus on the fiscal bottom line (Young & Allison, 1982). As a result, school districts are more likely to hire younger candidates than older ones, who typically have more experience and education, simply because the candidates with less experience and education will receive a lower salary (Young & Allison, 1982). If principals and superintendents are emphasizing monetary factors in hiring decisions, then a candidate for a teaching position who has a disability will be at a severe disadvantage. In some cases, hiring people with disabilities can result in costs to accommodate the disabled individual, and bias may cause all candidates with disabilities to be viewed as potential expenses.

School districts, in making all interviewing, hiring, and firing decisions, are bound by the rules of Section 504 of the Rehabilitation Act and the ADA. Section 504 of the Rehabilitation Act dictates that "[n]o otherwise qualified individual with a disability in the United States . . . shall, solely by reason of her or his disability, be excluded from the participation in, be denied the benefits of, or be subjected to discrimination under any program or activity receiving Federal financial assistance" (29 U.S.C.A. sec. 794). All public schools and school systems, at the local and at the state level, receive federal funding and are therefore subject to the regulations of the Rehabilitation Act. Under the act, "program or activity" includes all operations of state educational agencies and local educational agencies, regardless of whether the particular action involved directly received federal funding (29 U.S.C.A. sec. 794). Even if a state receives the direct financial support from the federal government and then distributes the funds to the local school systems, the local levels are still bound to the Rehabilitation Act as a recipient of indirect funding. Overall, the Rehabilitation Act establishes the basic employment rights of disabled individuals, including teachers, to fair and equitable treatment by employers, including public schools.

The Rehabilitation Act was designed to end laws and beliefs that deprived disabled individuals of rights and to alter the attitudes of a populace unfamiliar with and insensitive to the problems confronting individuals with disabilities. The Rehabilitation Act provides legal protections to anyone who "(i) has a physical or mental impairment which substantially limits one or more [of such person's] major life activities, (ii) has a record of such impairment, or (iii) is regarded as having such an impairment" (34 C.F.R. sec. 104.3(j)). As all public schools are covered by the requirements of the Rehabilitation Act, a public school cannot discriminate against an otherwise qualified teacher with a disability as a result of that disability. If a person with a disability is not hired or is fired "solely by reason of her or his disability," the requirements of the Rehabilitation Act have been violated (29 U.S.C.A. sec. 794(a)). A public school cannot refuse to hire, promote, or otherwise employ an otherwise qualified teacher with a disability because of the disability; further, an otherwise qualified teacher with a disability cannot be fired for the reason of having a disability. If an otherwise qualified teacher with a disability faces discrimination in the hiring or firing process, he or she can take legal action under the Rehabilitation Act.

The ADA works in conjunction with the rights and protections granted by the Rehabilitation Act. Enforcement of disability rights in employment derives from the ADA (42 U.S.C.A. sec. 12101 *et seq.*), the Department of Justice regulations for enforcement of the ADA (28 C.F.R. sec. 35 *et seq.*), Equal Employment Opportunity Commission regulations (29 C.F.R. sec. 1630 *et seq.*), and the Rehabilitation Act (29 U.S.C.A. sec. 701 *et seq.*) often with the requirements in each overlapping considerably. As with the chapter of the legal procedures required in IDEA, many statements in this chapter do not have a specific citation except for quotations. Once again, the reason is to avoid losing the reader in a deluge of section numbers. Unless otherwise noted, the material in this chapter is from at least one of the aforementioned sources.

The ADA, by itself, has not had a dramatic effect on the disabled in public schools. The primary reason for this limited impact is the substantial overlap between ADA and Section 504 of the Rehabilitation Act. When the ADA was enacted, the Rehabilitation Act already prevented discrimination against the disabled by any entity receiving federal financial assistance. As all public schools are partially funded by the federal government, they were already prohibited from engaging in discrimination against the disabled. The ADA, however, does add important structural, organizational, and administrative requirements with which school systems must comply that are important to teachers with disabilities. The ADA states that nothing in the ADA should be construed as anything but an enhancement of the protections provided by the Rehabilitation Act.

Under the ADA, a disability is a "physical or mental impairment that substantially limits one or more major life activities; a record of such an impairment; or being regarded as having such an impairment" (42 U.S.C.A. sec. 12102(2)). The Department of Justice regulations further elaborate that disabilities are "any physiological disorder or condition, cosmetic disfigurement, or anatomical loss" affecting, among other body systems, neurological functioning, and "[a]ny mental or psychological disorder" (28 C.F.R. sec. 35.104). The ADA prohibits employment discrimination against an individual with a disability by any state or local government agency, such as schools and school districts. The ADA instructs local and state governments that "no qualified individual with a disability shall . . . be excluded from participation in or be denied the benefits of the services, programs, or activities of a public entity" (42 U.S.C.A. sec. 12132). The Rehabilitation Act provides those same protections for federal agencies and any agency receiving federal assistance. These statutes are intended to prevent discrimination in government, employment, education, physical accessibility, health services, welfare, and social services, among others. Schools, school districts, and state educational agencies are bound by the requirements of the Rehabilitation Act and the ADA in making employment decisions.

According to the ADA, a person who has a "physical or mental impairment" which "substantially limits" any major life activity is considered disabled under the ADA (42 U.S.C.A. sec. 12102). When an individual cannot perform a major life activity, such as "caring for oneself, performing manual tasks, walking, seeing, hearing, speaking, breathing, learning and working," the individual is a member of the legally protected class of the disabled (29 C.F.R. sec. 1630.2). The ADA was enacted with several separate sections, known as Titles, meant to address the different areas of discrimination. Title I of the ADA prohibits employment discrimination (42 U.S.C.A. sec. 12111–12117). Covering "any State or local government" and "any department, agency, special purpose district, or other instrumentality of a State or States or local government," Title II serves to further prohibit discrimination in public schools (42 U.S.C.A. sec. 12131).

These laws specify what employers must do to guarantee rights of the disabled in employment decisions. If an employer takes discriminatory actions, the laws give the victims of discrimination the right to file suit. To qualify for protection under these laws, you must be disabled within the meaning of the laws. Though it may seem resplendently obvious, you must have an impairment that limits a major life function to be protected under the ADA and the Rehabilitation Act. If you have a condition that does not limit a major life activity, you cannot claim to have a disability, either to an employer or to a court (*Standard v. A.B.E.L. Services, Inc.*, 1998). Further, the standard used by courts to determine whether an employment decision was discrimination is not a subjective one but is based on the judgment of a reasonable person (*Doe v. DeKalb County School District*, 1998). This means that a subjective personal reason is not an adequate basis for claiming a decision of the employer to be discrimination.

Simply not getting the position you want is not enough to be the basis of a discrimination claim. If you want to teach seventh grade English and wind up teaching eighth grade English, that is not a case of employment discrimination. If one is given an undesirable teaching assignment, but one that any teacher in the same position, disabled or not, could expect, then there is no valid claim of discrimination. For example, a district has a policy of placing all new teachers in schools only after the current teachers have a chance to transfer to another school if they so desire. In this scenario, the majority of current teachers would do their best to get the positions in the newer, cleaner, safer, richer, or otherwise more preferable schools in the district. Most of the positions for new teachers would be in the older, poorer, or more dangerous schools. In that case, a new teacher with a disability could not claim employment discrimination for getting one of the less desirable positions. However, if a current teacher with a disability were the only teacher not allowed to transfer, that probably would be a case of employment discrimination.

If an individual with a disability is seeking legal protection under the procedural requirements of the Rehabilitation Act and the ADA, the disabled individual must establish a number of things in court. First, the teacher must demonstrate that he or she is, in fact, otherwise qualified for the position, with special needs the employer can reasonably accommodate (42 U.S.C. sec. 12131). The Equal Employment Opportunity Commission (EEOC) guidelines for the ADA define a qualified individual with a disability as someone "who satisfies the requisite skill, experience, education and other job-related requirements of the employment position . . . and who, with or without reasonable accommodation, can perform the essential functions of such position" (29 C.F.R. sec. 1630.2). The first half of this requirement is straightforward for teachers, since there are professional guidelines, certification requirements, and job requirements. A person who has graduated from an accredited college with a degree in education and teaching certificate (or received an advanced degree and certification or taken all the requirements after receiving a college degree and received certification) would likely meet the otherwise qualified requirement. The important part for being otherwise qualified is meeting the requirements of the job. If a teaching position is advertised for candidates with a teaching degree who have passed the state teacher's test, and you meet these criteria, then you are otherwise qualified for the position. Otherwise qualified is determined at the time of the employment decision and should not take speculation on future conditions into consideration. The employer should make such a decision based on relevant information, and cannot use fear of future insurance or workers' compensation costs to decide that someone is not otherwise qualified. Individuals with disabilities can only be considered otherwise qualified if they can "perform the essential functions of the position in question without endangering the health and safety of the individual or others" (*Wood v. Omaha School District*, 1994, p. 669).

Essential functions are job elements tasks that are "fundamental" and not "marginal" (29 C.F.R. sec. 1630.2). For example, an essential function of the job of an air traffic controller would be the ability to see very well. A blind person could be refused the job of air traffic controller and it would not be discrimination, since sight is fundamental to the job. However, employers cannot refuse to hire based on the inability to perform marginal, non-essential elements of a job. If a wheelchair user could perform every task in a complex office administrator position except refilling the cup dispenser at the water cooler every other week, then the individual cannot be refused employment simply over a minor task that is a minuscule element of the whole job. Essential functions are defined partly by the employer, especially in what is advertised in the job description, as well as amount of time spent performing the task, consequences if the employee does not do the task, and the work experiences of people in that job. How the employee performs a task is not relevant to considerations of essential function, only whether the employee can do the task at issue. Employers are not limited in what they establish as essential functions, but the essential functions must be consistently applied and cannot be used as a method of preventing otherwise qualified disabled individuals from getting a job. If an employer reasonably establishes speed or accuracy or the ability to proofread as essential functions of a job, the employer is not required to lower the standards of the job as an accommodation.

The safety issue is obviously of utmost importance in the context of education. An individual with a disability is not qualified for a job if the individual poses a direct threat, which is "a significant risk to the health or safety of others that cannot be eliminated by reasonable accommodation" (42 U.S.C.A. sec. 12111(3)). For example, a court could hold that it was not disability-based employment discrimination for a school district to demote a school van driver who had become insulin-dependant and prone to seizures. The court could find significant safety risk in allowing the man to continue as a driver responsible for transporting students, as he was prone to incapacitation at any time. In one case, a teacher was transferred from teaching students with severe behavioral disorders to students with mild behavior disorders when the teacher revealed he was HIV positive (*Doe v. DeKalb County School District*, 1998). The teacher sued, claiming discrimination against his disability, but the court determined the increased level of violence, and therefore increased chance of blood-to-blood contact, with students with severe behavioral disorders was a risk to the safety of the teacher and the students (*Doe v. DeKalb County School District*, 1998). The district felt that the teacher and students would be safer with him teaching students with mild behavior disorders where there was little chance of violence leading to blood-to-blood contact, and the court agreed (*Doe v. DeKalb County School District*, 1998). This case is illustrative of several important issues with safety and disability. The personal preferences of the disabled individual can be less important than general safety concerns. The teacher would rather have been working with the severely disturbed students, but it was safer for both the teacher and the students if the teacher worked with a better behaved and less volatile group. This outcome is correct, since the job of the teacher is to provide the best for students.

Special needs are usually considered reasonable accommodations if they do not result in prohibitive expense. A determination of reasonable accommodations for a disabled individual includes "the reasonableness of the cost of any necessary workplace accommodation, the availability of alternatives therefor, or other appropriate relief in order to achieve an equitable and appropriate remedy" (*Wood v. Omaha School District*, 1994, p. 669). An accommodation cannot be reasonable if it creates a situation "which would impose undue hardship on the operation of the program in question" (*Wood v. Omaha School District*, 1994, p. 669). To receive reasonable accommodations, the disabled employee must make the employer aware of the need for accommodation and provide reasonable documentation of the disability if the employer requests.

Employers should consult with the disabled employee to understand what accommodations are necessary, and employers can also seek guidance to appropriate accommodations from the EEOC, state or local rehabilitation agencies, and disability rights organizations. Determining the accommodations to be made is an "informal" and "interactive" process that involves the employer and the qualified individual with a disability (29

C.F.R. sec. 1630.2). Providing reasonable accommodation is "an individual process, geared to an individual with a disability, a job, and an employer" (Feldblum, 1996, p. 125). The employer, ultimately, makes the final decision as to what accommodation is to be provided. As long as the accommodation is appropriate and effective, the employer may choose the simplest, easiest, and least expensive method of accommodation. If the employer, without consulting the employee, offers an appropriate reasonable accommodation, the employee does not have the legal right to demand discussions about accommodations (*Barnett v. U.S. Air, Incorporated*, 1998). However, if the accommodations are unsatisfactory, the employee has the right to refuse the proffered accommodations and demand others.

As with the limitations on the extent of the substantive requirement in an FAPE under IDEA, reasonable accommodations are also, by definition, not necessarily intended to maximize benefits. The goal of making reasonable accommodation is to "determine if there are any modifications or adjustments to the job environment or structure that will enable the person to perform the job" (Feldblum, 1991, pp. 93–94). A reasonable accommodation is generally a modification or adjustment to an environment that allows a disabled individual to have similar benefits as non-disabled individuals, so long as the accommodation does not create undue hardship. School systems, like other employers, may be required to make reasonable accommodations in various circumstances. Reasonable accommodations can include, but are not limited to, provision of auxiliary aids, modification of equipment, adjustment of schedules, and making existing facilities readily accessible.

These types of accommodations are not required when they produce a burden of undue hardship on the party paying for them. Undue hardship is legally defined as "an action requiring significant difficulty or expense" (42 U.S.C.A. sec. 12111(10)(A)). When assessing whether an accommodation creates undue hardship, courts will examine the nature and cost of the accommodation, the impact of such an expense, the feasibility of less expensive alternatives, and other similar factors. Further, an accommodation that causes a fundamental or substantial alteration to the nature of the employer's business activities is considered a form of undue hardship. For example, an employer is not required to create a whole new type of job as an accommodation (*Terrell v. U.S. Air, Incorporated*, 1998).

The disabled individual must also establish to the court that the reason for the employment decision was a result of the disability. This requirement can be rather difficult, requiring a fairly precise demonstration of intent to discriminate by the employer (29 U.S.C.A. sec. 794). Courts, though, have often been willing to infer that negative employment decisions against disabled public school employees are a result of discrimination based on the individual's disability, unless the public school can clearly demonstrate to the contrary. In 1987, the Supreme Court unequivocally stated that a person with a disability who is otherwise qualified to teach should not be prevented from teaching simply due to the disability (*School Board of Nassau County v. Arline*, 1987). The cases of two disabled teachers display the range of possible outcomes for trying to prove employment discrimination by a school.

A blind English teacher, who had a Professional Certificate from the Pennsylvania Department of Education, twice won legal victories against the school district of Philadelphia, which claimed blindness excluded her from the right to teach (*Gurmankin v. Costanzo*, 1977; *Gurmankin v. Costanzo*, 1980). The Supreme Court held another teacher's firing was a violation of the Rehabilitation Act because the teacher was otherwise qualified to teach and the school district specified that it fired her because of her disability (*School Board of Nassau County v. Arline*, 1987). In that case, the school board actually stated that the teacher was discharged "not because she had done anything wrong," but because she had a "continued reoccurence [*sic*] of tuberculosis" (*School Board of Nassau County v. Arline*, 1987, p. 276). In both of these cases, the school district actually clearly stated that it was discriminating. Courts will generally not be as willing to find discrimination when a teacher with a disability claims a policy that is not overtly discriminatory led to a case of discrimination, especially when the school district offers accommodations.

Schools, of course, have the right to take adverse employment actions with due cause against any employee. Having a disability does not make an individual immune to discipline or dismissal. When a school district can show a rational relationship between a policy and its objective, it can justify an adverse employment action taken against a disabled employee. For example, a mobility-impaired teacher applies for a job in administration, which requires, among other things, superior communication skills for dealing with students, parents, and members of the community. As part of the selection process, each candidate must take an examination of oral and written communication skills. The teacher scores very poorly on the test and does not get the job. It goes to a candidate who has similar qualifications except that the other candidate scored well on the examination and that the other candidate is not disabled. Were the teacher to sue claiming disability discrimination, the district would only need to show the relationship between the examination and the job requirements, as well as the discrepancy in the scores of the candidates. In such a situation, the disabled teacher would not get the promotion, but it would be for reasons unrelated to the disability, so no employment discrimination would have occurred.

DISABILITY AND THE EMPLOYMENT PROCESS UNDER THE ADA

As should be clear from all of the requirements and protections discussed above, employers cannot legally make employment decisions that are discriminatory against individuals with disabilities. EEOC regulations specifically prohibit disability-based discrimination in:

1. Recruitment, advertising of jobs, and procedures to apply for a job;
2. Hiring, terminating, rehiring, promoting, demoting, transferring, and awarding tenure;
3. Rates of pay, compensation, and benefits;
4. Assignments, classifications, position descriptions, seniority, progression, and organizational structures;
5. All forms of leave, including sick leave and leave of absence;
6. Fringe benefits;
7. Training, apprenticeships, conferences, meetings, and professional activities;
8. Social and recreational activities sponsored by the employer; and
9. Any other term, condition, or privilege of employment. (29 C.F.R. sec. 1630.4)

The hiring process cannot be designed to keep out disabled individuals; promotion and firing decisions cannot be biased against disabled employees. The Rehabilitation Act and the ADA do not create any affirmative duty to hire disabled individuals. However, employers cannot make adverse employment decisions against an individual with a disability due to the disability unless the individual cannot perform an essential function of the job, the employment would create undue hardship on the employer, or the employee cannot be reasonably accommodated.

If the employment decision includes a test, the test should not be biased and accommodations, such as an alternate format or accessibility, should be provided as necessary. A test cannot be used to exclude an individual with a disability from consideration for a position unless the test measures an essential skill and no reasonable accommodation can be provided for the individual to successfully perform the function being tested.

Employers cannot ask directly about disabilities in a job interview. To this end, employers are not allowed to ask about disabilities, need of reasonable accommodation, medical histories, general health status, or workers' compensation history. If the employer asks each and every candidate about ability to perform the essential functions of the job, then such questions are acceptable. The employer may ask, so long as all job candidates are asked the same questions, how a potential employee would accomplish various job functions, with or without accommodations. If the job applicant voluntarily discloses a disability during the interview and wants to discuss potential reasonable accommodations, then the employer can discuss the issue. If the employer is aware of a disability because it is obvious, the employer may not make inquiries into the nature of the disability. For example, the EEOC pursued a discrimination claim against a company that repeatedly asked a potential employee numerous questions about his obvious facial deformities including whether his appearance would affect his ability to deal with customers (*EEOC v. Community Coffee*, 1995). The employer also cannot ask if the potential employee has had past substance abuse problems, but can ask if the employee is currently taking illegal drugs. The employer may not ask about or test for legal medications. Also, employers may not test for or ask about alcohol consumption. HIV/AIDS cannot be asked about or tested for prior to a conditional offer of employment.

Employment can be offered conditional to passing a drug test or a medical examination if every prospective employee must take it. These medical examinations can be comprehensive, testing for physical requirements, functional capacities, or measurable psychological traits that are necessary for performing essential functions of the job. If the medical examination reveals a disability, the employer cannot refuse to hire the individual unless the disability creates a direct threat to safety or renders the employee unable to perform the essential functions of the job, regardless of reasonable accommodations. If the medical examination includes a test for HIV/AIDS, the results cannot be used to deny employment unless the employee would pose a safety risk or could not perform an essential job function due to the disease. The information learned by the employer in the medical examination must be treated as confidential. It can only be disclosed to supervisors as relevant to accommodations, to safety personnel if the disability might necessitate first aid, or to government officials investigating compliance (42 U.S.C.A. sec. 12112(c)(3)(B)). In the post-conditional offer medical examination, the employer may also "inquire about a person's workers' compensation history" (EEOC *Technical Assistance Manual* sec. 9.3, p. IX-3). Any post-hiring medical examinations are subject to all the same restrictions as pre-employment examinations.

Physical agility tests are not considered the same as medical examinations by the EEOC. At any point during the employment process an employer may test for physical agility so long as it is job related and based on business necessity. If the physical agility test is used to disqualify an applicant with a disability, the employer must demonstrate that the physical trait is essential to the performance of the job and there is no reasonable accommodation that would allow the individual with the disability to do the job. EEOC also does not classify a polygraph as a medical examination, but since such tests can include prohibited questions, a polygraph test cannot be given prior to a conditional offer of employment.

The exact status of some kinds of tests is undetermined. Depending on the type of test and the conditions under which it is given, an examination of visual acuity may or may not be a medical examination. EEOC classifies some psychological tests as being medical examinations and other psychological tests as not being medical examinations. If someone who is not a medical professional gives a test intended to assess a mental aptitude, such as analytical thinking skills, rather than mental health, the test may be given prior to a conditional offer of employment. However, if the test is given by a medical professional or is intended to evaluate mental health, the test cannot be given prior to a conditional offer of employment.

Once an individual with a disability is hired, the ADA assures the right to a workplace free from harassment regarding disability. The ADA makes it "unlawful to coerce, intimidate, threaten, or interfere with" any disabled individual in performance of work activities (42 U.S.C.A. sec. 12203(b)). Employers are responsible to ensure that employees without disabilities are not harassing employees with disabilities. The employer also is forbidden from engaging in discrimination against the employees with disabilities. The laws prohibit intentional discrimination, which is known as disparate treatment, as well any policy that has the effect of creating discrimination, which is known as disparate impact. For disparate treatment, disability can play no part whatsoever in the discriminatory practice. An employer cannot justify a discriminatory action by claiming other factors also motivated the practice. Disparate impact can occur when the employer does not intend a practice to cause discrimination, but it does nonetheless. If an individual with a disability is adversely affected by a policy that results in either disparate treatment or disparate impact, that individual may seek to enforce the legal rights provided under the Rehabilitation Act and the ADA.

CROSS-EXAMINATIONS AND REBUTTALS

What are "essential functions?" How would you define the "essential functions" for a teaching position?

What is the EEOC? What protections does it provide?

What types of examinations are permissible throughout the hiring process?

What is disparate impact?

What is disparate treatment?

Chapter 11

Assistive Technology

Stephen Hawking, a professor at Cambridge University in Britain, is one of the great scientific minds of this century. He has made groundbreaking discoveries in quantum mechanics, gravity, and atomic behavior. Hawking is also one of the world's most recognized disabled persons, having suffered for three decades from Amyotrophic Lateral Sclerosis (ALS), a disease which progressively destroys neurons in the brain and spinal chord, killing 100,000 people worldwide each year. Symptoms of ALS include muscle weakness and paralysis, as well as impaired speaking, swallowing, and breathing.

Central to Hawking's work is his use of assistive technology. Due to his lack of muscular control, Hawking's speech became so slurred that few people could understand him and he gave seminars through an interpreter. For a time, he could only communicate by spelling out words letter by letter by raising an eyebrow when an assistant pointed to the right letter on a spelling card. Hawking uses an E Z Keys program which can predict and complete words in sentences, speeding up the ability of people with disabilities such as ALS to communicate. It can also convert text to speech with an integrated synthesizer program on any PC-compatible machine using Windows 95 or higher and a processor running at a minimum of 133 MHz. The program's word-prediction database holds up to 5,000 words and allows users to save thousands of set phrases that can be quickly retrieved and vocalized. Hawking can either use the voice synthesizer to speak what he writes or save it to disk. From there, Hawking can print out his thoughts or use the disc to speak them sentence-by-sentence. Using this method of communication, Hawking has written several books and numerous scientific papers and has given hundreds of talks.

Kent Cullers, a senior researcher at the Search for Extra-terrestrial Intelligence Institute (SETI) in Mountain View, California, has been blind since birth. Although he has never glimpsed the Milky Way or witnessed a full moon, Cullers has been a leader in the quest for life in the cosmos. Cullers develops, evaluates, and implements complex algorithms that allow scientists to sift through radio signals originating from distant star systems. He was the first blind student to earn a doctorate in physics in the United States and is also a leader in the field of envisioning and designing advanced radio telescopes that scan wider and wider swaths of the skies.

When it comes to communicating, Cullers uses a variety of assistive technology devices to get his ideas across. Graphically, Cullers uses a simple, raised-line drawing kit developed for blind people. He has used these drawings to convey ideas for designs of new scientific instruments. He also uses a system called Optacon, which consists of a photocell camera attached to an electronically controlled matrix of 144 vibrating pins that move up and down to represent letters. As he slowly moves the camera across the page, letters from words are translated into vibrating raised pins that cover about half the index finger. People with impaired vision can scan the camera over a document or computer screen and piece together an image in their mind. Cullers also uses two computers: a portable Windows laptop and a BrailleNote, a small computer the size of a mini-notebook that runs on WindowsCE and has a tactile input and output interface. The BrailleNote can connect to other Windows computers via serial or parallel ports as well as through PC cards and infrared ports. It has a built-in modem that makes it easy to log on to the Internet through a standard phone line. The device also easily converts to a Braille terminal for a standard PC. Additionally, Cullers uses a text-to-speech program on his Windows laptop. To do his calculations, Cullers uses a Braille code of mathematics, called the Nemeth Code. This system allows any print mathematical representation to be mapped into a tactile format. Cullers' achievements illustrate how using assistive technology can allow a person with disabilities to break into a rigorous, intellectual field.

Michael's parents bought him a three-wheeled recumbent wheelchair with large and colorful wheels, different gears, a flag strapped on the back, and the ability to go up and down hills just as fast as a regular bike. Soon, all the kids at school wanted to try it out, and Michael became a very cool adolescent to hang out with.

Parents and professionals realize that when it comes to adapting assistive technology to the classroom, peer acceptance matters. Some students with disabilities reject assistive technology out of fear of being seen as different even when the benefits are clear. Kids with disabilities want what all teens want, to fit in.

Many students with disabilities don't like the special communication equipment because the synthesized voice isn't their own. Others don't like the extra attention focused on them when they use it. Specialized assistive technologies become fully accepted in social settings just as the telephone, cell phone, laptop computer, and PDA have become socially accepted communication devices. The technology we use tells others about who we are, how we think, and what's important to us. Moreover, the design of the tool and the materials from which it is made can convey impressions about the device or the user in terms of viability, strength, and durability. Manufacturers of assistive technology are beginning to take these factors into consideration. As they create products that combine accessibility with style, they help destigmatize disabilities and make kids more receptive and willing to try assistive technology.

Examples of fun, accessible assistive technology include Motorola's new Talkabout T900. Motorola took the concept of text pagers, which were originally designed for the deaf and hard-of-hearing, and developed a "two-way personal interactive communicator" in colors such as "raspberry ice" and "mystic blue." Television ads show teens exchanging party invitations, jokes, and gossip over instant e-mail and text messaging. For people who are deaf or hard-of-hearing, this positive image is a breakthrough. Similarly, Nokia Mobile makes the Inductive Loopset for profoundly to severely hearing-impaired users with t-coil-equipped hearing aids. The t-coil drowns out feedback and surrounding sounds so the user only hears the other person's voice on the telephone. Nokia designed the coil to resemble the headsets that many hearing people use for hands-free conversation when they're driving. The difference between the two is barely noticeable and it comes in five interchangeable colors. Never before have the hearing-impaired been able to use the same trendy devices designed for hearing users.

The latest version of Encarta Encyclopedia is loaded with accessibility features such as narrator, sound sentry, and on-screen keyboard that synchronize with the Windows operating system. It's far easier for kids with disabilities to incorporate Encarta into their daily activities than use an individually tailored program that none of their classmates have seen before. Encarta does help integrate students with disabilities into mainstream education.

Lernout & Hauspie has an educational division and makes the Kurzweil 3000, a program that reads scanned or electronic text aloud to the blind or those with reading difficulties. Their efforts have helped humanize the software, making kids more receptive to the program. Kurzweil 3000 is used with earphones in a school or library setting, so most people assume the students are using a multimedia program. Some schools have adopted the software for all students, even those without learning disabilities.

IDEA requires public school districts to provide assistive technology devices and services to students, as determined by their IEP teams and teachers. The government set aside $7 billion in fiscal 2001 and $9 billion for fiscal 2002 to help fund states' assistive technology purchases. For someone with a speech impairment or hearing loss, assistive technology can make the difference between being able to participate in classroom discussions or sitting on the sidelines. The Department of Education statistics indicate 11 percent of the national student population from ages 6 to 17 falls under IDEA. Of those children, 96 percent go to regular public and private schools along with non-disabled peers. Visual aids, mouse trackers, and listening devices are vital to the daily lives of disabled students.

Educational technology plays an important role in improving learning for all students. However, students with disabilities frequently face basic physical and product access barriers that prevent them from using educational technology to benefit their learning. How does a student who is blind access the Internet? How does a student who is deaf receive information from the audio of a multimedia program? Access solutions are available. Screen readers that voice the text on the screen of each web page can overcome barriers to accessing the Internet encountered by students who are blind; captions built into multimedia programs can overcome barriers for students who are deaf. Some access solutions, using principles of universal design, are built right into the hardware or software, such as captions. Other solutions require add-ons, such as screen reader systems.

School districts need to ensure that the educational technology they purchase and use in their districts is accessible to all students, including students with disabilities. Purchasing and installing technology that is designed to be accessible is both responsive to students' needs and cost effective. It can help avoid the wasteful expenditure of time and money needed to retrofit systems that have not been planned to meet the accessibility and compatibility needs of all students. There are several points during the planning and implementation process that are key to assuring that educational technology is accessible.

- *Planning.* School districts and local school technology plans must address access issues to meet current and future needs of students with disabilities. It is imperative to include special education professionals on planning teams at both the district and individual school level. At all levels, questions should be asked about how students with disabilities will be able to use the technology.

- *Purchasing.* Accessibility should be a consideration when purchasing any educational technology (i.e., wiring, hardware, or software) for the school's instructional programs. Schools need to ask some basic questions to determine if the technology they are considering is powerful and flexible enough to support accommodation needs.

- *Support.* District teachers need not only awareness knowledge regarding technology accommodations but also hands-on familiarity with assistive technology. Schools that establish and maintain technology support services for teachers can boost adoption and integration of specific technology accommodations in class-rooms.

EXAMPLES OF TECHNOLOGY ADAPTATIONS

Over 4.3 million Americans have some type of visual impairment. Visual impairments include blindness and other disorders that may affect the central vision acuity, the field of vision, color perception, or binocular visual function. The American Medical Association defines legal blindness as visual acuity not exceeding 20/200 in the better eye with correction, or a limit in the field of vision that is less than a 20-degree angle (tunnel vision). Tumors, infections, injuries, retrolental fibroplasia, cataracts, glaucoma, diabetes, vascular impairments, or myopia may cause legal blindness. The resulting functional limitations will vary widely, as will the assistive technology and mobility aids recommended. Assistive technology for visual impairments includes:

- Screen reading program and speech synthesizer
- Braille embosser and printer
- Braille display processor
- Braille font program
- Braille graphics program
- Braille note writer
- Braille text translation system
- Copy machine for tactile relief images
- Extension keys for Braillewriter
- Paperless Braille machine
- Plastic sheets for Braille copier
- Thermal pen
- Translation program
- Braille alphabet cards
- Tactile paging system
- Television screen magnifier
- Voice output computer terminal
- Keytop overlay
- Audible keyboard signal
- Optical character recognition device
- Scanner
- Large print books
- Magnifiers

Students with motor impairments may experience limited muscle control of fine motor skills; limited muscle strength, coordination, range of motion, stability; limited use of hands to operate a computer; and limited gross motor skills. Over 70,000 students in United States public schools require such aids as:

- Alternative keyboard such as trackball or joystick
- Ultrasonic pointer device
- Voice recognition for input
- Book holders
- Page-turners
- Carts
- Manual wheelchairs
- Powered wheelchairs
- Sports wheelchairs
- Wheelchair accessories such as lapboards, arm rests, leg supports, batteries, carrying devices, hand rims, head supports, tires, seats, backs

Over 20 million Americans have a hearing impairment of some type. A hearing impairment is any type or degree of auditory impairment, while deafness is an inability to use hearing as a means of communication. Hearing loss may be sensorineural, which means one has difficulty in interpreting sounds; conductive, which means one has difficulty in hearing sounds; or a mixed impairment, involving both sensorineural and conductive. Hearing loss is measured in decibels and may be mild, moderate, or profound. A person who is born with a hearing loss may have language deficiencies and exhibit poor vocabulary and syntax. Many students with hearing loss may use hearing aids and rely on lip reading. Others may require an interpreter. For students with hearing impairments, the following are important accommodations:

- Visual icons that replace sound cues on the computer
- Video captioning

As we have learned, all recipients of federal funds, including local school districts, are subject to anti-discrimination legislation including IDEA that guarantees students with disabilities with a "free appropriate public education." School districts are required to provide assistive technology devices and services to individual students if a student's IEP team determines that the student needs them. Section 504 of the Rehabilitation Act states that no person with a disability shall be excluded from participation or denied benefits or otherwise be subjected to discrimination because of their disability. The ADA requires that local, county, or state governments must make facilities and services accessible when needed by people with disabilities. Students with disabilities must have an equal opportunity to participate in, and benefit from, a school district's programs and activities. If computer technology is part of a public school's education program, Section 504 and the ADA require a school to provide students with disabilities with accessible computer hardware and software so that they are not excluded from the education program. If technology is purchased that cannot be made accessible, it will have to be retrofitted, replaced, or some other adaptation will have to be made so that students with disabilities can have an equal opportunity to participate in the education program. If equal access to an education program can be provided through other means, a particular technology may not need to be fully accessible to every student. However, technology should be readily available that can provide access for individuals with all types of disabilities. Where technology is the only source of information or services, such as an electronic library system or a single station that provides Internet access, it must either be accessible or be able to be made accessible in order to provide students with disabilities with an equal opportunity to participate in the education program. In addition, the ADA and the Rehabilition Act require public elementary and secondary schools to take appropriate steps to ensure that communication with individuals with disabilities is as effective as communication with others.

Communication in the context of information technology means the transfer of information through computers, including the resources of the Internet. A school is required to provide appropriate auxiliary aids and services where necessary to ensure effective communication for individuals with disabilities. They are also required to make reasonable modifications in policies, practices or procedures when the modifications are necessary to avoid discrimination on the basis of disability. When making purchases and when selecting its resources, a school has a duty to solve barriers to information access that the school's purchasing choices create. If accessible computer technology or a particular assistive technology device or service is necessary for the provision of an FAPE to students with disabilities, federal laws require a school to provide that technology.

As with students, a school must make its technology systems and computer hardware and software accessible where necessary to ensure that it does not discriminate against its employees with disabilities in the terms and conditions of their employment. A school cannot discriminate against an employee based on his or her disability, and if job applicants, teachers, and other employees use technology provided by the school, the school must make that technology accessible so that employees with disabilities are not denied opportunities based on their disabilities. Employees with disabilities may also need particular assistive technology or access to standard technology as a reasonable accommodation. An employer need not provide a specific accommodation that is requested by an applicant or employee if an alternative means of accommodation that is less costly, but effective, is available. For example, although an individual with low vision may request a large computer monitor that would enable the individual to better view information on the computer screen, there may be situations in which an employer may not have to provide that monitor if a less expensive screen enlargement software can provide the same level of access to on-screen materials for that individual.

Many educational technology products on the market today have not been designed to provide or support full access for individuals with disabilities. There is currently no independent review entity that provides buyers with authoritative information regarding the accessibility of educational or other types of technologies or information on how products compare to each other concerning accessibility. Information on the accessibility of certain products is available, however, from the manufacturers themselves. In addition, when a school is procuring computer hardware and software, as well as entire systems of information technology and equipment, a school needs to add access considerations to the list of factors they use to make decisions about the purchase of educational technology, both for off-the-shelf products and for those systems that will be designed or created for a school's use. Best practice and common sense would advise that a school procure only products that are or can be made fully accessible. The following resource contains information that can be used to conduct a review of educational technology products for accessibility: The U.S. Department of Education's *Requirements for Accessible Software Design*. These requirements, adopted into the Department's contracts for software procurement, provide functional specifications that, if included in software design, will ensure minimum accessibility for individuals with disabilities. The requirements can be found via links on the Department's web site at http://www.ed.gov/offices/OCIO/asstech/ assi.html or at http://gcs.ed.gov.coninfo/clibrary/software.htm.

In addition, manufacturers of telecommunication equipment and service providers are subject to provisions of the Telecommunications Act of 1996 (47 U.S.C.A. sec. 225). This act requires manufacturers and service providers to address the access needs of people with disabilities as they design and fabricate equipment and services, if it is "readily achievable" (47 U.S.C.A. sec. 225). The act stipulates that input, controls, and mechanical functions shall be locatable, identifiable, and operable through at least one mode that complies with the following:

- Functions shall not require user vision.
- Functions shall not require user visual acuity better than 20/70 and shall not rely on audio output.

- Functions shall not require user color perception.
- Functions shall not require auditory perception.
- Functions shall not require fine motor control or simultaneous actions.
- Functions shall be operable with limited reach and strength.
- Functions shall not require a sequential response less than three seconds. Alternatively, any response time may be selected or adjusted by the user over a wide range.
- Functions shall not require speech.
- Functions shall minimize the cognitive, memory, language, and learning skills required of the user.

In addition, all information necessary to operate and use the product, including text, static or dynamic images, icons, or incidental operating cues, shall be provided through at least one mode that complies with the following:

- Information that is presented visually shall also be available in auditory form.
- Information that is provided through a visual display shall not require user visual acuity better then 20/70, and shall not rely on audio.
- Text, other than text output of a TTY, which is presented in a moving fashion shall be available in a static presentation mode at the option of the user.
- Information that is provided in auditory form shall be available in visual form and, where appropriate, in tactile form.
- Information that is provided in auditory form shall be available in enhanced auditory fashion (increased amplification or increased signal-to-noise ratio).
- Flashing visual displays and indicators shall not exceed a frequency of 3 Hz.
- Products which use audio output modes shall have an industry standard connector for headphones or personal listening devices (e.g., phone-like handset or ear cup) that cuts off speakers when used.
- Products shall not cause interference to hearing technologies (including hearing aides, cochlear implants, and assistive listening devices) of the user or bystanders.
- Products providing auditory output by an audio transducer that is normally held up to the ear shall provide a means for effective wiring coupling to hearing aids.
- Products shall be equipped with volume control that provides adjustable amplification ranging from 18–25 dB of gain.

Telecommunications equipment shall be compatible with peripheral devices and specialized equipment commonly used by individuals with disabilities to achieve accessibility and shall comply with the following provisions:

- Information needed for the operation of products (including output, alerts, icons, on-line help and documentation) shall be available in a standard electronic text format on a cross-industry standard port and all input to and control of a product shall allow for real time operation by electronic text input into a cross-industry standard external port and in cross-industry standard format. The cross-industry standard port shall not require manipulation of a connector by the user. Products shall also provide a cross-industry standard connector that may require manipulation.

- Products providing auditory output shall provide the auditory signal at a standard signal level through an industry standard connector.

- Touchscreen and touch-operated controls shall be operable without requiring body contact or close body proximity.

- Products which provide a function allowing voice communication and which do not themselves provide TTY functionality shall provide a standard non-acoustic connection point for TTYs.

SPECIFIC ASSISTIVE TECHNOLOGY DEVICES

It is estimated that between 15–20 percent of Americans have some type of learning disability. A learning disability is a permanent neurological disorder that affects the manner in which information is received, organized, remembered, and then retrieved or expressed. Students with learning disabilities possess average to above average intelligence. The disability is demonstrated by a significant discrepancy between expected and actual performance in one or more of the basic functions including memory, oral expression, listening comprehension, written expression, basic reading skills, reading comprehension, mathematical calculation, or mathematical reasoning.

ADD and ADHD are neurologically based medical problems characterized by inattention, impulsivity, and sometimes hyperactivity. The results can lead to lifelong problems. Learning disabilities, ADD, and ADHD vary from one person to another and are often inconsistent within an individual. Students may demonstrate one or more problem characteristics and the form may be mild, moderate, or severe. Assistive technology devices are aids that can help a person with a disability overcome functional limitations and perform tasks that might otherwise not be possible. A functional limitation exists when a task or tasks cannot be independently performed in a specific environment such as balance, behavior, bodily control, breathing, cognition, communication, coordination, seeing, hearing, smelling, tasting, touching, pain, and mobility. Task cueing systems include:

- PEAT—Assists with memory deficits by providing a system for cueing user while engaging in tasks.
- StepPAD—Plays pre-recorded messages when activated.
- The Jogger—Reminds user of an impending task, presents task, and records and transmits response to prompt.

Cognitive and behavioral software includes:

- Following Directions Series—Helps students learn to follow simple directions.
- Success CD-ROMs—Helps students learn proper behavior in social settings.
- Turn-Talking—Helps students develop communication skills.
- Working It Out Together CD-ROM—Helps students learn peer mediation techniques.

Reference tools for students with disabilities include:

- Franklin Speaking Language Master—Enables users with special needs to use a dictionary.
- Homework Wiz—Provides pronunciation and definitions of words.
- Merriam-Webster Speaking Dictionary and Thesaurus—Provides definitions and synonyms for words.
- Speaking Language Master—Provides auditory feedback of words and definitions.
- Webster's Spelling Corrector Plus—Corrects spelling and provides synonyms.

Language development software includes:

- Labeling Tutor—Teaches students to associate written words, sounds, and pictures.
- Swim, Swam, Swum—Helps students understand irregular verbs in the past, present, and future tenses.
- Word Hound—Promotes word recognition.
- WordQ Writing Aid Software for Learning Disabilities and ESL—Suggests words while students write and provides text-to-speech feedback.
- Ace Detective—Supports reading for detail, drawing conclusions, and making inferences.
- All My Words—Provides language activities and games.
- Clicker Plus—Helps students create words, phrases, and sentences.
- Imagination Express Series—Develops language skills.
- Learning Well—Promotes reading comprehension and cooperative learning.
- Nouns & Sounds—Builds auditory awareness and development.

Concept teaching aids include:

- Concrete to Abstract Kit—Helps students develop higher-order thinking skills.
- Magnetic Boards—Helps students with a variety of cognitive and/or motor disabilities improve language skills.

- School Passport—A communication board which teaches school-related vocabulary.
- Touch 'N Feel Box—Develops sense of touch, imagination, and thinking skills.
- Visual Motor Skills Easel—Improves visual motor integration skills.

Voice input systems include:

- D1000 Recorder—Allows users to record and play messages.
- L & H Voice Xpress—Allows user to access computer applications through spoken commands.
- Naturally Speaking—Allows word processing by dictating into computer.

Reading systems include:

- CAST eReader—Reads electronic text aloud.
- DECTalk—Speaks text sent by computer and provides computer speech output.
- IntelliTalk II—A talking word processor.
- Keynote Gold Multimedia—A speech synthesizer that provides high-quality voice speech output.
- Kurzweil 3000—Reads and highlights scanned or electronic text aloud.
- Optical Character Readers (OCR)—Scans printed text and outputs as speech.
- Verbal Eyes—Helps user complete electronic forms with voice output software.
- Vocal Eyes—Processes screen and keyboard output from software into speech.

Common barriers to educational technology access for all students include costs associated with obtaining equipment, difficulty connecting rural locations, lack of funding to train personnel to use technology, and so on. For students with disabilities, more basic access barriers are encountered in interacting with the educational technology product. Motor disabilities may limit a student's ability to use a standard keyboard, the standard monitor display may not be usable by students with visual impairments, and students with a hearing impairment may not understand the speech output of an instructional program. Alternative input and output features are frequently needed by students with disabilities to allow them to interact with the educational technology on an equal basis with other students. Such features are critical for educational technology "product access" just as ramps and lever door handles are critical for building access.

These access features also provide benefits for individuals without disabilities. Just as curb cuts accommodate not only individuals who use wheelchairs but also individuals pushing shopping carts and baby strollers, many educational technology access features support students with a variety of learning needs. Alternative input options allow preschool children to use a computer effectively when they do not yet have the motor skills to use a standard keyboard. Voice output systems not only provide access for individuals who cannot see text on a screen display, but also support effective technology use by individuals with limited reading skills. Text display of speech output can foster literacy development and efforts to learn new languages, in addition to providing access for individuals who cannot hear. As the developers of computer hardware and software recognize the benefit that can be derived from all individuals (those with and without disabilities) being able to use the same computer equipment and software applications, the concept of universal design in the development of new products becomes more accepted and built-in access should become more readily available.

As a school district purchases technology for the schools, several methods can be used to ensure that the educational technology products or systems provide the accessibility a school needs. School staff that has familiarity with the access standards can directly review products and/or product specifications. This review should definitely include the expertise of special educators and educational technology specialists. Community resources and individuals who are users of adaptive technology and are familiar with access features can be asked to assist in product reviews. In addition, vendors can be asked to provide a review of their products in reference to the access standards to demonstrate how their products conform to these standards. Asking vendors to review or demonstrate the accessibility of their products provides an added benefit of increasing awareness to access issues that can be addressed by the manufacturer during future product development.

There are three main areas where disabled people need assistive technology: in independent-living situations, education, and employment. The scarcity of funding for assistive technology prevents too many disabled students from getting an appropriate education and too many unemployed adults with a disability from being hired. As you know, students with disabilities are covered under IDEA. Disabled students can have assistive-technology products included in their IEPs. The school system is required under the law to purchase the products for them; however, the device becomes the property of the school system. Many schools will not allow the student to take the products home with them; when the students graduate, they can't take the device with them. State disability offices are mandated by federal law to advocate for assistive technology for state residents with disabilities, including students. If you are receiving Supplemental Security Income under Social Security and you need a talking computer or some other assistive-technology device, you can submit an invoice to the federal government for payment with certification from a doctor or rehabilitation counselor that you need the device for everyday living. For more severe disabilities, funding for assistive technology can be obtained through the

Supplemental Security Disability Insurance program of Social Security. Persons with disabilities and advocates must explore every potential source of support.

FUTURE SHOCK?

Assistive technology (AT) supports students with disabilities and provides a means for people with differences to accomplish specific tasks on their own. AT helps increase the independence of persons with learning differences. Often, these individuals rely on parents, teachers, friends, and siblings for help. Yet, overreliance on others may slow the transition into adulthood and independence. It may also lower self-esteem. The development of products cited throughout this chapter as well as thousands of other valuable resources promotes equality for persons with disabilities. A glimpse into the future reveals even more "techie" aids including:

- IBot—In standard mode, it functions like a regular powered wheelchair. The wheels can swivel into several other configurations to enable different activities. To climb stairs, the two large wheels rotate around each other in a circular motion that slowly moves the chair upwards while keeping the seat level and stable. The chair also has an upright balance mode where the two sets of big wheels are stacked vertically and the seat is elevated several feet.
- ICommunicator—This combination of hardware and software converts real-time speech into three separate formats. For the deaf it renders speech as on-screen text. For the hearing impaired, it converts the spoken word into computer-enhanced speech that can be digitally amplified. For those who sign, it translates speech into sign-language symbols displayed on the computer screen.
- VVT—The VisAble Video Telescope is a palm-held video camera with a high-powered image-processing unit and a single eyepiece. It is used as a small telescope and focuses automatically for long-, mid-, and short-range viewing.

Only 25 percent of individuals with disabilities who work and 40 percent of individuals with disabilities who want to work say they need special equipment or technology to perform effectively the kind of job they prefer. Half of the people with disabilities who work full- or part-time use computers at work. Those who work full-time (60 percent) are more likely to use a computer than those who work part-time (35 percent). More than 28 percent of people with disabilities own special equipment or technology to assist them because of their disability. The number has risen significantly and is expected to steadily increase. Those who describe their disability as very or somewhat severe (33 percent) are more likely to own special equipment than those who characterize their disability as slight or moderate (19 percent). Fifteen percent of people with disabilities who work full- or part-time, or would like to be working, need a personal computer. As researchers continue to explore and adapt artificial intelligence, space exploration, and other technologies, we will continue to develop aids for living and learning.

Concerned educators must support the inclusion and strengthening of technology-focused language and initiatives in all relevant legislation; however, issues related to technology and disability are continually emerging. Forward thinking and planning must characterize efforts to anticipate and act on such needs. Legislation to promote and improve the expanded utilization of technology is included in various existing public laws as well as bills under consideration. While the expanding use of technology has benefits for all citizens, it can be particularly beneficial for people with disabilities; however, it can also result in additional barriers that limit access by others with certain types of disabilities. To ensure the benefits of technology for all persons with disabilities, we must be proactive, work with other organizations, and take a comprehensive approach to requests for support, testimony, or promotion of any assistive technology legislation under consideration. Input should be actively solicited from the field. It should be cross-disability in nature, and should include teachers, administrators, service providers, policy makers, consumers with disabilities and their families, and advocates.

CROSS-EXAMINATIONS AND REBUTTALS

Find web sites that promote assistive technology devices and choose one device that you could use to provide a "level playing field" for all your students.

What are some important considerations for your school to consider when purchasing hardware/software systems?

What technologies for the visually impaired would you hope to have available as a teacher? Why?

What assistive technology would you include in an IEP for a student with a learning disability?

Chapter 12

Disabilities and the Media

People with disabilities face many barriers every day, from physical obstacles to systemic barriers in employment and civic programs. Often, the most difficult barriers to overcome are attitudes other people carry regarding people with disabilities. Whether born from ignorance, fear, misunderstanding or hate, these attitudes keep people from appreciating and experiencing the full potential a person with a disability can achieve. Fifty-four million Americans have one or more physical or mental disabilities, and this number is increasing as the population as a whole is growing older. Studies have documented that people with disabilities, as a group, occupy an inferior status in our society and are severely disadvantaged socially, vocationally, economically, and educationally. Society doesn't expect people with disabilities to perform up to standard, and when people with disabilities do, they are perceived as heroic or courageous. This attitude has the effect of patronizing people with disabilities rather than empowering them to demand equal pay, equal benefits, equal opportunity, and equal access to the workplace.

Marlee Matlin, a 35-year-old Academy Award–winning actor, is one of the world's most renowned deaf persons as White House adviser on the TV drama *The West Wing*. Matlin lost her hearing to a fever when she was 18 months old. The actor has been signing since she was 5 years old. Matlin has a Telecommunications Device for the Deaf, or TDD, and a television with closed-caption technology. She also has a series of signaling devices to alert her when the doorbell rings, the phone rings, or when her baby cries.

She sees the Internet as putting people with disabilities on the same footing as everybody else. Matlin says she can't imagine a deaf person surviving without access to assistive technology. She notes that Vinton Cerf, one of the Internet's founders, helped to develop e-mail as a way to communicate with his deaf wife, Sigrid.

In a time when 70 percent of working-age people with disabilities are jobless, Matlin says she does not recall being discriminated against because of her deafness when working; however, she does not understand why employers fear hiring deaf people.

People with quadriplegia can drive cars and have children, people who are blind can tell time on a watch and visit museums, people who are deaf can dance and enjoy music, and people with developmental disabilities can be creative and maintain strong work ethics. Unfortunately, people with disabilities are often subtly dismissed; for example, many people shout at people who are blind or don't expect people using wheelchairs to have the intelligence to speak for themselves. As educators, we must work to counter this type of prejudice.

> Pelswick Eggert is like most 13-year-old boys; he wears his baseball hat backward and is starting to notice girls. But Pelswick gets around via a wheelchair. Also, he's the main character in an animated comedy series, *Pelswick*, on the Nickelodeon cable network. Pelswick easily finds himself in trouble and is far more believable than most past TV portrayals of wheelchair-using youths.
>
> Executive producer, cartoonist John Callahan, is paralyzed from the armpits down and uses a wheelchair. From his own experience, Callahan knows how little others, especially children, understand about the lives of people in wheelchairs. Since more than 1 million Americans use wheelchairs, including 90,000 high-school kids, Pelswick can help impressionable kids and teens better understand the lives and needs of the "permanently seated." The plots often hinge on Pelswick's disability and directly address the attitudinal and physical barriers that people using wheelchairs face every day.

How someone with a disability is portrayed in the mass media can have a powerful effect on people. Much of what we know of people, places, and events comes from what we see on TV and in movies or read in the papers. Currently in film and television, persons with disabilities are portrayed stereotypically, characters created by someone with little knowledge of the attitudes and abilities of an individual with a disability.

While the media causes these misrepresented notions of persons with disabilities, mass media may also be the best solution to true understanding. More and more we are seeing disabled actors in commercials and roles in the mainstream media. The disabled characters are much better written and not so much "about the disability." It is up to disabled actors, musicians, writers, producers, and directors to work toward better and more abundant representation in movies and TV.

Recent examples of positive portrayals of persons with disabilities in the movies include:

- *The Bone Collector*, based on Jeffrey Deaver's novel, stars Denzel Washington as a quadriplegic detective on the trail of a serial killer. There is absolutely no sign of patronization, condescension, or any self-pity beyond an understandable-under-the circumstances attempted try at a suicide pact (Washington is afraid one of his seizures will turn him into a vegetable). He does all his investigative work by a voice-activated computer from a large hospital bed. His prodigy is Angelina Jolie, who does the work at the actual crime scene. He is portrayed as intelligent, capable, and passionate.
- *Notting Hill*, starring Hugh Grant and Julia Roberts, features a woman in a wheelchair played by Gina McKee. McKee's acting is quite poignant, and her loving relationship with her husband illustrates her personal qualities, not her disability.
- *Nell*, starring Jodie Foster, is set in the beautiful Blue Ridge Mountains. Foster is a young woman who has been brought up by her mother who had suffered a stroke in the backwoods. A doctor, Liam Neeson, finds her after her mother has died but she is unable to speak except in a language known only to her mother. The doctor becomes her teacher; however, she becomes our teacher as we learn about learning disabilities and autism.
- *The Mighty*, starring Sharon Stone is the story of Kevin (Freak), a 13-year-old boy with Morquios Syndrome. He walks with braces on his legs and crutches. At school he faces prejudice and has no friends. Then along comes Max, who is exceedingly large for his age and has learning difficulties. Freak's sharp intellect and Max's ability to protect him are the beginnings of a beautiful adolescent friendship. From the book *Freak the Mighty* by Rodman Philbrick.
- *The Mask*, starring Cher and Eric Stolz, is the story of a teenage boy with craniodiaphyseal dyaplasia. This is an absorbing and enlightening film that is unsentimental and realistic. Cher, as the mother, reveals the real conflicts of a single parent struggling to care for her son while living her own life.
- *Mr. Holland's Opus*, starring Richard Dreyfuss, is the story of a man who wants to be a composer. He takes a job as a music teacher thinking it will be temporary, but for 30 years he is devoted to his teaching yet still ambitious to compose. Unfortunately, his son is deaf and won't be able to hear his "Opus".
- In *As Good As It Gets*, Jack Nicholson plays a romance novelist with obsessive compulsion disorder. He carries out meaningless repetitive actions and is very rude to everyone, especially women. The only person who tolerates him is a waitress (Helen Hunt) who has a son with chronic asthma.
- *My Left Foot*, starring Daniel Day-Lewis, is a triumph of adapting a book written with one left foot to a film made by hundreds of people. Christy is disabled from birth with cerebral palsy and the portrayal of his disability is honest and multi-faceted.

- *The English Patient* is the story of a badly burned victim, Ralph Fiennes, after an air crash in the desert during World War II, being cared for by a Canadian nurse, Juliette Binoche.
- *The Horse Whisperer*, starring Robert Redford and Kristin Scott Thomas, is the story of two girls hit head-on by a Mack truck on an icy road. This accident causes the death of one girl and her horse and severe injury to a second girl and her horse. The survivor, Grace, has lost the lower half of one leg and she and her horse are severely traumatized. Her parents have difficulty coping with her condition, so her mother decides to travel to Montana to see a "horse whisperer" hoping he can help the horse and her daughter.

A person with a disability has the potential to present a visually provocative image and the choice to use such a character provides a powerful tool for the dramatic narrative. Unfortunately, the media often unintentionally perpetuate stereotypes through characters with disabilities portrayed as evoking pity, as bitter and unhappy, or as inspirational heroes. But perhaps the most significant advances in the mass media portrayal of people with disabilities comes from advertisers, who see these people as something much more than disabled; they are seen as consumers. Ads that show people with disabilities playing sports, shopping, teaching, driving, and eating at McDonalds make society aware that people with disabilities do the same things everyone else does.

Television is also taking a lead in programming that portrays disability in an honest, realistic manner. Shows such as Frasier, Providence, and Port Charles have major characters with disabilities who are gifted professionals, possess a wide array of emotions, are involved in romantic relationships, enjoy friends and adventure, and have common, recognizable flaws.

The National Arts and Disability Center (NADC) is the national information dissemination, technical assistance, and referral center specializing in the field of arts and disability. Dedicated to promoting the full inclusion of children and adults with disabilities into the visual arts, performing arts, media, and literary arts communities, the NADC serves to advance artists with disabilities and accessibility to the arts. Their web site, http://nadc.ucla.edu, provides access to its resource directories, annotated bibliographies, and conferences.

A witty and satirical cartoon about disability can be found at http://www.dizabled.com. The site, created by John and Claire Lytle, features the adventures and misadventures of Leeder, a wheelchair user. Even though the cartoons, on the surface, poke fun at disabilities, the humor is in the universality of life's ups and downs.

Van Gogh, a band from Atlanta, will release in 2002 a documentary, featuring the brothers Heisner and the band with concert footage. The musicians in this unusual group perform in wheelchairs on stages across the country and work in music studios to score videos and films on disabilities. More about the group can be found at their web site, http://www.vangoghmusic.com.

Contemporary media is a powerful catalyst for social change. Educators need to use this power to initiate discussions in schools and homes across the country about disability. Through reading, students can begin to identify with someone similar to themselves who has a disability.

LITERATURE SUGGESTIONS FOR SCHOOL MEDIA SPECIALISTS

Literature is a powerful tool for discovering ourselves and our relationships with others, a useful resource for helping students learn the realities of living with a disability. The more opportunities students have to openly share and discuss perceptions of disability, the more understanding they will possess as adults. The following novels deal with a variety of disabilities in realistic portrayals suitable for class discussions and independent reading.

Brown, C. (1991). *My left foot*. Portsmouth, NH: Heinemann. Christy Brown is born with cerebral palsy in Dublin, Ireland. His mother teaches him to write with his left foot.

Eliot, G. (1987/1860). *The mill on the floss*. New York: Penguin. Her brother forbids Maggie to associate with Philip, a hunchback who loves her.

Voigt, C. (1986). *Izzy, willy-nilly*. New York: Atheneum. Isobel wakes up in a hospital after a car accident, to discover her leg will have to be amputated.

Johnston, J. (1993). *Hero of lesser causes*. Boston: Joy Street Books. Keely is devastated when her older brother Patrick is paralyzed by polio, but the love of siblings strengthens both of them.

Konigsburg, E.L. (1996). *The view from Saturday*. New York: Atheneum. Four students develop a special bond with their teacher, a paraplegic, who supports them in an academic bowl.

Paulsen, G. (1991). *The monument*. New York: Delacorte Press. Thirteen-year-old Rocky is self-conscious about the braces on her legs and has her life changed when an artist comes to town to design a monument.

Covington, D. (1991). *Lizard*. New York: Delacorte Press. Lizard, a bright, deformed boy, is sent to live in a Louisiana home for the retarded. The friendship of a visiting actor changes his life.

Paterson, K. (1978). *The great Gilly Hopkins*. New York: Harper Trophy. A child of the foster care system, Gilly finds a new family with Mr. Randolph, a blind African-American man.

Taylor, T. (1995). *The cay*. New York: Flare. Philip is blinded by a torpedo accident and is helped by Timothy, an elderly West Indian sailor.

Armstrong, J. (1996). *Mary Mehan awake*. New York: Alfred A. Knopf. The story of Mary's spiritual journey through the loss of her brother paralleled with a young man deafened in the war.

McCullers, C. (1983). *The heart is a lonely hunter*. New York: Bantam Books.

John Singer, a deaf mute in the rural South, and his relationships with the townspeople is chronicled in this classic novel.

Janover, C. (1997). *Zipper, the kid with ADHD*. Bethesda, MD: Woodbine. Zipper has to learn behavior management if he wants to play drums with his new friend Pete.

Crutcher, C. (1987). *The crazy horse electric game*. New York: Greenwillow Books. The people in a special school where he enrolls help a high school athlete back to physical and mental health.

SUGGESTED VIDEOS FOR MEDIA CENTERS

Aquarius Productions (1995). *My body is not who I am*.
Brodie, J. (1990). *As I am*.
Human Relations Media (1990). *Just like anyone else: Living with disabilities*.
PBS Series (1995). *People in motion: Changing ideas about physical disability*.
Texas Scottish Rite Hospital for Children (1994). *Withstanding ovation*.
United Artists (1962). *The miracle worker*.
Tristar (1984). *Places in the heart*.
Paramount (1986). *Children of a lesser god*.

INTERNET RESOURCES

A multitude of web sites exist which discuss disabilities, but it is important to remember that web sites are in a constant state of flux. A few suggestions for student exploration include:

• The American Disability Association, http://www.ADANET@SISONLINE.COM
• The Beach Center on Families and Disability, http://www.beach@dole.lsi.ukans.edu
• The National Health Information Center, http://www.nhicinfo@health.org
• The National Information Center for Children and Youth with Disabilities, http://www.nichcy@aed.org

As most of us who work or have worked with children know, being accepted by others and "fitting in" can be a daunting process. Adults who as children were placed in the lower level reading group or were the last person chosen for the baseball team have recalled countless stories of damaged self-esteem. Having a disability that separates one from his or her peers in terms of appearance can have a significant impact on self-image. There are several good books and videos available that address a number of self-esteem issues. Steering young people with disabilities to resources that speak of them and to them can be beneficial in helping them recognize that they are not alone. Open discussion and reflective writing can help students process and consider the material in these books and/or films in a more in-depth manner. Helping students focus on the strengths they possess can give them a sense of empowerment and allow them to confront a difficult subject with confidence that they could also handle such difficulties. Through this type of discussion, students may also come to appreciate the struggles and hardships their peers with disabilities face and increase their sensitivity to disability issues. Adolescence is a time of major adjustments and personal and emotional growth and change. Disability complicates this difficult period, bringing to the forefront issues of identity, self-worth, acceptance, and relationships. As a society we need to eradicate the fear and stigma of disability and promote understanding, awareness, and caring. We need to provide positive role models for our students as well as positive support for those adolescents with disabilities.

Postscript 1

And in the End, Hope Remains

I have need to be all on fire, for I have mountains of ice about me to melt.

—William Lloyd Garrison, 1871

Having come to the end of this book, you hopefully have a better understanding of disability laws and of disability culture, not only in schools, but also in society as a whole. Tremendous progress has been made in some areas of life for individuals with disabilities, but there are many fights that remain. In a quarter century, individuals with disabilities have made immense gains in the field of education and in-roads into many other areas of basic civil rights. The key, however, is to be found in education. Today's young adults with disabilities are the first generation of disabled people to benefit from increased educational opportunities provided by the laws described in this book.

Equal access to, and subsequent success in, education is the gateway to changing many other areas of life for individuals with disabilities. Nothing will change society's attitudes about disabilities more than educational access leading to educational success leading to career success. People with disabilities can hardly be pitied if they are established in fields requiring training, skill, and intelligence. An M.D. in a wheelchair will change many attitudes, as will a deaf lawyer. A general education teacher with a disability can change the attitudes of innumerable children, parents, colleagues, and community members. World-renowned physicist Dr. Stephen Hawking, who has a severe degenerative motor neuron disease, has explained the situation brilliantly: "The way for disabled people to be appreciated is to be successful. For the physically disabled, this means being smarter than the next guy. No one is going to be impressed if you are a Paralympic champion. You have to be outstanding in absolute terms" (Hain, 1997, p. 14). Equal educational access and opportunity lead to the ability to excel in these absolute terms, to be a better teacher, better doctor, better lawyer than someone who doesn't have a disability.

The research and the writing of this book were highly complex. Fortunately, the benevolence of many professors along the way helped in the writing of this book before anyone knew this book would ever be written. My research on the topic began simply as graduate work and kept growing from there. I must thank those professors who allowed me to research disability law and education over the course of a number of degrees as I worked to come to an understanding of these issues. I am particularly grateful to, in alphabetical order: Professor Terry Coonan (Director, Florida State University's Human Rights Center), Dr. Elinor A. Scheirer (University of North Florida), Professor Lois J. Shepherd (Florida State University College of Law), Dr. G. Pritchy Smith (University of North Florida), Dr. Michael P. Smith (University of North Florida), and Professor Harold P. Southerland (Florida State University College of Law). This does not mean that any of the above individuals necessarily agree with the content of this book, or would admit they ever met me, but each has given me the chance to research or to teach about matters central to this text. For that I am ineluctably grateful.

The necessity of a text like this became apparent to me some years ago, when, as an idealistic young graduate student, I first attempted to teach the requirements of IDEA to undergraduate general education majors. It was an eye-opening experience. There are so many things teachers should know about disabled students but that too often just don't get taught. So often people seem very disinclined to address disability issues, due in no small part to the fact that it is an uncomfortable topic for many people. It shouldn't be. Sadly, the avoidance of discussion of disability issues leads to a complete lack of understanding. If you do have trouble discussing disability issues or dealing with disabled individuals, I sincerely hope this book will assist you in interacting with the disabled. If you are a teacher with a disability, I hope this book will help you understand your legal rights and allow you to use them. For all readers, I hope this book provides insight into and understanding of the rights of the disabled in schools and gives you the knowledge you need to ensure that those rights are available to all disabled members of your school community. And, hopefully, it will even inspire you to want to continue the progress that has been made.

Individuals with disabilities are only starting to feel the societal effects of no longer being bound by unchecked social oppression in the most important areas. Education is the key to positive change, the key to providing hope, and the key to opening the future wide for people with disabilities. In spite of all the negatives, it is a time of hope.

Paul T. Jaeger
January 2002

Postscript 2

Creating Caring Communities through Education

Teachers have the ability to make the most significant improvements in the world today, and preparing future teachers to educate for global understanding is professionally and personally essential. We know, firsthand, how necessary awareness, understanding, and knowledge of disability issues are for every educator. Both of us have experienced attending public schools, university teacher education programs, and doctoral degree programs with a disability. We have both taught with a unique awareness of students with disabilities in our classes. One of us chose to pursue a career in teacher preparation and the other a career in law and research, each hoping to impact educational policy as advocates of students and teachers with disabilities.

It was in school where I found refuge, a place where I could be successful, a place where I was known for something other than my disability. It was tough, though, because I felt like a normal kid and wanted to be a normal kid. I loved the teachers who punished me for talking or passing notes and worked much harder for those who didn't appear to notice my disability. In school I could be smart, not handicapped. I became a voracious reader, hungry to live vicariously for a few hours without pain, without feeling awkward or different. I devoured biographies of famous women, convinced I could make a difference some day. I was going to accomplish this goal as a teacher.

What my students and I share is complicated, changing, and challenging. It is the soul of education, a concept which crosses the boundaries of time and space; it is community. Education must embrace a spirit of community based on acceptance, affirmation, encouragement, support, and renewal where children feel comfortable to explore the treasure within themselves and where teachers can find a renewed wholeness in the teacher/student partnership. For these reasons, I have begun each new school year/semester by explaining my disability to my students so they have a better understanding of me as both their teacher and as a person. Authenticity is a responsibility to self, an awareness of the person one ought to be which creates an enduring bond supporting the potential and growth of the other. Community nurtures the authenticity of the other. The companion to authenticity is vulnerability. It hurts to be vulnerable; yet as teachers, we cannot remove boundaries without becoming vulnerable. Through this pain develops a sense of common humanity which can inspire love, courage, humility, and hope. This partnership allows for a shared learning experience, provides opportunities for personal relevance, lets go of control, and enhances caring. A structure for community must be built on dialogue and reflection. True learning is a function of experience which takes place in the connections of human beings with one another in community. True community happens only when caring happens. Psychologists, sociologists, and anthropologists have measured care and love, finding ratios strong in relation to physical and mental health.

Using this text will help develop communities in classrooms, communities where respect, understanding, and acceptance can grow. Everyone needs community, and teachers have the opportunity to inspire all students to achieve academically, socially, and morally. Many thanks to the Conference on English Education of the National Conference of Teachers of English who established a Commission on the Preparation of Teachers with Disabilities to make educators aware of disability issues. Participation on this commission motivated me to help all educators understand disability.

Cynthia Ann Bowman
January 2002

How to Understand and Use Legal Sources

The history of the efforts to use litigation to achieve equal educational opportunity teaches that when a social problem is addressed through litigation, lawyers and judges redefine the terms of debate about the problem, and non-lawyers lose control over the resulting public discourse. Those outside the legal system lose the power to frame the questions asked about the problem and to provide the analytical framework for understanding and remedying it. In that way, litigation can deflect attention away from the root causes and problems that prompted the litigation and motivated the resort to the law in the first place. (Halpern, 1995, p. 317)

So what on earth does the above quote have to do with finding and using legal resources? Everything, valiant reader, everything. Like it or not, law defines our society and frames every public debate. Being able to find, understand, and employ the law is empowerment to affect real change. When someone who is not a lawyer or politician knows what to do with the law, then that person has the opportunity to have a genuine voice in the dialogue on vitally important issues. Education is one of those vitally important issues. Knowing how to find education law, and what to do with the law when you do find it, allows you to help shape the public debate and the implementation of the law that arises from the debate.

If you have read this book straight through to this appendix, and praise to those who have, you already have become aware of the range of sources in which law can be found. The variety of legal sources cited in this text probably came as somewhat of a surprise to many of you. Oftentimes the law can sound like it comes from one place, completely unified and uniform. The true nature of the situation is a lot more oblique.

THE FEDERAL SYSTEM AND THE SEPARATE STATES

Failure to understand the nature and function of the national and state governments is rampant in our country, even among politicians, who really ought to know better. As such, we will start by discussing the basics of the U.S. government and the state governments.

Begin by noting the actual name of this nation: the United States of America. The name indicates a group of separate states that are functioning in a collective. The way this nation is designed, the federal government (the one operating out of Washington, D.C.) has power on the national level. In the process of creating and implementing law, the legislative branch creates the law, the executive branch enforces the law, and the judiciary interprets the law. Each state also has its own government. In each individual state, the government of that state has to follow and implement the federal laws, but the state government also has the power to add further laws that address issues not covered by federal law, as well as laws that enhance federal laws. When the federal government sets a legal standard, it is usually a standardizing requirement, allowing the states to enhance the standard if so desired. The roles of the three branches of government play similar roles in states as in the federal government.

Laws come from several sources. First, the Constitution provides the backbone for all federal power, as well as establishing the separation of powers between the three branches of government and enumerating the different roles of the federal and the state governments. The constitutional government was actually the second national government of the United States, the first being the preposterously unsuccessful and oft forgotten Articles of Confederation government. The Articles of Confederation created a system where the national government had little power and the states had nearly unlimited power, creating competition between the states that the national government was powerless to stop. Fortunately, the authors of the Constitution learned a bevy of important lessons from the first government, most significantly that power must be balanced between the national government and the state governments.

The second place law comes from is statutes. When the legislature creates law, it ultimately takes effect in the form of statutes. The Congress determines a legal need must be met and creates legislation to remedy the situation. The laws passed by the legislature are codified as statutes. The laws in statutes lead to another source of law: regulations. When the legislature passes a statute, the lawmakers often cannot foresee every possible application of the law. Statutes are usually quite broad and general. Regulations are specific, fleshing out the statutes. Administrative agencies create regulation to ensure that statutes are implemented properly. Federal statutes and regulations are the law in the entire country. Each individual state also has statutes and regulations that comprise the laws of that state. The state laws cannot contradict federal law, but can address areas not covered by federal law or enhance the federal laws. The laws of a particular state are only in effect in that state. The state laws of Arkansas generally do not affect the residents of New Jersey.

Finally, and perhaps most prodigiously, law comes from the decisions of the courts, often called case law. The judiciary interprets the Constitution, statutes, and regulations. These interpretations of the law create new meanings and applications of the laws, making the judiciary a further source of law. When it comes to interpreting the Constitution, courts have pretty much the final say on legal matters. However, when a court interprets a statute, the legislature can later alter the statute as a result of the court's opinion. The federal system has courts in levels. The three levels, from lowest to highest, are the U.S. District Court, the U.S. Court of Appeals, and the U.S. Supreme Court. A holding at a higher level supercedes a holding at a lower level. After one court has made a decision, that ruling may be appealed to the next highest level. State courts have different names, but all follow a similar structure of lower, middle, and highest courts. Most states have district, appeals, and supreme courts in that order. However, not all follow that pattern. Some states call the middle level courts Superior Courts and other states call the lower level courts Circuit Courts. New York, apparently just to be completely contrary, calls its lowest level courts the Supreme Courts. The highest court in New York is the Court of Appeals.

In the federal system, the district courts are fairly localized, with a number of U.S. District Courts in most states. An appeal from a U.S. District Court goes to the appropriate U.S. Court of Appeals. There are 13 Courts of Appeals, known as federal judicial circuits. The first 11 of the circuits each include a number of states and territories, while the District of Columbia has its own Twelfth Circuit, and the lucky Thirteenth Circuit is for specialized matters from across the country, such as the Bankruptcy Court. The 11 state circuits are as follows:

- First Circuit: Maine, Massachusetts, New Hampshire, Puerto Rico, and Rhode Island;
- Second Circuit: Connecticut, New York, and Vermont;
- Third Circuit: Delaware, New Jersey, Pennsylvania, and the Virgin Islands;
- Fourth Circuit: Maryland, North Carolina, South Carolina, Virginia, and West Virginia;
- Fifth Circuit: Louisiana, Mississippi, and Texas;
- Sixth Circuit: Kentucky, Michigan, Ohio, and Tennessee;

- Seventh Circuit: Illinois, Indiana, and Wisconsin;
- Eighth Circuit: Arkansas, Iowa, Missouri, Minnesota, Nebraska, North Dakota, and South Dakota;
- Ninth Circuit: Alaska, Arizona, California, Guam, Hawaii, Idaho, Montana, Nevada, the Northern Mariana Islands, Oregon, and Washington;
- Tenth Circuit: Colorado, Kansas, New Mexico, Oklahoma, Utah, and Wyoming;
- Eleventh Circuit: Alabama, Georgia, and Florida.

The Fifth Circuit was split in the early 1980s, resulting in the creation of the Eleventh Circuit. The "Old Fifth Circuit" included all the states currently in the circuit, as well as all the states that are now in the Eleventh Circuit. Cases from the Fifth Circuit before the split are considered the law in both circuits. However, a case decided in either circuit since the split has no force of law in the other circuit. One of the important things to remember is that each court at each level has separate jurisdiction. And that's the really hard part.

JURISDICTION AND THE COURTS: THE CONFUSING STUFF

Jurisdiction is literally the area in which a court has power to hear a case and make a decision about that case. Some jurisdictions are based on geography (such as a federal circuit court), some on the type of the case involved (such as a criminal case), and others based on the amount of money that is at issue (such as a dispute involving a sum over $50,000). The jurisdiction of a court is the area where the decisions of that court have power of law. A state district court has jurisdiction over part of a state, so it can hear matters from that area and its decisions as force of law are limited to that same area. On the other hand, the United States Supreme Court has jurisdiction over the entire country, so it can hear cases from any part of the country and its decisions have force of law throughout the entire nation. Sounds easy enough, right? Unfortunately, since there are so many levels of courts in both the states and the federal system, jurisdiction is a Byzantine concept that can even be baffling for experienced lawyers. Entire classes in law school are devoted to jurisdiction. And we're going to cover it in a couple pages. So fasten your seatbelts and keep your hands and feet inside the car.

One of the problems with jurisdiction is that there are so many kinds of jurisdiction, including ancillary, concurrent, subject matter, coordinate, limited, and summary. That's just a small part of the list. To keep this discussion as clear and useful as possible, we are to focus on understanding what courts have jurisdiction over educational matters and how appeals on educational matters can wind through the various jurisdictions.

A large of number of different courts, from low-level state courts to the United States Supreme Court, can play a role in issues about education. Education is matter of concern in every part of the country, affecting virtually all people in society at some level. Because of its omnipresence and immense importance, education is continually an issue in the public dialogue at the local, state, and national levels. Many different facets and concepts in education are perpetually being debated. Since so many people who are not educators feel they have a stake in education, it is an area of public importance that attracts considerably more debate and legal maneuvering than virtually any other public issue. As an experiment, try to get a group of people to engage in a serious debate about the proper role of the United States in shaping the lending policies of the World Bank. You likely won't find many people with any sort of opinion, unless you happen to spend your free time with bankers, economists, and overzealous political junkies. However, simply mention an educational issue, such as achievement testing, in any context and everyone in earshot has opinions that they not only will readily share but they will be more than happy to yell, harangue, and otherwise vehemently express these opinions. Everyone has opinion on issues involving education. The nature of education directly affecting so many people in so many different ways leads both to constant debate and to truckloads of lawsuits.

Suits involving education can start at either the lowest level of state courts or the lowest level of federal courts, depending on the circumstances. If the issue involves state education law, it will most likely start in state court, while controversies involving national education laws often would begin in federal courts. However, in some cases, federal laws specify what courts have jurisdiction over the laws. The discussions of the various laws in this book note the laws that have the proper jurisdiction specified within the law. Federal laws protecting disabled students can actually lead to suits in both state and federal courts. If a state refused to provide special education to any students with disabilities, the inevitable lawsuit would likely be filed in federal court. If the parents of a particular student were disputing the IEP of that student with the school district, the resulting legal action would probably occur in state courts.

When a court makes a ruling, that decision is only valid in the jurisdiction of that particular court. A state district court holding is only the law in the jurisdiction of that court. A holding by the Tenth Circuit Court is good law in that entire circuit, but does not directly affect the law in any other circuit. However, the decision of one court often will have a great deal of influence on other courts. If a court has held on a particular issue, that opinion may be quite persuasive to other courts that later consider the same issue. However, it is entirely possible, and in fact often happens, that the circuit courts are in disagreement with each other on a particular issue. When the circuit courts disagree on a legal issue, the Supreme Court will often ultimately resolve the dispute. The jurisdiction of the United States Supreme Court is, of course, the United States. When looking at case law, it is important to pay particular attention to what court the law comes from.

FINDING CASES AND LAWS

Now that you know where laws come from and what laws are relevant to you, it is time to find out where to find the texts of the laws. Statutes, regulations, and cases, for both the federal government and the state governments, are all reported in several ways and are available at many academic libraries. Depending on the resources of the library in which you are doing your research, several electronic search engines for the law may be available. Lexis-Nexis, Westlaw, and Academic Universe all offer easy to use and thorough legal search engines. These search engines allow the user to search legal national and state materials by topic, by case name, by case citation, by statute number, and a number of other options. Each service costs money, however, and not all libraries will necessarily have these electronic options. Fortunately, looking up the materials in print volumes is also a fairly simple process. To facilitate the process of finding print materials in doing legal research, we will examine a statute citation and a case citation.

A statute citation is 42 U.S.C.A. sec. 12101–12213. That is the citation for the Americans with Disabilities Act. U.S.C.A. stands for United States Code Annotated, where all the statutory laws of the United States are collected. Forty-two is volume number of the United States Code Annotated where the law is catalogued. The section numbers indicate the part of the volume where the law is. If you wished to read the ADA, you would pull the 42 volume of the United States Code Annotated off the shelf and read sections 12101 to 12213. The same laws are available in the U.S.C., the United States Code. The annotated edition has the laws as well as commentaries and references to relevant cases, references, books, scholarly writings, and other materials. Throughout this text, references are to the annotated code as the additional information and references are of significant utility to both the novice and the experienced legal researcher.

A citation for a case is *Brown v. Board of Education*, 347 U.S. 483 (1954). The names are of the parties involved in the action. The U.S. indicates the particular case reporter series where the case may be found. The U.S. series is for all United States Supreme Court cases. Cases from federal district and circuit courts are found in reporters like F., F.2d, F.3d, F. Supp., and F. Supp.2d. Each series is a different federal reporter. The highest number of a volume and of a series contains the most recent cases. Cases from state courts are available in reporters for the individual states, as well as in reporters for the relevant regions of the country, such as the Atlantic

Reporter and the Southern Reporter. The first number in the citation (i.e., 347) is the volume number of the case reporter. The second number in the citation (i.e., 483) is the page number in the volume where the case starts. Sometimes the page number in a case citation is followed immediately by a comma and another number, which is a page number within the case of particular interest. The final number (i.e., 1954) is year the case was decided. So to find *Brown v. Board of Education*, you would start reading at page 483 in volume 347 of the United State Supreme Court Reporter. Another reporter series of United States Supreme Court cases is S.Ct.; both series contain the same cases.

The regional case reporters and the states they include are as follows:

- Atlantic Reporter: Connecticut, Delaware, the District of Columbia, Maine, Maryland, New Hampshire, New Jersey, Pennsylvania, Rhode Island, and Vermont;
- Northeastern Reporter: Illinois, Indiana, Massachusetts, New York, and Ohio;
- Northwestern Reporter: Iowa, Michigan, Minnesota, Nebraska, North Dakota, South Dakota, and Wisconsin;
- Pacific Reporter: Alaska, Arizona, California, Colorado, Hawaii, Idaho, Kansas, Montana, Nevada, New Mexico, Oklahoma, Oregon, Utah, Washington, and Wyoming;
- Southeastern Reporter: Georgia, North Carolina, South Carolina, Virginia, and West Virginia;
- Southern Reporter: Alabama, Florida, Louisiana, and Mississippi;
- Southwestern Reporter: Arkansas, Kentucky, Missouri, Tennessee, and Texas.

The names of the regional reporters and the states in each reporter reflect the fact that this nation has been in a process of growth. At this point, it is pretty hard to think of Michigan as a part of the Northwestern United States, but when the reporter began, Michigan was considered to be in that region. The names and divisions of states within the reporters is an amusing reminder of the history of this nation.

WHY YOU SHOULD DO LEGAL RESEARCH

Hopefully this text has inspired you to become more interested in education law, both for how it affects the teacher and for how it affects the students. The more you know about the laws in a classroom, the better you can apply them and the better voice for change you can be if you see a need for the laws to be improved. The first step in being able to know and use the law, as well as to become a voice for change, is being able to find the laws. Now that you know how to find laws, you can learn all about the laws of your state and your country to try to improve the classroom and the world for your students.

Appendix B

A Guide to Relevant Legal
Acronyms and Abbreviations

ADA: The Americans with Disabilities Act, a federal law.

Ann.: Annotated.

CFR: The Code of Federal Regulations, the publication that documents the guidelines and regulations related to federal statutes.

DOE: The Department of Education, a federal agency.

DOJ: The Department of Justice, a federal agency.

EAHCA: The Education for All Handicapped Children Act, the earliest version of the federal law now known as IDEA.

EEOC: Equal Employment Opportunity Commission, a federal agency.

EHA: The Education for the Handicapped Act, a federal law supplanted by IDEA.

ESEA: The Elementary and Secondary Education Act, a federal law.

Et al.: "And others," an abbreviation of the Latin phrase *et alia*. Primarily used when a document has a large number of authors.

Et seq.: "And the following," an abbreviation of the Latin phrase *et sequentia*. Primarily used in references to statutes to indicate that the section cited and all the following sections of statute are being referenced.

Ex parte: "On behalf of," used to indicate a party taking a legal action for someone else. Often used when a party is a minor.

Ex rel: "Upon relation," an abbreviation of the Latin phrase *ex relatione*. Used when an action is brought by the state based on information from a private individual.

F.: Federal, a federal case law reporter.

F.2d: Federal Second, a federal case law reporter.

F.3d: Federal Third, a federal case law reporter.

FAPE: A Free Appropriate Public Education, as mandated by IDEA.

Fed. Reg.: The Federal Register, a publication that documents official federal government announcements, postings, and records.

FERPA: The Family Educational Rights and Privacy Act, a federal law.

F. Supp.: Federal Supplement, a federal case law reporter.

F. Supp.2d: Federal Supplement Second, a federal case law reporter.

Id.: The citation is the same as the previous citation.

IDEA: The Individuals with Disabilities Education Act, a federal law.

IDELR: Individuals with Disabilities Education Law Report, a case reporter.

IEP: An Individualized Education Program, as mandated by IDEA.

In re: "In the matter of," usually used for a judicial disposition of a matter that is not adversarial.

LEA: A Local Education Agency, such as a school district.

L. Ed.: Lawyer's Edition, a Supreme Court case law reporter.

LRE: A Least Restrictive Environment, as mandated by IDEA.

Nat'l. Disab. L. Rep.: National Disability Law Reporter, a case law reporter.

OCR: The Office of Civil Rights, a federal government agency.

Rehab. Act: The Rehabilitation Act, a federal law.

SEA: A State Education Agency, such as a state department of education.

S.Ct.: Supreme Court, a Supreme Court case law reporter.

Sec.: Section.

See, e.g.: "See, for example."

Sess.: Session.

U.S.: United States, a Supreme Court case law reporter.

References

Allis, S. (1996, November 4). The struggle to pay for special ed. *Time*, 82–83.

Arnold, J. B. & Dodge, H. W. (1994, October). Room for all. *The American School Board Journal, 181(10)*, 22–26.

Ballard, J., Ramirez, B. A., & Weintraub, F. J. (Eds.). (1982). *Special education in America: Its legal and governmental foundations*. Reston, VA: Council for Exceptional Children.

Bartlett, L. (1993). Economic cost factors in providing a Free Appropriate Public Education for handicapped children: The legal perspective. *Journal of Law & Education, 22*, 27–60.

Bates, M. W. (1994, Spring). Free Appropriate Public Education under the Individuals with Disabilities Education Act: Requirements, issues and suggestions. *Brigham Young University Education & Law Journal*, 215–222.

Beyer, J. A. (1999). A modest proposal: Mediating IDEA disputes without splitting the baby. *Journal of Law & Education, 28*, 37–60.

Bowe, F. (1979). Handicapping America: Barriers to disabled people. In J. P. Hourihan (Ed.), *Disability: Our challenge* (pp. 87–104). New York: Teachers College Press.

Bruser, S. (1998). Parents: The best source to help children succeed in school. *Enable, 2(4)*, 82–83.

Bunch, E. A. (1998). School discipline under the Individuals with Disabilities Education Act: How the stay-put provision limits schools in providing a safe learning environment. *Journal of Law & Education, 27*, 315–321.

Burgdorf, M. & Burgdorf, R. (1975). History of unequal treatment: The qualifications of handicapped persons as a "suspect class" under the equal protection clause. *Santa Clara Law Review, 15*, 855–910.

Burkhauser, R. V. & Daly, M. C. (1996). The potential impact on the employment of people with disabilities. In J. West (Ed.), *Implementing the Americans with Disabilities Act* (pp. 153–192). Cambridge, MA: Blackwell Publishing.

Colker, R. & Tucker, B. P. (1998). *The law of disability discrimination* (2nd ed.). Cincinnati, OH: Anderson.

Comenius, J. A. (1910). *The great didactic* (2nd ed.). London: A. & C. Black.

Crawford, C. H. (1999, April). What to do when they play the disability card. *The Braille Forum*, 5–9.

Curoe, P.R.V. (1926). Educational attitudes and policies of organized labor in the United States. *Contributions to Education, 201*, 33.

Dagley, D. L., McGuire, M. D., & Evans, C. W. (1994). The relationship test in the discipline of disabled students. *Education Law Reporter, 88*, 13–31.

Davies, N. (1998). *Europe: A history*. New York: HarperPerennial.

Dupre, A. P. (1997). Disability and the public schools: The case against "inclusion." *Washington Law Review, 72*, 775–858.

Fay, G. O. (1899). Hartford and the education of the deaf. *American Annals of the Deaf, 44*, 419–435.

Feldblum, C. R. (1991). Employment protections. In J. West (Ed.), *The Americans with Disabilities Act: From policy to practice* (pp. 81–102). New York: Milbank Memorial Fund.

Feldblum, C. R. (1996). The employment sector: Medical inquiries, reasonable accommodation, and health insurance. In J. West (Ed.), *Implementing the Americans with Disabilities Act* (pp. 81–152). Cambridge, MA: Blackwell Publishing.

Fleischer, D. Z. & Zames, F. (2001). *The disability rights movement: From charity to confrontation*. Philadelphia: Temple University Press.

Fuchs, D. & Fuchs, L. (1994). Inclusive schools movement and the radicalization of special education reform. *Exceptional Children, 60(4)*, 294–309.

Gallimore, R. & Goldenberg, C. (1996, Fall). Accommodating cultural differences and commonalties in educational practice. *Multicultural Education*, 16–19.

Gatto, J. T. (2000, November). Hector isn't the problem. *The Sun*, 5–10.

Gill, C. J. (1995). A psychological view of disability culture. *Disabilities Studies Quarterly, 15(4)*, 16–19.

Greenwood, C. D. (1992, Spring). Congress' new IDEA in special education: Permitting a private right of action against state agencies. *Brigham Young University Education & Law Journal*, 49–73.

Gubernick, L. & Conlin, M. (1997, February 10). The special education scandal. *Forbes Magazine*, 66–70.

Hahn, H. (1997). New trends in disability studies: Implications for educational policy. In D. K. Lipsky & A. Gartner (Eds.), *Inclusion and school reform: Transforming America's classrooms* (pp. 315–328). Baltimore: Paul H. Brooks.

Hain, H. B. (1997, October). Light years ahead: One-on-one with Stephen Hawking. *WE*, 14.

Hallenbeck, B. A. & Kauffman, J. M. (1994). Integrated special education: United States. In K. Mazurek & M. A. Winzer (Eds.), *Comparative studies in special education* (pp. 403–419). Washington, DC: Gallaudet University Press.

Halpern, S. C. (1995). *On the limits of the law: The ironic legacy of Title VI of the 1964 Civil Rights Act*. Baltimore: Johns Hopkins University Press.

Handel, R. C. (1975). The role of the advocate in securing the handicapped child's right to an effective minimal education. *Ohio State Law Journal, 36*, 349–378.

Hansen, A. (1916). The education of the deaf in the Scandinavian countries. *Volta Review, 18*, 407.

Harry, B., Allen, N., & McLaughlin, M. (1995). Communication versus compliance: African-American parents' involvement in special education. *Exceptional Children, 61(4)*, 364–377.

Heumann, J. E. (1979). Handicap and disability. In J. P. Hourihan (Ed.), *Disability: Our challenge* (pp. 7–31). New York: Teachers College Press.

Hill, K. D. (1986). Legal conflicts in special education: How competing paradigms in the Education for All Handicapped Children Act create litigation. *University of Detroit Law Review, 64*, 129–170.

Hobbs, T. & Westling, D. L. (1998). Inclusion, inclusion, inclusion: Promoting successful inclusion through collaborative problem solving. *Teaching Exceptional Children, 31(1)*, 12–19.

Howard, P. K. (1994). *The death of common sense: How law is suffocating America*. New York: Warner Books.

Huefner, D. S. (1993, Spring). Revisiting Congress' new IDEA in special education. *Brigham Young University Education & Law Journal*, 169–182.

Huefner, D. S. (1998). The Individuals with Disabilities Education Act amendments of 1997. *Education Law Reporter, 122*, 1103–1122.

Jensen, G. (1996). Disciplining students with disabilities: Problems under the Individuals with Disabilities Education Act. *Brigham Young University Journal of Law & Education*, 34–54.

Kirp, D., Buss, W., & Kuriloff, P. (1974). Legal reform of special education: Empirical studies and procedural proposals. *California Law Review, 62*, 40–156.

Kitchin, R. (1998). "Out of place," "knowing one's place": Space, power, and the exclusion of disabled people. *Disability & Society, 13*, 343–356.

Kriegel, L. (1982). Claiming the self: The cripple as American male. In M. G. Eisenberg, C. Griggins, & R. Duval (Eds.), *Disabled people as second-class citizens* (pp. 52–63). New York: Springer Publishing.

Ladurie, E. L. (1979). *The territory of the historian* (B. Reynolds & S. Reynolds, Trans.). Hassocks, Sussex: Harvester Press. (Original work published 1973.)

Landes, D. S. (1998). *The wealth and poverty of nations: Why some are so rich and some so poor*. New York: Norton.

Lankford, H. & Wycoff, J. (1999). The allocation of resources in special education and regular instruction in New York State. In T. B. Parrish, J. G. Chambers, & C. M. Guarino (Eds.), *Funding special education* (pp. 147–175). Thousand Oaks, CA: Corwin Press.

Leonard, J. (1996). Judicial deference to academic standards under Section 504 of the Rehabilitation Act and Titles II and III of the Americans with Disabilities Act. *Nebraska Law Review, 75*, 27–90.

Macht, J. (1998). *Special education's failed system: A question of eligibility*. Westport, CT: Bergin & Garvey.

McCarthy, M. M. (1993). Can costs be considered in special education placements? *Journal of Law & Education, 22*, 265–282.

McClung, M. (1974). Do handicapped children have a legal right to a minimally adequate education? *Journal of Law & Education, 3*, 153–173.

McLesky, J., Henry, D., & Hodges, D. (1998). Inclusion: Where is it happening? *Teaching Exceptional Children, 31(1)*, 4–10.

McLesky, J., Henry, D., & Hodges, D. (1999). Inclusion: What progress is being made across disability categories? *Teaching Exceptional Children, 31(3)*, 60–64.

Meyen, E. L. (1995). Legislative and programmatic foundations of special education. In E. L. Meyen & T. M. Skrtic (Eds.), *Special education and student disability, an introduction: Traditional, emerging, and alternative programs* (pp. 33–95). Denver, CO: Love Publishing Company.

National Council on Disability. (1995). *Improving the implementation of the Individuals with Disabilities Education Act: Making schools work for all of America's children.* Washington, DC: Author.

NCES Fact Sheet. (2000).

Neal, D. & Kirp, D. (1986). The allure of legalization reconsidered: The case of special education. In D. Kirp & D. Jensen (Eds.), *School days, rule days: The legalization and regulation of education* (pp. 343–367). London: Falmer Press.

Nelson, T. D. (1997). Congressional attention needed for the stay-put provision of the Individuals with Disabilities Education Act. *Brigham Young University Education & Law Journal*, 49–68.

Parrish, T. B., & Wolman, J. (1999). Trends and new developments in special education funding: What the states report. In T. B. Parrish, J. G. Chambers, & C. M. Guarino (Eds.), *Funding special education* (pp. 203–229). Thousand Oaks, CA: Corwin Press.

Perlin, M. L. (1992). On "sanism." *Southern Methodist University Law Review, 46(2)*, 373–407.

Rachelson, A. D. (1997). Expelling students who claim to be disabled: Escaping the Individuals with Disabilities Education Act's "stay-put" provision. *Michigan Law & Policy Review, 2*, 127–158.

Ramsingh, O. M. (1995). Disciplining children with disabilities under the Individuals with Disabilities Education Act. *Journal of Contemporary Health Law & Policy, 12*, 155–181.

Rebell, M. (1986). Structural discrimination and the rights of the disabled. *Georgetown Law Journal, 74*, 1435–1489.

Rippa, S. A. (1992). *Education in a free society: An American history* (7th ed.). New York: Longman.

Roberts, R. & Mather, N. (1995). The return of students with learning disabilities to regular classrooms: A sellout? *Learning Disabilities Research and Practice, 10(1)*, 46–58.

Rothstein, L. F. (1994). College students with disabilities: Litigation trends. *Review of Litigation, 13*, 425–445.

Salder, J. E. (1966). *J. A. Comenius and the concept of universal education.* New York: Barnes & Noble.

Schoenfeld, B. N. (1980). Civil rights for the handicapped under the Constitution and Section 504 of the Rehabilitation Act. *University of Cincinnati Law Review, 49*, 580–610.

Scotch, R. K. (2001). *From goodwill to civil rights: Transforming federal disability policy* (2nd ed.). Philadelphia: Temple University Press.

Scruggs, T. E. & Mastropieri, M. A. (1995). What makes special education special? Evaluating inclusion programs with the pass variable. *Journal of Special Education, 29(2)*, 224–233.

Scruggs, T. E. & Mastropieri, M. A. (1996). Teacher perceptions of mainstreaming/inclusion, 1958–1995: A research synthesis. *Exceptional Children, 63(1)*, 59–74.

Shapiro, J. P. (1993). *No pity: People with disabilities forging a new civil rights movement.* New York: Times Books.

Shapiro, J. P. (1997, April 14). The strange case of somnolent Samantha. *U.S. News and World Report*, 31.

Shapiro, J. P., Loeb, P., & Bowermaster, D. (1993, December 13). Separate and unequal. *U.S. News and World Report*, 46–60.

Shemberg, A. (1997). Mediation as an alternative method of dispute resolution for the Individuals with Disabilities Education Act: A just proposal? *Ohio State Journal on Dispute Resolution, 12*, 739–757.

Siegel, L. M. (1994). *Least Restrictive Environment: The paradox of inclusion.* Boston: Allyn & Bacon.

Smith, D. D. (2001). *Introduction to special education: Teaching in an age of opportunity.* Boston: Allyn & Bacon.

Smith, G. P. (1999). Knowledge bases for diversity in teacher education. *Multicultural Perspectives, 1*, 49–51.

Special Ed. (1996, June 6). *60 Minutes.*

Spring, J. (1993). *Conflict of interests: The politics of American education* (2nd ed.). New York: Longman.

Stick, R. S. (1976). The handicapped child has a right to an appropriate education. *Nebraska Law Review, 55*, 637–682.

Szasz, T. (1971). *The manufacture of madness: A comparative study of the Inquisition and the mental health movement.* New York: Harper & Row.

Tweedie, J. (1983). The politics of legalization in special education reform. In J. G. Chambers & W. T. Hartman (Eds.), *Special education policies: Their history, implementation, and finance* (pp. 48–73). Philadelphia: Temple University Press.

United States Commission on Civil Rights. (1997). *Equal educational opportunity and nondiscrimination for students with disabilities: Federal enforcement of Section 504.* Washington, DC: Author.

United States Department of Education. (1995). *Digest of Education Statistics.* Washington, DC: Author.

United States Department of Education. (1997). *The Individuals with Disabilities Education Act amendments curriculum.* Washington, DC: Author.

Vanderwood, M., McGrew, K. S., & Ysseldyke, J. E. (1998). Why we can't say much about students with disabilities during education reform. *Exceptional Children, 64*, 359–370.

Wang, M. C., Reynolds, M. C., & Walberg, H. J. (1986, September). Rethinking special education. *Educational Leadership, 44(1)*, 26–31.

Weintraub, F. J. & Ballard, J. (1982). Introduction: Bridging the decades. In J. Ballard, B. A. Ramirez, & F. J. Weintraub (Eds.), *Special education in Amer-*

ica: Its legal and governmental foundations (pp. 1–10). Reston, VA: Council for Exceptional Children.

Wenkart, R. D. (1993). The Americans with Disabilities Act and its impact on public education. *Education Law Reporter, 82,* 291–302.

Winzer, M. A. (1993). *The history of special education: From isolation to integration.* Washington, DC: Gallaudet University Press.

Yell, M. L. (1998). *The law and special education.* Upper Saddle River, NJ: Merrill.

Young, I. P. & Allison, B. (1982). Effects of candidate age and teaching experience on school superintendents and principals in selecting teachers. *Planning & Change, 13(4),* 245–256.

Young, I. P. & Prince, A. L. (1999). Legal implications for teacher selection as defined by the ADA and the ADEA. *Journal of Law & Education, 28,* 517–530.

Zettel, J. J. & Ballard, J. (1982). The Education for All Handicapped Children Act of 1975 (P. L. 94–142): Its history, origins, and concepts. In J. Ballard, B. A. Ramirez, & F. J. Weintraub (Eds.), *Special education in America: Its legal and governmental foundations.* Reston, VA: Council for Exceptional Children.

Zirkel, P. A. (1996). The substantive standard for FAPE: Does Section 504 require less than IDEA? *Education Law Reporter, 106,* 471–477.

Table of Legal Authorities

Air Carrier Access Act, 49 U.S.C.A. sec. 41705.
Alamo Heights Independent School District v. State Board of Education, 790
F.2d 1153 (5th Cir. 1986).
Albertsons, Inc. v. Kirkingburg, 527 U.S. 555 (1999).
Alexander v. Choate, 469 U.S. 287 (1985).
Americans with Disabilities Act (ADA), 42 U.S.C.A. sec. 12101 *et seq.*
Americans with Disabilities Act (ADA) regulations, 28 C.F.R. sec. 35 *et seq.* &
29 C.F.R. 1630 *et seq.*
A. W. v. Northwest R-1 School District, 813 F.2d 158 (8th Cir.) *cert. denied* 484
U.S. 847 (1987).
Babb v. Knox County School System, 965 F.2d 104 (6th Cir. 1992).
Barnett v. Fairfax County School Board, 927 F.2d 146 (4th Cir. 1991).
Barnett v. U.S. Air, Incorporated, 196 F.3d 979 (9th Cir. 1998).
Bartlett v. New York State Board of Law Examiners, 970 F. Supp. 1094 (S.D.
N.Y. 1997).
Battle v. Pennsylvania, 629 F.2d 269 (3rd Cir. 1980).
Beattie v. Board of Education of City of Antigo, 172 N.W. 153 (Wis. 1919).
Board of Education v. Holland, 786 F. Supp. 874 (E.D. Cal. 1992).
Board of Education v. State ex rel. Goldman, 191 N.E. 914 (Ohio Ct.App.
1934).
Board of Education of the County of Cabell v. Dienelt, 843 F.2d 813 (4th Cir.
1988).
Board of Education of the Hendrick Hudson Central School District v. Rowley,
458 U.S. 176 (1982).
Board of Trustees of the University of Alabama v. Garrett, 531 U.S. 356 (2001).
Bonnie Ann F. v. Calallen Independent School District, 835 F. Supp. 340 (S.D.
Tex. 1993).

Borough of Palmyra Board of Education v. Hurley, 2 F. Supp.2d 637 (D. N.J. 1998)

Breece v. Alliance Tractor-Trailer Training II, Inc., 824 F. Supp. 576 (E.D. Va. 1993).

Brown v. Board of Education, 347 U.S. 483 (1954).

Buck v. Bell, 274 U.S. 200 (1927).

Burke County Board of Education v. Denton, 895 F.2d 973 (4th Cir. 1990).

Campbell v. Talladega County Board of Education, 518 F. Supp. 47 (N.D. Ala. 1981).

Cedar Rapids Community School District v. Garrett F., 526 U.S. 66 (1999).

Cherry v. Matthews, 419 F. Supp. 922 (D. D.C. 1976).

Christopher W. v. Portsmouth School Committee, 877 F.2d 1089 (1st Cir. 1989).

City of Cleburne v. City of Cleburne Living Center, Inc., 473 U.S. 432 (1985).

Civil Rights Act, 42 U.S.C.A. sec. 1981 *et seq.*

Clevenger v. Oak Ridge School Board, 744 F.2d 514 (6th Cir. 1984).

Clovis Unified School District v. California Office of Administrative Hearings, 903 F.2d 635 (9th Cir. 1990).

Clyde K. and Sheila K. ex re. Ryan D. v. Puyallup School District, 35 F.3d 1396 (9th Cir. 1994).

Coleman v. Zatechka, 824 F. Supp. 1360 (D. Neb. 1993).

143 Cong. Rec. S4295 (1997).

Cordrey v. Euckert, 917 F.2d 1460 (6th Cir. 1990).

Corey H. v. Board of Education, 995 F. Supp. 900 (N.D. Ill. 1998).

Craig v. Boren, 429 U.S. 190 (1976).

Crawford v. Pittman, 708 F.2d 1028 (5th Cir. 1983).

Dade (FL) County School District, 20 IDELR 267 (OCR 1993).

Daley v. Koch, 639 F. Supp. 289 (D. D.C. 1986).

D'Amico v. New York State Board of Bar Examiners, 813 F. Supp. 217 (W.D. N.Y. 1993).

Daniel R. R. v. Texas Board of Education, 874 F.2d 1036 (5th Cir. 1989).

Darian v. University of Massachusetts Boston, 980 F. Supp. 77 (D. Mass. 1997).

DePaul University (IL), 4 Nat'l. Disab. L. Rep. 157 (1993).

Department of Public Welfare v. Haas, 154 N.E.2d 265 (Ill. 1958).

DeVries v. Fairfax County School Board, 882 F.2d 876 (4th Cir. 1989).

Doe v. Defendant I, 898 F.2d 1186 (6th Cir. 1990).

Doe v. DeKalb County School District, 145 F.3d 1441 (11th Cir., 1998).

Doe v. Koger, 480 F. Supp. 225 (N.D. Ind. 1979).

Doe v. Washington University, 780 F. Supp. 628 (E.D. Mo. 1991).

Doe v. Withers, 20 IDELR 442 (W.Va. Cir. Ct. 1993).

Doe by Gonzales v. Maher, 793 F.2d 1470 (9th Cir. 1986)

Drew P. v. Clarke County School District, 877 F.2d 927 (11th Cir. 1989).

Education for All Handicapped Children Act: see Individuals with Disabilities Education Act.

E. E. Black Limited v. Marshall, 497 F. Supp. 1088 (D. Hi. 1980).

EEOC Compliance Manual No. 198.

EEOC Technical Assistance Manual.

EEOC v. Community Coffee, Civ. No. H-94-1061 (S.D. Tex. 1995). Cited in: Miller, P. S. (1998). The EEOC's enforcement of the Americans with

Disabilities Act in the Sixth Circuit. *Case Western Reserve Law Review,* 48, 217–261.

Elementary and Secondary Education Act of 1965, 20 U.S.C.A. sec. 6301 *et seq.*

Equal Opportunity Act of 1992, 42 U.S.C.A. sec. 1885 *et seq.*

Expansion of Teaching in the Education of Mentally Retarded Children Act of 1958, 72 Stat. 1777.

Ex Parte Zeigler, 15 N.W.2d 34 (Wis. 1944).

Fair Housing Act of 1988, 42 U.S.C.A. sec. 3602.

Family Educational Rights and Privacy Act, 20 U.S.C.A. sec. 1232g.

56 Fed. Reg. 35544 (1991).

Florence County School District Four v. Carter, 510 U.S. 7 (1993).

Flour Bluff Independent School District v. Katherine M., 24 IDELR 673 (5th Cir. 1996).

Gadsby v. Grasmick, 109 F.3d 940 (4th Cir. 1997).

Galloway v. Superior Court of District of Columbia, 816 F. Supp. 12 (D. D.C. 1993).

G. D. v. Westmoreland School District, 930 F.2d 942 (1st Cir. 1991).

Gladys J. v. Pearland Independent School District, 520 F. Supp. 869 (S.D. Tex. 1981).

Graham v. Richardson, 403 U.S. 365 (1971).

Greer v. Rome City School District, 950 F.2d 688 (11th Cir. 1991).

Guckenberger v. Boston University, 957 F. Supp. 306 (D.C. Mass. 1997).

Guckenberger v. Boston University, 974 F. Supp. 106 (D.C. Mass. 1997).

Gun-Free School Act of the Goals 2000: Educate America Act, 20 U.S.C.A. sec. 7151.

Gurmankin v. Costanzo, 556 F.2d 184 (3rd Cir. 1977).

Gurmankin v. Costanzo, 626 F.2d 1115 (3rd Cir. 1980).

Halasz v. University of New England, 816 F. Supp. 37 (D. Me. 1993).

Handicapped Children's Protection Act, 20 U.S.C.A. sec. 1400, 1415.

Hayes v. Unified School District No. 377, 877 F.2d 809 (10th Cir. 1989).

Helms v. Independent School District #3, 750 F.2d 820 (10th Cir. 1985).

Honig v. Doe, 484 U.S. 305 (1988).

Hurry v. Jones, 734 F.2d 879 (1st Cir. 1984).

Individuals with Disabilities Education Act (IDEA), 20 U.S.C.A sec. 1400 *et seq.*

Individuals with Disabilities Education Act (IDEA) regulations, 34 C.F.R. sec. 300 *et seq.*

In re Masters, 13 N.W.2d 487 (Minn., 1944).

In re Moe, 432 N.E.2d 712 (Mass. 1982).

In re Smith, 926 F.2d 1027 (11th Cir. 1991).

In re Terwilliger, 450 A.2d 1376 (Pa. Super.Ct. 1982).

Irving Independent School District v. Tatro, 468 U.S. 883 (1984).

Jackson v. Franklin County School Board, 806 F.2d 623 (5th Cir. 1986).

Jefferson County Board of Education v. Breen, 694 F. Supp. 1539 (N.D. Ala. 1987), *aff'd*, 853 F.2d 853 (11th Cir. 1988).

Johnson v. Independent School District Number 4, 921 F.2d 1022 (10th Cir. 1990).

Kari H. v. Franklin Special School District, 1997 U.S. App. Lexis 21724 (6th Cir. 1997).

Kari H. v. Franklin Special School District, 1999 U.S. App. Lexis 15158 (6th Cir. 1999).

Korematsu v. United States, 323 U.S. 214 (1944).

Kruelle v. New Castle County School District, 642 F.2d 687 (3rd Cir. 1981).

Lachman v. Illinois State Board of Education, 852 F.2d 290 (7th Cir. 1988).

Lane v. Pena, 867 F. Supp. 1050 (D. D.C. 1994), *aff'd* 518 U.S. 187 (1996).

Light v. Parkway School District, 21 IDELR 933 (8th Cir. 1994).

Lunenberg School District, 22 IDELR 290 (1994).

Lyons by Alexander v. Smith, 829 F. Supp. 414 (D. D.C. 1993).

Mavis v. Sobol, 839 F. Supp. 968 (N.D. N.Y. 1993).

Max M. v. Illinois State Board of Education, 629 F. Supp. 1504 (N.D. Ill. 1986).

McGregor v. Louisiana State University Board of Supervisors, 3 F.3d 850 (5th Cir. 1993).

Mesa (AZ) Unified School District No. 4, EHLR 312:103 (OCR 1988).

Miener v. Missouri, 800 F.2d 749 (8th Cir. 1986).

Mills v. Board of Education of the District of Columbia, 348 F. Supp. 866 (D. D.C. 1972).

Morton Community School District No. 709 v. J. M., 152 F.3d 583 (7th Cir. 1998), *cert. denied* 119 S.Ct. 1140 (1999).

Mr. X v. New York State Education Department, 20 F. Supp.2d 561 (S.D. N.Y. 1998).

Murphy v. United Parcel Service, 527 U.S. 516 (1999).

Murray v. Montrose County School District, 22 IDELR 558 (10th Cir. 1995).

Myles S. v. Montgomery County Board of Education, 824 F. Supp. 1549 (M.D. Ala. 1993).

National University (CA), 5 Nat'l. Disab. L. Rep. 82 (1993).

N.C. Gen. Stat. 115–165 (1963).

N.C. Sess. Laws, Ch. 584 (1965).

New Mexico Association for Retarded Citizens v. The State of New Mexico, 678 F.2d 847 (10th Cir. 1982).

Oberti v. Board of Education of the Borough of Clementon School District, 995 F.2d 1204 (3rd Cir. 1993).

Ohio Civil Rights Commission v. Case Western Reserve University, 666 N.E.2d 1376 (Ohio 1996).

Ohio Rev. Code Ann. Sec. 3321.04.

Pennsylvania Association for Retarded Children (PARC) v. Commonwealth of Pennsylvania, 334 F. Supp. 1257 (E.D. Pa. 1971).

People v. Caldwell, 603 N.Y.S.2d 713 (N.Y. App. Term., 1993).

Petition of Rubenstein, 637 A.2d 1131 (Del. Supr. 1994).

Philadelphia (PA) School District, 18 IDELR 931 (OCR 1992).

Plyler v. Doe, 457 U.S. 202 (1982).

Poe v. Lynchburg Training School and Hospital, 518 F. Supp. 789 (W.D. Va. 1981).

Polk v. Central Susquehanna Intermediate Unit 16, 853 F.2d 171 (3rd Cir. 1988).

Poolaw v. Bishop, 23 IDELR 407 (9th Cir. 1995).

Pregnancy Discrimination Act of 1978, 42 U.S.C.A. sec. 2000e *et seq.*

Providence College (RI), 6 Nat'l. Disab. L. Rep. 89 (1994).

Pushkin v. Regents of the University of Colorado, 658 F.2d 1372 (10th Cir. 1981).

Rapid City School District v. Vahle, 922 F.2d 476 (8th Cir. 1990).

Rehabilitation Act, 29 U.S.C.A. sec. 701 *et seq.*

Rehabilitation Act regulations, 34 C.F.R. sec. 104 *et seq.*

Roncker v. Walter, 700 F.2d 1058 (6th Cir. 1983).

Rothman v. Emory University, 828 F. Supp. 537 (N.D. Ill. 1993).

Rothschild v. Grottenhaler, 725 F. Supp. 776 (S.D. N.Y. 1989), *affirmed in part, vacated in part*, 907 F.2d 286 (2nd Cir. 1990).

S-1 v. Turlington, 635 F.2d 342 (5th Cir. 1981), *cert. denied* 454 U.S. 1030 (1981).

Sacramento City Unified School District v. Rachel H., 14 F.3d 1398 (9th Cir. 1994).

San Jose State University (CA), 4 Nat'l. Disab. L. Rep. 358 (1993).

Sanders by Sanders v. Marquette Public Schools, 561 F. Supp. 1361 (W.D. Mich. 1983).

Saunders v. Horn, 959 F. Supp. 689 (E.D. Pa. 1996).

School Board of Nassau County v. Arline, 480 U.S. 273 (1987).

School Board of Prince William County v. Malone, 762 F.2d 1210 (4th Cir. 1985).

School Committee, Town of Burlington v. Department of Education of Massachusetts, 471 U.S. 359 (1985).

Schuldt v. Mankato Independent School District No. 77, 937 F.2d 1357 (8th Cir. 1991).

Sean R. v. Town of Woodbridge Board of Education, 794 F. Supp. 467 (D. Conn. 1992).

Shanahan v. Board of Education of the Jamesville-Dewitt School District, 953 F. Supp. 440 (N.D.N.Y. 1997).

Shook v. Gaston County Board of Education, 882 F.2d 119 (4th Cir. 1989).

Smith v. Robinson, 468 U.S. 992 (1984).

Southeastern Community College v. Davis, 442 U.S. 397 (1979).

Springdale School District v. Grace, 494 F. Supp. 266 (W.D. Ark. 1980).

Standard v. A.B.E.L. Services, Inc., 161 F.3d 1318 (11th Cir. 1998).

Stemple v. Board of Education, 623 F.2d 893 (4th Cir. 1980).

Students of California School for the Blind v. Honig, 736 F.2d 538 (9th Cir. 1984).

SUNY Health Science Center at Brooklyn-College of Medicine (NY), 5 Nat'l. Disab. L. Rep. 77 (1993).

Sutton v. United Air Lines, Inc., 527 U.S. 471 (1999).

Tatum v. Andalusia City School, 977 F. Supp. 1437 (M.D. Ala. 1997).

Taylor v. Board of Education, 649 F. Supp. 1253 (N.D. N.Y. 1986).

Telecommunications Act of 1996, 47 U.S.C.A. sec. 225.

Terrell v. U.S. Air, Incorporated, 132 F.3d 621 (11th Cir. 1998).

Timothy W. v. Rochester, New Hampshire, School District, 875 F.2d 954 (1st Cir. 1989).

Trimble v. Gordon, 430 U.S. 762 (1977).

United States v. Tennessee, 798 F. Supp. 483 (W.D. Tenn. 1992).

University of California, San Diego, 5 Nat'l. Disab. L. Rep. 163 (June 24, 1993).

Waechter v. School District No. 14-030, 773 F. Supp. 1005 (W.D. Mich. 1991).

Watson v. City of Cambridge, 32 N.E. 864 (Mass. 1893).

W. G. v. Board of Trustees of Target Range School District, 960 F.2d 1479 (9th Cir. 1992).

Wood v. Omaha School District, 25 F.3d 667 (8th Cir. 1994).

Wynne v. Tufts University School of Medicine, 976 F.2d 791 (1st Cir. 1992).

Yaris v. Special School District of St. Louis, County 558 F. Supp. 545 (E.D. Mo. 1983), *aff'd* 728 F.2d 1055 (8th Cir. 1984).

Index

About the Authors

PAUL T. JAEGER is a Research Associate at the Information Use Management and Policy Institute of the School of Information Studies at Florida State University, where he researches the legal and policy aspects of information issues such as privacy, e-government, accessibility, and the digital divide. He has earned a Juris Doctor with Honors and a Master of Education. His primary research interest is disability law and its relationships to education and information policies. His scholarly publications have addressed issues of disability law, education law, accessibility, privacy law, e-government, and constitutional law.

CYNTHIA ANN BOWMAN is an Assistant Professor of English Education at Florida State University, where she teaches undergraduate and graduate courses in teaching methods, literacy, technology, and curriculum issues. A member of the National Council of Teachers of English, the Conference on English Education, the International Reading Association, and the American Educational Research Association, she has made presentations and published numerous articles and book chapters on creating classroom communities, infusing technology into the curriculum, language arts collaborations, teacher research, critical literacy, and students with disabilities.